Beautiful Bundts

Beautiful Bundts

100 Recipes for Delicious Cakes & More

JULIE ANNE HESSION

Robert ROSE

For Gigi

Design and production: Kevin Cockburn/PageWave Graphics Inc.

Editor: Sue Sumeraj

Copy editor: Kelly Jones

Recipe editor: Jennifer MacKenzie

Proofreader: Wendy Potter

Indexer: Gillian Watts

Image prepress and color correction: Pixel Ink Retouching

Cover image: Classic Pound Cake (page 34)
Page 2: Triple Coconut Bundt (page 44)
Page 288: Lemon Poppy Seed Bundts (page 220)

Published by Robert Rose Inc.
120 Eglinton Avenue East, Suite 800, Toronto, Ontario, Canada M4P 1E2
Tel: (416) 322-6552 Fax: (416) 322-6936
www.robertrose.ca

Printed and bound in China

3 4 5 6 7 8 9 LEO 25 24 23 22 21

Contents

Introduction

When I told people I was working on a Bundt cookbook, I received a number of different reactions. Some told me how much they love Bundts, and to remember them any time I needed a taste tester. Some offered recipe suggestions (*Make sure to include something with pistachios!*). Some clearly wondered how many different recipes I could create using a Bundt pan. The most common response, however, was something like this: "Bundts always make me think of that great scene from the movie *My Big Fat Greek Wedding*!"

If you are not familiar with the popular comedy, that scene involves two mothers, one of the bride and one of the groom. The groom's mother brings a Bundt cake as a hostess gift, which she presents to the bride's mother, the matriarch of a traditional Greek family. The following conversation ensues:

"What is it?"

"It's a Bundt."

"A boont?"

"Bundt."

"A bonk!"

The groom's mother is noticeably frustrated: "Bundt! Bundt!"

The bride's mother's expression changes to one of understanding: "Oh! It's a *cake*!"

As the bride's mother walks away, she whispers to her friend, "There's a *hole* in this cake!"

Bundt cakes are an American tradition, which may be why they evolve but never really go out of style. I'm not sure when I was served my first slice, but growing up I always associated Bundt cake with my mom's afternoon bridge group or our church bake sale. The Bundts were usually flavored simply with chocolate, vanilla or lemon, but occasional fancier ones featured two marbled batters or (my favorite) a cinnamon streusel swirl.

Today, amidst a sea of labor-intensive fondant-covered cakes, specialty cake pops and beautifully decorated cupcakes, Bundts offer a bit of a rewind to baking that is classic, uncomplicated and nostalgic.

Despite having European roots, the Bundt pan, as most of us know it, was created in the United States. There are even a few of the original pans on display at the Smithsonian Institution in Washington, DC. In the early 1950s, Minnesota businessman H. David Dahlquist and his brother Mark Dahlquist (cofounders of Nordic Ware) were approached by a group of local Jewish women who were looking for someone to create a modernized version of the gugelhupf pan, used to make a ring-shaped yeast cake containing dried fruit and nuts that was popular among Jewish communities in Germany, Austria, Poland and Switzerland.

Instead of traditional cast iron, the new pan was made from aluminum — as many pans still are (along with silicone and steel). When deciding what to call their pan, the creators drew from the German word *bundkuchen*, which links the words *bund* ("group" or "bundle") and *kuchen* ("cake"). Hoping that these new cakes would bring people together as a group, they simply added a "t" to *bund* and (wisely!) trademarked their new word.

The original Bundt pan featured fluted, or grooved, sides, which served as markers for even slices, and a central tube or "chimney," which created a hole through the center of the cake. This shape allowed more batter or dough to come into contact with the pan's surface than in traditional round or rectangular cake pans, encouraging even distribution of heat during the baking process and eliminating the jiggly center often associated with deeper pans.

Perhaps surprisingly, the Bundt pan was not an instant success. After a modest initial production run, sales were so bad that it was almost discontinued. Luckily, in 1966, a Texas woman named Ella Helfrich used her Bundt pan to create the now-famous Tunnel of Fudge cake as her entry into the Pillsbury Bake-Off. The chocolate cake was sliced to reveal a fudgy filling made from a packet of Pillsbury frosting that was piped into the center of the batter before baking. The recipe earned a $5,000 second-place prize, and the cake was an overnight sensation — in today's terms, it "went viral"! Suddenly, cooks and bakers everywhere wanted a Bundt pan so that they, too, could make this innovative cake. As a result, millions of pans were sold in the following years.

Today, Bundt pans come in a wide variety of shapes, from the classic ring with fluted sides to pans shaped like holiday-inspired wreaths, hearts and stars and pans with names like "Stained Glass" or "Fleur de Lis." There is also a variety of sizes, from bite-size baby Bundts and mini Bundts to half-size Bundts and oversized Bundts for a crowd.

Just as there is no one "right" shape or size for a Bundt pan, there is no one "right" cake to bake in it. There are many, many types of recipes that can be created in a Bundt pan — even macaroni and cheese! My goal, when creating the recipes, was to think outside the typical Bundt box and include not only popular cake flavors, such as banana or vanilla, but also recipes that are usually baked in other types of pans. In addition to one-bowl cakes, you'll find cakes that are layered, swirled or filled with gooey centers. There are Bundts best served for breakfast or brunch (although I'll certainly understand if you want to eat a slice of Glazed Cinnamon-Raisin Roll Bundt at midnight), and there are individual mini Bundts for a fun ending to a dinner party. You can go around the calendar with my holiday-inspired Bundts or go around the world with the international Bundts. And you'll be delighted by the delectable savory Bundts, from pull-apart Savory Cheese and Herb Monkey Bread Bundt to Baked Sausage Rigatoni Bundt.

Because of their curved and slanted edges, Bundt cakes are more difficult to frost than traditional layer cakes, so most of the cakes in this book are coated with poured glazes or glossy ganaches, sprinkled with powdered sugar or occasionally left undecorated.

Each beautiful Bundt is accompanied by a photo to give you a mouthwatering glimpse of what you can look forward to when you complete the recipe. In addition, I've included four sets of step-by-step photos to guide you through some of the more advanced techniques.

I'm hoping your Bundt pan will earn a spot of honor in your kitchen cabinets so that it is easily reached when you create one of the over 100 original recipes in this book. Or maybe, like me, you'll end up with an entire Bundt pan section in your pantry!

Peppermint Chocolate Mocha Bundt

PART 1

All About Bundts

Equipment and Tools

The process of baking beautiful Bundts will be much easier with help from this list of equipment and tools, most of which you probably already have in your kitchen (or in your toolbox, in the case of measuring tape)!

BUNDT PANS

When I was growing up, the Bundt pan came in one shape: a ring with rounded, scalloped edges that could easily be cut into 12 to 16 neat slices. Today, this is fittingly known as a "traditional" Bundt pan. Keeping it company are dozens of pans with unique shapes, from holiday-inspired stars and hearts to deep gugelhupf pans and ridged Bavarian-style models. Bundt pans also come in a variety of sizes, materials and colors, making for an overwhelming number of options. Here's what you need to know to choose the best pans and, as needed, adapt the recipes to work with the pans you have.

Shape

The Bundts for this book were baked in about 15 different pans (you should see my collection!), depending on size requirement, toppings (some shapes are better than others for glazing) or "theme." Depending on which shape of pan you choose for your Bundt, you may need to increase or decrease the baking time by 5 to 10 minutes to accommodate the varying width and/or height. The doneness tests indicated in the recipe will help you determine when the cake is done; keep checking on the cake, and remove it from the oven when it passes the specified doneness tests (see box, below).

Size

Traditional Bundt pans are about 10 inches (25 cm) in diameter and $3\frac{1}{2}$ to 4 inches (8.5 to 10 cm) deep, with a volume of 10 to 15 cups. But just as they come in a variety of shapes, the world of Bundt pans also offers an array of size options for you to consider, from bite-sized 2-oz cakelets to massive 16-cup party Bundts. If you have two or three Bundt pans in the following sizes, you will be able to prepare all of the recipes in this book:

- **Minimum 15-cup Bundt pan:** This pan will work for every regular-size (not mini) Bundt in this book. Some cakes will only fill the pan about two-thirds full after baking, but several, including most of the yeast Bundts, will rise up and over the top.
- **10-cup Bundt pan:** If you want to incorporate a uniquely shaped Bundt, such as a crown or cathedral style, into your collection, most of these pans have a capacity of 10 cups.
- **Mini Bundt pan(s):** Good things come in small packages, so there is an entire chapter in this book devoted to individual-size mini Bundts (as well as several more minis in other chapters.) These recipes were tested in molds that range in capacity from about 5 oz (150 mL) to 8 oz (250 mL) per cake.

Checking for Doneness

Baking times can vary. To prevent overbaking, keep an eye on your Bundt as it nears the last quarter of the baking process, and check for doneness using the tests specified in the recipe. For example, the recipe might say to bake the cake "until the top is puffed and golden brown and a tester inserted in the center comes out clean." When you first start baking recipes from this book, set the timer to about 10 minutes before the earliest time in the range and, when it goes off, open the oven door just wide enough to take a peek; if it looks puffed and golden brown, use a tester to check the inside. If it doesn't, close the door and reset the timer for 5 to 10 minutes (or more if the cake looks very underdone). Take care not to open the oven too much or too often, or you'll lose heat.

Check Your Volume

The recipes in this book call for pans by volume capacity in cups. If your pan is not already stamped with its volume (check around the rim or outer surface), you can determine how much batter it will hold by pouring in measured water by the cupful until the pan is filled to the brim. Keep in mind that you want the pan to be no more than two-thirds to three-quarters full of batter, to allow the batter room to rise as it bakes. When baking foods other than batters, such as pasta, you can fill the pan almost to the top.

Depending on the volume of your mini Bundt pan, you may get fewer or more cakes when you follow a recipe's guideline on how full the molds should be for optimal baking. To cover this, there is range in yield (e.g., 8 to 10 mini Bundts) for those recipes.

Material

The pans used to create these beautiful Bundts were made from heavy, nonstick cast aluminum, which conducts heat evenly during the baking process. Most nonstick aluminum or steel pans will work equally well. Although silicone Bundts pans are now readily available, I do not recommend them because they have a somewhat wobbly structure and do not conduct heat as well as their metal counterparts.

Color

The choices continue when it comes to color! Aluminum and steel Bundt pans are available in both light and dark colors. Darker varieties are either black or dark gray, and light varieties can be light gray, silver, cream-colored on the inside with vivid color on the outside, or even gold.

Because darker colors absorb heat faster, you will need to make some oven temperature and/or baking time adjustments when using a dark gray or black pan, or the exterior may get too dark before the interior of the Bundt is fully baked:

- For Bundts baked at 325°F (160°C), use the same temperature but start checking for doneness (see box, page 10) about 10 minutes before the earliest time specified in the recipe.
- For Bundts usually baked at 350°F (180°C), reduce the temperature to 325°F (160°C).
- For Bundts baked at 375°F (190°C), reduce the temperature to 350°F (180°C).
- Non-cake Bundts, such as pasta and stuffing, aren't affected as much by pan color. Bake them at the temperature specified, but start checking for doneness about 15 minutes before the earliest time specified in the recipe and keep a close eye on your Bundt to make sure the crust doesn't get too dark. If you find that the crust is getting dark before the center is hot, reduce the oven temperature by 25°F (10°C).

STAND MIXER

Most of the recipes in this book use a stand mixer fitted with the paddle attachment to create a smooth, evenly blended batter or dough. For yeast recipes, the dough hook attachment simulates kneading with minimal effort on your part. Most doughs can be kneaded by hand on a floured work surface, but it will take a bit longer to achieve the desired texture. For extremely sticky dough, a stand mixer yields best results.

Nonstick Baking Spray with Flour

Before filling pans, it is important to make sure they are evenly sprayed with nonstick baking spray with flour, which replicates the traditional greasing and flouring process. Common brands are Pam for Baking and Baker's Joy, both of which were used with great nonstick success in these recipes. See page 20 for acceptable alternatives to this spray.

HANDHELD MIXER

Although it requires a bit more effort, a handheld electric mixer can be used instead of a stand mixer to mix batter or dough, so don't despair if you don't own a stand mixer — you don't need to run out and buy one to prepare the recipes in this book. A handheld mixer is also beneficial when multiple batters or whipped egg whites are involved in the recipe, so that you don't need to clean out your stand mixer bowl mid-recipe.

FOOD PROCESSOR

Finely ground graham crackers for the S'mores Bundt Cake (page 102) and perfectly puréed ripe bananas for the Peanut Butter Banana Swirl Bundt (page 128) both require the use of a food processor fitted with a metal blade, as do various fillings, streusels and toppings. For recipes such as the Zucchini Apple Nut Bundts (page 232), use the food processor's grating disk to create evenly shredded fruit and vegetables in seconds.

I don't generally recommend using a blender in place of a food processor, as mixtures tend to get stuck or clump in the bottom of the container, which is not fun to clean!

KITCHEN SCALE

A small kitchen scale is helpful to have whether you're baking Bundts or brownies. Many recipes call for certain ingredients, such as chopped chocolate, by weight, as this is a more accurate way of measuring than by volume.

In addition, for recipes that require you to divide dough or batter in halves or thirds (or sixths, as in the Rainbow Swirl Bundt on page 124), you can determine precise measurements by weighing the batter (see the box, below, for detailed instructions on weighing batter) and dividing by the number of portions you need. Repeat the weighing process with another bowl, or bowls, to divide the batter into portions.

WHISK

Recipes often call for dry ingredients to be sifted together, but I find this process tedious, and usually messy. In this book, most dry ingredients are whisked to blend before they are added to the batter. (The exceptions are cocoa powder and cake flour, both of which can form clumps that are eliminated by sifting them through a fine-mesh sieve or flour sifter.)

MICROPLANE-STYLE GRATER

Bakers and cooks are often asked to list their favorite kitchen tools. In addition to my workhorse of an immersion blender, I always include my fine rasp grater, made by Microplane, in this list. For recipes that call for grated zest, such as the Lemon Lover's Bundt (page 42), this handy tool finely grates flavorful citrus peel in seconds while avoiding the bitter white pith underneath.

Two Ways to Weigh Batter

- **For a digital scale:** Before you start mixing your batter, place the empty mixer bowl on the scale to weigh it, and write down the weight. Once the batter is mixed, place the bowl back on the scale and note the total weight, then subtract the weight of the empty bowl to determine the weight of the batter. If you have a digital scale with a memory function, you can place the empty bowl on the scale, press Tare, then activate the memory function. Follow the manufacturer's instruction to retrieve the memory, which will automatically subtract the weight of the empty bowl when you put the filled bowl back on the scale.
- **For an analog scale:** Place the empty mixer bowl on the scale and turn the dial to zero (then don't move the dial). Once the mixed batter is in the bowl, place it back on the scale and it will tell you the weight of the batter without the bowl.

ROLLING PIN

Almost all of the yeast-raised Bundts in this book require the use of a rolling pin after the initial rise to shape the dough into an even rectangle. Because many of the doughs are sticky, you should lightly sprinkle both the work surface and the top of the dough with flour so that the dough doesn't stick to the rolling pin.

MEASURING TAPE

Whether you're measuring the length and width of your Babka Dough (page 78) or the diameter of a baking pan, there are many occasions when you will want your tape measure to be within reaching distance. Here's a tip: If you only have one tape measure, and it's in the garage, buy yourself a second one to keep in your utensil drawer. It will take some of the guesswork out of baking!

PASTRY BRUSH

Just as a painter can't work without a paintbrush, I couldn't have created these beautiful Bundts without my trusty pastry brush. Not only did I use it to brush egg wash or melted butter onto yeast-raised Bundts before baking, but it came in handy when nonstick baking spray pooled in the crevices of a Bundt pan: a quick once-over with a natural bristle or nylon/plastic fiber brush ensures an evenly coated pan. Silicone bristle brushes are also available, but they aren't my favorite type, as ingredients don't cling to them as well as they do with the other materials.

CAKE TESTER

When you're testing traditional layer cakes for doneness, a toothpick works every time. In the case of Bundts, however, a standard toothpick is barely long enough to reach the center. Use a metal cake tester (found in baking supply stores), a long, thin skewer or a thin knife to accomplish this task.

COOLING RACKS

Although with many recipes you are given the option to invert the Bundt cake onto either a wire cooling rack or a plate after baking, my preference is the cooling rack, as it offers an open, slightly raised platform on which the cake can thoroughly cool while allowing steam to escape. Cooling warm Bundts on a plate can result in a moist underside (because the steam had nowhere to go) and cakes that stick when you try to move them. Exceptions to this rule are Bundts that are served still warm from the oven, such as many of the savory Bundts or the Mini Chocolate Lava Bundts (page 108).

Other Necessary Tools

The following is a list of everyday kitchen tools that you will need for most (if not all) of these recipes:

- Measuring cups (dry and liquid)
- Measuring spoons
- Fine-mesh sieve or flour sifter
- Mixing bowls
- Spatulas
- Offset spatula/palette knife (optional, but helpful for smoothing batters)
- Large spoons (for transferring batters to pans)
- Oven mitts
- Small, medium and large saucepans
- Large skillet
- Plastic wrap

Key Ingredients

As with equipment, most of the ingredients used for Bundt cakes are similar to those used to bake your favorite birthday cake or yeast-raised pastry. That said, Bundts can be more temperamental than a standard round cake layer, due to their depth, longer baking times and unique shapes, so there are some key things to know about the ingredients used in these recipes, including how to select them, how to prepare them and substitution options.

FLOURS

With the exception of a few recipes that use bread flour (which adds springiness and chew to the texture of the Garlic Knot Pull-Apart Bundt, page 156) or whole wheat flour (which brings a heartier texture to the Healthy Start Bundt, page 72), the Bundts in this book are made with either all-purpose flour or cake flour. Cake flour contains less protein than all-purpose flour, producing cakes with a tender, more delicate texture.

If you don't have cake flour in your pantry, you can add cornstarch to all-purpose flour to replicate the tender, delicate texture of cake flour. Spoon the amount of cornstarch specified in the chart below into a dry measuring cup, then spoon in all-purpose flour to the top of the cup and level it off. Continue to measure all-purpose flour, on its own, until you have the total amount of flour called for.

For example, if the recipe calls for 1½ cups (375 mL) cake flour, spoon 3 tbsp (45 mL) cornstarch into a ½-cup (125 mL) dry measuring cup, top it up with all-purpose flour and level it off to make ½ cup (125 mL), then measure another 1 cup (250 mL) plain all-purpose flour.

Total Amount of Flour	Amount of Cornstarch
1 cup (250 mL)	2 tbsp (30 mL)
1½ cups (375 mL)	3 tbsp (45 mL)
2 cups (500 mL)	¼ cup (60 mL)
2¼ cups (550 mL)	4½ tbsp (67 mL)
2½ cups (625 mL)	5 tbsp (75 mL)

BUTTER AND VEGETABLE OIL

Use unsalted butter, not salted butter, for your beautiful Bundts, as this allows you to control the amount of salt in the finished product. I also commonly use vegetable oil in place of or in addition to unsalted butter in my baking recipes, because I find that it helps to create a moist texture in cakes that may otherwise be too dry.

SOUR CREAM/BUTTERMILK/YOGURT

Dairy products, such as sour cream, buttermilk or yogurt, are typically incorporated into a cake batter at the end of the mixing process, alternating with the flour mixture. These acidic ingredients produce a fine crumb and add moisture and flavor to the cake.

Using full-fat sour cream or Greek yogurt will result in a denser, moister cake, because they contain more fat than buttermilk. I love using plain Greek yogurt in recipes, as it is extra-thick and rich. You can replace whole-milk sour cream and Greek yogurt with low-fat varieties, but I don't recommend fat-free options. If you cannot find Greek yogurt, you can use plain or vanilla-flavored full-fat regular yogurt instead. Flavored yogurts usually contain added sugar.

How to Soften Butter

Many recipes require butter to be softened, which helps it blend smoothly with sugar and develop the ideal "light and fluffy" texture when beaten. An easy way to soften butter is to cut it into 1- to 2-tbsp (15 to 30 mL) chunks and microwave it on Low (10%) power in 15-second intervals until it reaches the desired consistency. But don't let it melt.

Make Your Own Buttermilk

You can make your own version of buttermilk with plain milk (not fat-free/skim) and vinegar. For each cup (250 mL) of buttermilk called for, stir 1 tbsp (15 mL) white or apple cider vinegar into 1 cup (250 mL) milk and let stand at room temperature for 15 minutes before using.

SUGAR

In addition to granulated sugar's use in batters, you'll often see it used as a coating for yeast Bundts, such as Spiced Apple Hazelnut Monkey Bread (page 142), creating a caramelized, textured exterior after baking. For these recipes, when you're preparing the pan before mixing your batter, coat the pan with nonstick baking spray with flour, then sprinkle a small amount (about 2 tbsp/30 mL) of sugar into the pan and shake to coat evenly.

In a few recipes, brown sugar replaces granulated sugar in the batter or as a coating. All brown sugar (light and dark) should be measured firmly packed into a dry measuring cup. Sift it to make sure it is clump-free before coating the pan or adding it to batters.

MAPLE SYRUP

Be sure to use pure maple syrup, not imitation pancake or table syrup. Look for grade A syrup, as it will have the most concentrated maple flavor.

Measuring Sticky Sweets

Maple syrup, honey and corn syrup can be a challenge to measure accurately, thanks to their (frustrating!) tendency to stick to the measuring cup. To prevent this from happening, lightly spritz your measuring cups with nonstick spray before filling them. The sticky ingredient will slide right out of the cup and into the batter!

EGGS

Most of the non-savory recipes in this book require the eggs to be at room temperature before they are beaten into batters. Why? Well, like softened butter, room temperature eggs mix more easily into batter and help increase volume. To bring cold eggs to room temperature quickly, place them in a bowl, cover them with warm tap water and let them stand for 5 to 10 minutes to warm up.

When you're adding multiple eggs to a batter, add them one at a time, making sure each egg is fully incorporated before adding another and scraping down the sides of the bowl as necessary.

Whipped egg whites are occasionally added to batters separately from yolks to create a light, airy texture. It's easier to separate cold eggs, so separate them as soon as you remove them from the refrigerator, then bring them to room temperature for whipping. To quickly bring egg whites to room temperature, place the bowl of egg whites in a larger bowl of hot water and let stand for 5 minutes.

Always use a clean, dry bowl for whipping egg whites, as moisture or traces of oil or other fats will inhibit the whipping process. Choose a metal, glass or even copper bowl; plastic or wooden bowls can store particles of fat or moisture.

When whipping, start with your mixer on a lower speed and gradually increase to high speed as the whites start to firm. Perfectly whipped egg whites should be smooth and glossy, but not dry. If you overwhip the whites until they are dry, they will likely break down when they are folded into the batter, creating a heavier Bundt instead of the intended lighter, fluffier cake.

Cream of Tartar

In some recipes, cream of tartar is added to egg whites to stabilize them when whipped, keeping them from collapsing, enhancing their volume and giving them a bright white sheen.

YEAST

Use active dry yeast, not "instant" or rapid rise yeast, for your yeast-raised beautiful Bundts. Many recipes in this book call for a ¼-oz (8 g) package, which is equivalent to 2¼ tsp (11 mL) should you buy yeast in jars. Yeast loses potency as it ages, resulting in longer rising times, so always check the "use by" date on your yeast package or jar before use, to make sure it has not expired (discard it if expired).

As you follow the recipes, you will be mixing the yeast with warm water and a small amount of sugar to "proof" the yeast, making sure it is still alive. If the mixture doesn't foam, throw the yeast out — it's likely no good and your dough won't rise properly. Start again with a fresh package or jar of yeast.

VANILLA

Pure vanilla flavoring comes in several forms, including vanilla extract, vanilla beans and ground vanilla bean. I prefer pure vanilla extract to its artificial, or "imitation," counterpart, because it lends a more intense, complex vanilla flavor to batters and glazes.

Most of the recipes in this book call for vanilla extract, but a handful capitalize on the visual beauty added by the pretty black specks that dot slices of cake, custards and glazes made with vanilla bean seeds. Look for a vanilla bean that is plump, glossy and fragrant, and not dry, and store it in an airtight container in a cool, dark place.

Ground vanilla bean (also called vanilla bean powder) is available in jars in specialty baking and spice shops, and makes a good substitute for vanilla beans. Use 1½ tsp (7 mL) ground vanilla bean as a substitute for 1 vanilla bean, or follow the directions on the label.

COCOA POWDER

Because unsweetened cocoa powder is the dominant flavor in several of the cakes and glazes in this book, the quality of the ingredient is very important. Good-quality cocoa will shine through in the finished product. Premium cocoa powder is generally 22% to 24% fat, which you can verify on nutritional labels. Look for cocoa powder that has at least 1 gram of fat per 5-gram serving. It is important to sift cocoa before adding it to batter, to avoid bitter-tasting clumps.

CHOCOLATE

Stock up on semisweet or dark (also called bittersweet) chocolate the next time you see it on sale! These are the varieties of chocolate most commonly called for in this book. I prefer dark chocolate when baking, as it is slightly less sweet than semisweet and has a more intense chocolate flavor.

When selecting chocolate, look for a glossy surface without any blemishes or a cloudy film, which can be a sign that it's too old. The chocolate should have a strong chocolate aroma — this seems obvious, but some brands smell more like additives or other ingredients. Finally, taste the chocolate and savor it (all in the name of research!). The texture should be smooth and velvety when melted, without any unpleasant granules or residue. If you enjoy the flavor of a chocolate on its own, you will likely enjoy it in a Bundt, glaze or ganache.

Some recipes in this book call for traditional chocolate chips, while others call for irregularly shaped chocolate chunks, which (I think) add a more interesting appearance when they're baked into a cake. In most cases,

How to Scrape the Seeds from a Vanilla Bean

Use a paring knife to split the vanilla bean down its length. Press one end of the bean against a cutting board or other flat surface and, using the dull side of the knife, scrape the seeds from the pod, moving from the tip down the length of the pod and flattening the bean as you go. Use the seeds and reserve the pod for another use, such as making vanilla sugar.

How to Melt Chocolate

Melt chocolate in a saucepan over medium-low heat, stirring constantly until smooth. Alternatively, place it in a microwave-safe bowl and microwave it on Medium (50%) power in 30-second intervals, stirring between each interval.

these two ingredients are interchangeable, so use whichever you prefer. The two types of chocolate do melt differently, though, so it's best not to substitute one for another in recipes that call for the chocolate to be melted.

FRUIT

There is no shortage of fruit in these recipes: fresh, frozen, dried, juiced and zested! Where fresh fruit is called for, as in the Strawberries and Cream Bundt (page 114), I've tried to offer a variation using frozen fruit, including instructions for measuring (thawed, drained, etc.).

A few recipes, such as the Healthy Start Bundt (page 72) call for grated apples with the liquid squeezed out, so that excess moisture isn't added to the batter. To remove liquid from apples, use your hands to gently squeeze portions of the grated apple over a bowl or sink.

NUTS

Many of the batters, fillings and toppings in these recipes call for toasted walnuts, hazelnuts, almonds or pecans. To toast nuts (whole or halves), spread them in an even layer on a baking sheet and bake them in a 350°F (180°C) oven, checking often, for 8 to 10 minutes or until the nuts are fragrant and lightly browned. Immediately transfer the nuts to a cutting board or plate and let cool, then chop as directed.

Basic Bundts, Start to Finish

Creating beautiful Bundts involves several key steps, some of which are used to make every Bundt in this book. In this chapter, you'll find a comprehensive list of essential Bundt-baking techniques, from properly preparing pans to storing your cakes.

Read It Through!

The first thing I always tell bakers, from novice to advanced, is to read recipes through, from start to finish, before they turn on their oven or plug in their stand mixer. That way, there will be no surprises as far as timing (several Bundts take more than 1 day to prepare), necessary equipment or ingredients.

PREPARING THE PAN

For those new to baking Bundts, one of the most intimidating factors is removing the baked cake from the pan. *What if it sticks?* Although I discuss this in detail in "Cooling and Releasing the Bundt" (page 22), one way to prevent cakes from sticking is to prepare the pan correctly.

For most of the Bundts in this book, the pans are sprayed with an even coating of nonstick baking spray before the batter, dough or filling is added. I prefer to use nonstick baking spray with flour, which quickly and easily replicates the traditional greasing and flouring process. Alternatively, you can use standard nonstick baking spray or a mister filled with vegetable oil to coat the pan, or you can use a pastry brush to spread a thin layer of vegetable oil over the pan. For extra insurance that the cake won't stick, you can dust the sprayed pan lightly with flour, using a sieve or a shaker with a fine-mesh top. Just be sure there are no clumps of flour that will spoil the look of the baked Bundt.

For specially shaped pans with deep crevices, nonstick baking spray with flour works best. If your spray pools in crevices or in the bottom of the pan, simply use a pastry brush to distribute the spray in an even layer.

PREHEATING THE OVEN

Some of the recipes in this book instruct you to preheat your oven before you start combining ingredients, while others require a few hours (or even a few days) of preparation before baking begins. In the latter cases, the recipe steps will tell you when to preheat the oven.

Before preheating, you'll want to make sure your oven rack is in the right position. For most Bundts, the rack should be positioned in the center of the oven. Some Bundts, however, have dough that rises over the top rim of the pan. For these recipes, lower the oven rack one notch so that the top of the pan isn't too close to the top of the oven.

Some Bundts, such as the Maple Bacon Monkey Bread (page 144), have very sticky components that may bubble up and out of the pan during the baking process. For these Bundts, line the oven rack below the one on which your Bundt will sit with foil or a baking sheet to catch any drips (and save you from a mess to clean up later).

Oven Temperature Accuracy

It is important to make sure your oven is heating accurately to prevent overbrowning or underbaking. To double-check, place an oven thermometer on the middle rack of your preheated oven for 15 minutes, then read the temperature. If the reading is significantly higher or lower than the temperature your oven says it's at, your oven needs to be calibrated.

MEASURING INGREDIENTS

A common baking mistake is not measuring ingredients properly. Accurate measurements are an integral part of creating perfectly textured, perfectly filled and perfectly glazed Bundts.

Dry ingredients, such as flour, should be measured using the "spoon and level," or "spoon and sweep," method. Use a large spoon to gradually fill the appropriate dry, nesting-style measuring cup or measuring spoon with the ingredient, without packing or shaking the cup, then level off the top with a flat edge, such as a knife blade or offset spatula. This prevents ingredients from becoming compacted, as occurs when you use the measuring cup as a scoop, potentially adding more than is necessary for the recipe. Light and dark brown sugars are the exception to this rule, as they are always measured "packed" into the measuring cup or spoon.

Measure liquid ingredients in a clear glass or plastic measuring cup with the quantities marked by lines on the side. Set the cup on a level surface before adding the liquid, and read it at eye level to make sure you have an accurate read.

MIXING THE BATTER OR DOUGH

For most of the recipes in this book, you'll get the best results by mixing the batter or dough with a stand mixer. When incorporating ingredients like softened butter, sugar and eggs, the stand mixer's powerful paddle attachment creates a smooth, even batter with volume. It also enables the baker to walk away from the mixer while it's mixing. (But don't walk too far away — always check in on the beating process to see how your batter is coming along!)

When mixing, or "creaming," butter and sugar, you are aerating the ingredients, which helps to create Bundts with a lighter texture and finer crumb. A butter and sugar mixture that has been creamed properly should be pale yellow in color and light and fluffy in texture, and should not "cling" to the side of the bowl. If you rub the mixture between your fingers, it should feel just slightly rough, signifying that most of the sugar has dissolved.

Gradual additions are recommended when you're adding any liquid ingredient to a fat, so with most batters, the eggs are added one at a time during the mixing process. This allows the mixture to properly emulsify and thicken slowly. Wait until the previous egg has been fully incorporated into the batter before you add another. I like to slow the mixer down to medium-low speed while I add the egg, so that it doesn't splatter against the sides of the bowl, and then increase the speed to medium to mix the egg into the batter. During this process, you may need to stop the mixer and scrape down the sides of the bowl if you notice the batter clinging to the sides; otherwise, you will likely find clumps of butter and sugar in your finished batter.

The last step of mixing a basic Bundt batter is to mix in the dry ingredients along with an additional fat, such as milk, buttermilk, sour cream or yogurt. Dry ingredients are added at the end of the mixing process so that the flour is not overmixed, which would result in a dense, tough cake. You can also prevent overmixing by gradually adding the dry ingredients to the batter and alternating with one of the additional fats. Always start and end the alternating process with dry

Using a Handheld Mixer and Kneading by Hand

If you don't have a stand mixer, in most cases a handheld electric mixer will work just as well for mixing your batter or dough, though a little more effort on your part will be required. Do note, however, that many handheld mixers are not strong enough to incorporate the flour mixture, so that should be done by hand if the motor feels or sounds like it's working too hard.

You can knead dough by hand on a lightly floured work surface. This can take one-and-a-half to two times as long as kneading with a powerful stand mixer. Look and feel for the cues given in the recipe ("smooth and elastic"; "sticky"; etc.) to help you determine when your dough is ready.

ingredients, mixing on low until each addition is incorporated before adding the next portion, and mixing *just* until the batter is smooth.

Most of the yeast-raised Bundts also use the dough hook attachment for your stand mixer, which simulates kneading while giving your back and forearms a break! Ingredients are usually mixed first with the paddle attachment, to form the dough, and then the dough hook is attached to knead the dough for the time stated in the recipe.

FILLING THE PAN

Thin batters can be carefully poured into the prepared pan. For thick batters, spoon large portions into the pan, spreading the batter to pack it so there are no large air pockets. Once all of the batter has been added to the pan, smooth the top with the back of a spoon or a spatula. If you notice any air bubbles in the batter, give the pan a few firm taps on the counter to release them.

BAKING AND TESTING FOR DONENESS

There are only three Bundts in this book that do not require the use of an oven. One is steamed in a pot (page 208), and two are cooked on the stove and chilled in the pan (pages 174 and 210). All of the other Bundts are baked in an oven that has been preheated as instructed in the recipe.

The recipes offer a range in baking time to account for variations in oven temperatures and pan size, shape and color. To prevent overbaking, keep an eye on your Bundt as it nears the last quarter of the baking process, and check for doneness at the earliest time in the range (or even earlier — see "Checking for Doneness," page 10). Most fully baked Bundts have tops that are puffed and golden, and that spring back when lightly pressed. In many cases, a tester inserted in the center of the Bundt should come out clean (test a few different spots around the Bundt), although this doesn't apply to some yeast-raised Bundts (which could still be underbaked even though the tester comes out clean) or savory or filled Bundts (which could have fully baked fillings that still cling to the tester). Use the "press" test and visual tests on these Bundts.

COOLING AND RELEASING THE BUNDT

I know, I know — that Bundt looks and smells so good you want to devour it straight from the oven. Not so fast! While some Bundts are indeed best served warm from the oven, many develop their best flavor and texture when given a little time to cool.

After baking, most Bundts are cooled for 10 to 20 minutes in the pan, giving them time to settle and shrink back a bit from the sides of the pan. After this initial cooling process, place an inverted plate or a cooling rack over the pan and, holding both sides firmly with oven mitts, carefully flip the pan over to release the Bundt.

If, by chance, the Bundt doesn't release with a big "Ta-da!", don't panic! Simply invert the pan again, so that it is back on the counter, as it was when it came out of the oven. Use an offset spatula or a thin knife to carefully loosen around the outer and inner edges of the pan (being careful not to scratch the pan), then invert it once more over the plate or rack. If the Bundt *still* doesn't release, leave it as is for up to 10 minutes and let gravity work its magic.

Still no luck? Just because that Bundt is being stubborn and sticking doesn't mean it's not worth serving. Use a knife to cut the Bundt into sections and carefully pry them out with an offset spatula or the knife. If possible, piece the sections back together and proceed with "strategic glazing" — positioning the glaze to cover any breaks in the cake.

Depending on the recipe, the released Bundt might be eaten warm, it might be glazed, or it might be cooled completely, wrapped and stored overnight before glazing. For many Bundts, wrapping and storing the cake overnight not only develops its flavor, but also tightens the crumb, making the cake easier to slice and serve.

GLAZING

After the cakes have cooled, either a bit or completely (each recipe tells you which), many of them receive a smooth coating of glaze or ganache, which decoratively drips down the sides in a beautiful pattern. Basic confectioners' (icing) sugar glazes come together in a snap and tend to coat the cake on their own when poured over top. These glazes should be thick and glossy but pourable, with a consistency similar to corn syrup.

Thicker glazes, such as a ganache or the Salted Caramel Glaze (page 273), have the consistency of a thick sundae sauce, so some coaxing might be required to nudge the glaze down the sides of the Bundt. After pouring the glaze over the Bundt, firmly tap the plate or wire rack a few times on the counter to draw the glaze down the sides and create an even, glossy texture.

How to Thicken a Thin Glaze

Glazes that are too thin fail to cling to the top and sides of the Bundt and end up in a pool on the plate. If you've accidentally added too much liquid to your glaze mixture, simply whisk in more confectioners' sugar, 2 tbsp (30 mL) at a time, until you've achieved the desired thickness.

STORING

Many Bundts are best served warm from the oven or at room temperature the same day they are baked. But some reach their full flavor and texture potential after they are cooled completely, wrapped tightly in plastic wrap and stored at room temperature or in the refrigerator overnight before they are glazed or served.

Some Bundts are best stored in the refrigerator, including those with glazes or fillings that contain cream, eggs and yogurt, savory Bundts, and Bundts that may lose their structure if kept warm, such as the Retro Cranberry Mold (page 174). For others, such as the "World's Best" Brownie Bundts (page 230), the desired texture is created when they are chilled.

Yeast-based Bundts are generally best stored, tightly covered, at room temperature, as refrigeration can make them go stale quite quickly.

If you happen to have leftovers (not likely!), cakes that have been glazed are best stored in a cake container or something similar, as plastic wrapping is likely to stick to the glaze and peel it off when uncovered.

Make Aheads

If time is an issue and you need to prepare your Bundt in advance, each recipe offers "Make Ahead" advice, including reheating instructions where relevant.

Specialty Bundts

Most of the Bundt recipes you have seen up to now, whether in cookbooks and magazines or on websites, are likely traditional one-bowl cakes with fairly straightforward ingredients and steps. In addition to a collection of basic Bundts, this book includes a wide array of unique recipes, from yeast-raised holiday treats and pull-apart crowd pleasers to beautifully swirled batters and savory casseroles, all of which will (hopefully!) make you regard your Bundt pan as the useful and versatile tool it really is.

YEAST-RAISED BUNDTS

From breakfast pastries like cinnamon rolls to international specialties like buttery Belgian craquelin, yeast-raised Bundt recipes are found in multiple chapters in this book. While working with yeast may be daunting to novice bakers, it's really quite simple, and the method for achieving perfectly puffed dough is similar in every recipe. But when working with yeast Bundts, there are a few key things to keep in mind.

Proofing

At the start of each recipe, the yeast is proofed, or "proven" to still be alive. During this step, warm water or milk and a small amount of sugar are mixed with the active dry yeast. After 5 to 10 minutes, the mixture should be foamy and fragrant. If it isn't, the yeast is no longer active and should be discarded.

Mixing

When mixing ingredients to form a yeast dough, you want to make sure that they are all at least at room temperature, as cold ingredients will retard the proofing process. For most yeast doughs, the ingredients are initially mixed with the paddle attachment to form a dough, after which the dough hook is attached to the mixer to simulate the kneading process.

Look for the kneading time estimates and visual cues given in each recipe to help you determine when your dough is ready for the next step. In many cases, you are looking for dough that is smooth, soft and slightly sticky.

Some recipes offer a range of flour amounts (e.g., 4 to $4\frac{1}{2}$ cups/1 to 1.125 L). If the dough you are kneading is too sticky and is clinging to the dough hook or the sides of the bowl, add flour, 1 tbsp (15 mL) at a time, until the correct texture is achieved.

Rising

The dough is usually left to rise once or twice during a recipe: definitely after it is mixed and possibly after it is arranged in the Bundt pan, before baking. For the initial rise, the dough is transferred to an oiled bowl and turned to coat with oil so that it can be easily turned out of the bowl for the next step. The bowl should be covered in plastic wrap to prevent the dough from drying out during the rising process.

For best rising, dough should be placed in a warm, draft-free location. A good place is in your oven. Turn the oven on at the lowest temperature setting for 30 seconds, just to infuse a bit of warmth, then turn it off before placing the bowl in the oven.

Some dough may take a little less or more time to rise than is estimated in the

How to Warm Water or Milk

Warm water or milk in a small saucepan over medium-low heat, checking with a thermometer until the ideal temperature of 100°F to 110°F (38°C to 43°C) is reached. If using a microwave, heat the water or milk on Medium (50%) power in 10-second intervals, stirring between each interval, until the ideal temperature is reached. If you don't have a thermometer, the liquid should feel hot to the touch, but not so hot that you have to pull your finger away.

recipe, depending on where you live and the temperature or humidity in your kitchen that day. With most recipes, you are looking for the dough to double or almost double in size. Not sure if the dough has risen enough? Use the poke test: simply poke the dough with two fingers (gently, but enough to make an impression). If it holds the indentation, the dough is ready.

After the second rise, the top of the dough should be just above the top of the Bundt pan at most, as it will rise more while baking. For recipes where the dough may rise quite high, lower your oven rack one notch down from the center to keep the top of the Bundt from overbrowning.

Baking

The standard doneness test of inserting a tester into the center to see if it comes out clean will not work for yeast Bundts, as dough that is underbaked can still produce a clean tester. To test these Bundts, look for a puffed, deep golden brown top that springs back when lightly pressed.

Cooling

As with most Bundts, yeast Bundts are cooled for 10 to 20 minutes in the pan before they are inverted onto a plate or wire rack to cool for a few minutes longer (if served warm) or completely (if served at room temperature.) Because they are more visually pleasing to serve "upside down," so that the puffed and textured side of the Bundt is facing up, some Bundts are inverted again onto a second plate or platter immediately after they are removed from the pan.

LAYERED AND SWIRLED BUNDTS

Layered and swirled Bundts are visually stunning and are, therefore, some of my favorites to slice and serve. The bright Rainbow Swirl Bundt (page 124), for example, is always a showstopper! Some of these Bundts feature two or more different batters, while others feature a single batter plus a filling, such as streusel, that is decoratively swirled in before baking.

Layered Bundts seemingly act as your sous-chef and do a bit of work for you, magically creating swirls on their own out of neatly arranged layers during the baking process, due to batters rising at various rates.

For a swirled Bundt, two batters, or a batter and filling, are swirled together with a thin knife or skewer. When swirling a Bundt batter, drag the knife or skewer back and forth in a medium-width "S" motion several times around the pan. This helps to create a pretty swirl without mixing the colors together completely.

For more detailed instructions on making a swirled Bundt, see the variation on page 33.

FILLED BUNDTS

There are two types of filled Bundts in this book. One type is baked with the filling already inside, such as the German Chocolate Bundt (page 92). The other type is filled after the Bundt is baked and cooled, as with the Key Lime Bundt (page 106). In the latter case, the filling is usually too delicate for baking (such as a custard) and would not retain its consistency once in contact with heat.

Baking Bundts with the filling already inside is the less technical approach, whereas the idea of filling Bundts after baking is likely to beg the question "How did you do that?" I'll teach you how in the step-by-step instructions and photos on page 88.

Inverting a Filled Cake

After filling a cake with custard, cream or curd, it's best to invert it onto a serving plate instead of a wire rack. Because sections of the cake have been removed and replaced, the cake should be moved as little as possible so that they don't fall out.

PULL-APART BUNDTS

Whether you're hosting a brunch or a poker night, there is nothing more fun to serve to a crowd than pull-apart Bundts. Yes, each of these Bundts can be sliced and served like traditional Bundts, but it's so much more enjoyable to simply set the Bundt in the center of the table and let people tear pieces away. There is one thing that all of the pull-apart recipes have in common: it is *impossible* to eat just one piece!

Two types of pull-apart Bundts appear in this book:

• **Monkey bread:** Featuring dozens of pieces of pillow-soft yeast dough coated with toppings and arranged in a Bundt pan, monkey bread (also called "*pluck it bread*") can be sweet or savory. Best served warm, these Bundts are inverted directly onto a plate or platter (alongside plenty of napkins for sticky fingers!). Although they are not technically monkey bread, a few recipes in this book, such as Garlic Knot Pull-Apart

Bundt (page 156) or Hot Cross Bun(dt)s (page 168), follow the same basic model, so I've included them in this category.

• **Accordion-style Bundts:** I call some of the pull-apart Bundts "accordion-style" because, after baking, the tops look like a round accordion! These Bundts are arranged in thin vertical layers around the Bundt pan, rather than in pieces. The layers can be pulled apart one at a time or in sections. While assembling accordion Bundts is definitely somewhat of a messy experience, the end results are well worth the extra cleanup! Like monkey bread, these Bundts are best served warm the day they are baked.

The step-by-step instructions and photos on pages 138–141 show you exactly how to make both types of pull-apart Bundts.

Figgy Pudding

PART 2

Beautiful Bundts

Pecan Praline Bundt

Basic Bundts

Basic Bundts, Step by Step

1 Spray the Bundt pan evenly with nonstick baking spray. If using a pan with odd angles or crevices, evenly distribute the spray with a pastry brush.

2 In a medium bowl, whisk the dry ingredients together.

3 In the bowl of a stand mixer fitted with the paddle attachment (or in a large bowl, using a handheld electric mixer), beat sugar and butter or oil until light and fluffy.

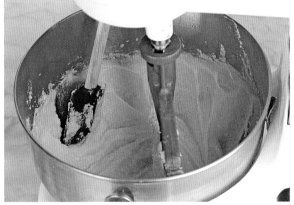

4 Beat in eggs, one at a time, making sure each egg is fully incorporated before adding another and scraping down the sides of the bowl as necessary.

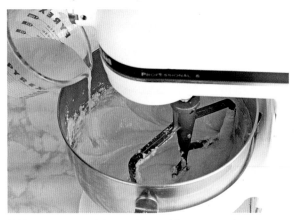

5 Beat in any additional liquid flavorings (such as vanilla or lemon juice), if applicable, until smooth.

6 With the mixer on low speed (or using a rubber spatula), beat or stir in the dry ingredients in 3 additions, alternating with 2 additions of the dairy ingredient, until all is well incorporated.

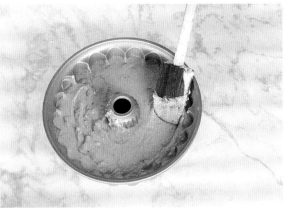

7 Beat or stir in any additional textural ingredients (such as nuts or chocolate chips), if applicable.

8 Pour or spoon batter into the prepared pan and smooth the top with the back of a spoon or a spatula. (Or, to make a swirled Bundt, see the variation, below.)

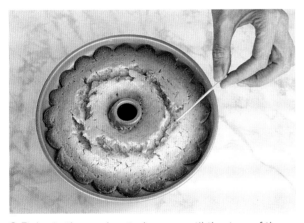

9 Bake in the preheated oven until the top of the Bundt is puffed and golden brown and a tester inserted in the center comes out clean.

10 Let the Bundt cool for 10 minutes, then place an inverted plate or cooling rack over the pan and, holding both sides firmly with oven mitts, carefully flip the pan over to release the Bundt.

Variation: Making a Swirled Bundt

8a Transfer half the batter to another bowl and stir in added ingredients for the second batter. Spoon large dollops (about ¼ cup/60 mL each) of both batters into the prepared pan, alternating between them, until you have used all the batter.

8b Marble the batters by dragging a thin knife or skewer back and forth in a medium-width "S" motion several times around the Bundt. Smooth the top and continue as directed in step 9.

Classic Pound Cake

The original pound cake earned its name because it was made from 1 lb (500 g) each of butter, eggs, flour and sugar. Throughout the years, there have been many variations of this recipe, both its ingredients and technique. This recipe uses smaller quantities, as the full amounts would overflow in a Bundt pan, and adds some flavoring via vanilla extract and a splash of brandy. This cake is best served the next day, with freshly whipped cream and berries or a dusting of confectioners' sugar.

MAKES 12 TO 14 SERVINGS

Tips

If you don't have cake flour, you can make a substitute. See page 16 for more information.

Because eggs are the only leavening in this batter, it is important to carefully follow the mixing times outlined in the method, as they help to create volume in the cake.

This cake is fantastic served sliced and toasted in a skillet or on a griddle, similar to French toast. Lightly butter and heat until golden brown on both sides.

Make Ahead

You can prepare this cake up to 4 days in advance. Tightly wrap the undusted cooled cake in plastic wrap and store at room temperature.

- Preheat oven to 325°F (160°C)
- Minimum 10-cup Bundt pan, sprayed

2½ cups	cake flour, sifted	625 mL
½ tsp	salt	2 mL
1½ cups	unsalted butter, softened	375 mL
1½ cups	granulated sugar	375 mL
6	large eggs, at room temperature	6
3	large egg yolks, at room temperature	3
2 tbsp	brandy	30 mL
2 tsp	vanilla extract	10 mL
	Confectioners' (icing) sugar, sifted	

1. In a medium bowl, whisk together flour and salt.
2. In the stand mixer bowl, beat butter on medium speed for 2 to 3 minutes or until light (see tip). Gradually add granulated sugar and beat for 6 to 8 minutes or until very light and fluffy.
3. In another medium bowl, whisk together eggs, egg yolks, brandy and vanilla.
4. With the mixer on medium speed, add egg mixture to butter mixture in a slow stream and beat for 3 minutes, scraping down the sides of the bowl as needed, until batter is smooth.
5. Using a spatula, gradually fold flour mixture into egg mixture. Transfer batter to prepared pan and smooth the top.
6. Bake in preheated oven for 45 to 65 minutes or until puffed and golden and a tester inserted in the center comes out clean. Let cool in pan for 10 minutes, then carefully invert cake onto a wire rack to cool completely.
7. Wrap cooled cake tightly in plastic wrap and store at room temperature overnight. Serve dusted with confectioners' sugar.

Variations

Incorporate additional flavor into the cake by adding grated zest from 1 lemon or orange, 1 tsp (5 mL) almond extract, or 1 tbsp (15 mL) orange liqueur (such as Grand Marnier) or rum in step 3.

If you don't have brandy, substitute an equal amount of freshly squeezed orange or lemon juice.

Vanilla Bean Bundt with Butter Rum Glaze

Although this cake might seem simple, the resulting flavors are anything but! Grinding an entire plump vanilla bean into the sugar ensures maximum vanilla flavor in every bite. A double dose of butter rum glaze, absorbed through both the bottom and top of the cake, creates a dessert that is rich and light at the same time.

MAKES 12 TO 14 SERVINGS

Tips

If you don't have cake flour, you can make a substitute. See page 16 for more information.

Look for a vanilla bean that is plump, glossy and fragrant, not dry. Store in an airtight container in a cool, dark place.

This cake is best prepared using full-fat sour cream, as it helps to keep it moist, but you can also use a lower-fat version (not fat-free).

Make Ahead

You can prepare this cake up to 4 days in advance. Tightly wrap the cooled glazed cake in plastic wrap or store in a cake container and store at room temperature or in the refrigerator.

- Preheat oven to 325°F (160°C)
- Food processor
- Minimum 10-cup Bundt pan, sprayed

2 cups	cake flour, sifted	500 mL
1 tsp	baking soda	5 mL
½ tsp	salt	2 mL
1	vanilla bean, split and ends trimmed	1
1½ cups	granulated sugar	375 mL
1 cup	unsalted butter, softened	250 mL
4	large eggs, at room temperature	4
2 tbsp	dark rum	30 mL
½ cup	full-fat sour cream	125 mL
1	recipe Butter Rum Glaze (page 275)	1

1. In a medium bowl, whisk together flour, baking soda and salt.
2. In food processor, process vanilla bean and sugar until vanilla is finely ground.
3. In the stand mixer bowl, beat sugar mixture and butter on medium speed for 4 to 5 minutes or until very light. Beat in eggs, one at a time, then beat for 2 minutes. Beat in rum.
4. With the mixer on low speed, alternately beat in flour mixture and sour cream, making three additions of flour and two of sour cream, and beating until incorporated. Transfer batter to prepared pan and smooth the top.
5. Bake in preheated oven for 40 to 55 minutes or until golden brown and puffed and a tester inserted in the center comes out clean.
6. Using a pastry brush, brush the cake with half the warm glaze and let stand for 10 minutes. Carefully invert cake onto a wire rack set over a baking sheet or paper towels.
7. Using a toothpick or the tines of a fork, poke 15 to 20 small holes in the top of the cake. Drizzle or brush the remaining glaze over the top of the cake. Let cool completely. Wrap cake tightly in plastic wrap and store at room temperature overnight before serving.

Variation

You can replace the rum with an equal amount of freshly squeezed orange juice in both the cake and glaze.

Rich Chocolate Bundt

Your search for *the* chocolate Bundt can stop with this recipe! I know that's a big statement, but I've been making a variation of this cake, in layer and sheet forms, for years, and it never fails to get rave reviews — and requests for the recipe! Using oil instead of butter helps to keep the cake extra-moist, and the addition of espresso powder provides a boost to the chocolate flavor. Although this cake stands well on its own (or maybe with a scoop of ice cream), true chocoholics will love it covered with a dense chocolate glaze.

MAKES 12 TO 14 SERVINGS

Tips

If you can't find espresso powder, use ¾ cup (175 mL) strong brewed coffee in place of the espresso powder and hot water.

It's important to sift cocoa powder before adding to dry ingredients, to avoid bitter-tasting clumps.

For best results, wrap the cooled cake tightly in plastic wrap and store at room temperature or in the refrigerator overnight before glazing.

Refrigerating the glazed cake creates a fudgy texture that tastes great alongside a scoop of vanilla ice cream!

Make Ahead

You can prepare this cake up to 2 days in advance. Store the cooled glazed cake in a cake container at room temperature or in the refrigerator.

- Preheat oven to 325°F (160°C)
- Minimum 10-cup Bundt pan, sprayed

2 tsp	espresso powder (see tip)	10 mL
¾ cup	hot water	175 mL
2 cups	all-purpose flour	500 mL
1 cup	unsweetened cocoa powder, sifted	250 mL
1 tsp	salt	5 mL
½ tsp	baking powder	2 mL
½ tsp	baking soda	2 mL
2½ cups	granulated sugar	625 mL
⅔ cup	vegetable oil	150 mL
5	large eggs, at room temperature	5
2 tsp	vanilla extract	10 mL
1¼ cups	sour cream (not fat-free)	300 mL
1	recipe Chocolate Glaze (page 270)	1

1. In a small bowl, stir together espresso powder and hot water.
2. In a medium bowl, whisk together flour, cocoa, salt, baking powder and baking soda.
3. In the stand mixer bowl, beat sugar and oil on medium speed for 2 minutes. Beat in eggs, one at a time. Beat in vanilla and espresso mixture.
4. With the mixer on low speed, alternately beat in flour mixture and sour cream, making three additions of flour and two of sour cream, and beating until incorporated. Transfer batter to prepared pan and smooth the top. Tap the pan on the counter a few times to remove any air bubbles.
5. Bake in preheated oven for 50 to 60 minutes or until puffed and firm and a tester inserted in the center comes out with only a few moist crumbs attached. Let cool in pan for 15 minutes, then carefully invert cake onto a wire rack to cool completely (see tip).
6. Pour the slightly cooled glaze over the cooled cake, using an offset spatula or knife to coax it down the sides if necessary. Let glaze cool completely or refrigerate cake to set the glaze before serving.

Chocolate Chip Cream Cheese Bundt

I'll be the first to admit I'm not a huge fan of cream cheese (I'm a butter-and-jam-on-a-bagel girl!), except when it comes to desserts. Incorporating it into the batter results in a dense, rich and beautiful cake that is textbook old-fashioned comfort food. The key to success with this cake is making sure all of the ingredients — especially the cream cheese — are well incorporated. It takes a bit longer to bake than other Bundts, but the end result is well worth the wait!

MAKES 12 TO 14 SERVINGS

Tips

Use full-fat cream cheese for this recipe, as lower-fat varieties will affect the texture and moisture level of the finished cake.

Wider Bundt pans will bake the batter more quickly, while cakes in narrower, deeper pans will need more time to bake through.

For best results, wrap the cooled cake tightly in plastic wrap and store at room temperature or in the refrigerator overnight before glazing.

Make Ahead

You can prepare this cake up to 2 days in advance. Store the cooled glazed cake in a cake container at room temperature or in the refrigerator.

- **Preheat oven to 325°F (160°C)**
- **Minimum 10-cup Bundt pan, sprayed**

2½ cups	cake flour, sifted	625 mL
1 tsp	baking powder	5 mL
½ tsp	salt	2 mL
2¼ cups	granulated sugar	560 mL
1¼ cups	unsalted butter, softened	300 mL
8 oz	brick-style cream cheese, softened (see tip)	250 g
5	large eggs, at room temperature	5
2 tsp	vanilla extract	10 mL
1½ cups	dark or semisweet chocolate chips	375 mL
1	recipe Cream Cheese Glaze (page 276)	1

1. In a medium bowl, whisk together flour, baking powder and salt.

2. In the stand mixer bowl, beat sugar, butter and cream cheese on medium speed for 4 minutes or until light and very fluffy. Beat in eggs, one at a time then beat for 4 minutes. Beat in vanilla.

3. With the mixer on medium-low speed, beat in flour mixture in three additions until fully incorporated. Beat in chocolate chips. Transfer batter to prepared pan and smooth the top.

4. Bake in preheated oven for 45 to 65 minutes or until puffed, firm and deep golden brown and a tester inserted in the center comes out clean. Let cool in pan for 15 minutes, then carefully invert cake onto a wire rack to cool completely (see tip).

5. Pour glaze over the cooled cake, letting it drip down the sides. Let glaze set for at least 20 minutes before serving.

Variation

Replace chocolate chips with other chip flavors, such as peanut butter or butterscotch. Use chocolate chunks or freshly chopped chocolate for a less uniform appearance.

Lemon Lover's Bundt

This bright, cheerful Bundt is a variation on the popular lemon loaf pound cake we used to make at my bakery. The tangy citrus glaze is the perfect complement to the dense, moist cake. With a Meyer lemon tree in our backyard that produces hundreds of lemons each year, I'm happy to have plenty of "excuses" to make this cake, over and over again.

MAKES 12 TO 14 SERVINGS

Tips

If you don't have cake flour, you can make a substitute. See page 16 for more information.

Meyer lemons and regular lemons can be used interchangeably in this recipe. Meyer lemons, with their deep yellow to orange color and sweeter, less acidic flavor, are usually available between December and May.

One medium lemon yields about 1 tbsp (15 mL) grated zest and 2 to 3 tbsp (15 to 45 mL) juice. You'll need 5 to 7 lemons for this recipe. Extra zest can be wrapped well and frozen for up to 6 months.

Make Ahead

You can prepare this cake up to 2 days in advance. Store the cooled glazed cake in a cake container at room temperature or in the refrigerator.

- Preheat oven to 325°F (160°C)
- Minimum 10-cup Bundt pan, sprayed

2½ cups	cake flour, sifted	625 mL
½ tsp	baking soda	2 mL
½ tsp	salt	2 mL
¼ tsp	baking powder	1 mL
1 cup	unsalted butter, softened	250 mL
1¾ cups	granulated sugar	425 mL
5	large eggs, at room temperature	5
2 tbsp	grated lemon zest (see tip)	30 mL
½ cup	freshly squeezed lemon juice	125 mL
1 tsp	vanilla extract	5 mL
1 cup	sour cream (not fat-free)	250 mL
1	recipe Lemon Glaze (page 272)	1

1. In a medium bowl, whisk together flour, baking soda, salt and baking powder.

2. In the stand mixer bowl, beat butter on medium speed for 2 minutes or until light. Gradually add sugar and beat for 3 to 4 minutes or until mixture is very fluffy. Beat in eggs, one at a time, then beat for 2 minutes. Beat in lemon zest, lemon juice and vanilla.

3. With the mixer on low speed, alternately beat in flour mixture and sour cream, making three additions of flour and two of sour cream, and beating until well incorporated. Transfer batter to prepared pan and smooth the top.

4. Bake in preheated oven for 45 to 60 minutes or until puffed and a tester inserted in the center comes out clean. Let cool in pan for 15 minutes, then carefully invert cake onto a wire rack to cool completely (see last tip, page 40).

5. Pour glaze over the cooled cake, letting it drip down the sides. Let glaze set for at least 15 minutes before serving.

Triple Coconut Bundt

As the recipe name indicates, this Bundt boasts three layers of coconut goodness through a glaze, a soaking syrup and the cake itself (which, on its own, contains three types of coconut). Topped with a sprinkling of lightly toasted large-flake coconut, this beautiful white cake would be the perfect dessert for a dinner party or a bridal or baby shower.

MAKES 12 TO 14 SERVINGS

Tips

If you don't have sticks of butter with tablespoon (15 mL) markings, measure ¾ cup + 2 tbsp to equal 14 tbsp (205 mL).

To toast coconut, spread in an even layer on a baking sheet and bake in a 300°F (150°C) oven, stirring occasionally, for 8 to 10 minutes or until golden brown. Watch carefully, as coconut can burn quickly.

Full-fat coconut milk is the best option for this recipe, as it creates a thicker glaze, but lower-fat coconut milk can be used in a pinch. Whisk the can of coconut milk well before measuring to make sure you evenly blend the cream and the milk, which tend to separate in the can.

Look for unsweetened large-flake coconut flakes in the baking or bulk bins sections of your grocery store or natural foods store.

- Preheat oven to 350°F (180°C); dark pan, 325°F (160°C)
- Minimum 10-cup Bundt pan, sprayed

CAKE

2½ cups	cake flour, sifted	625 mL
2 tsp	baking powder	10 mL
½ tsp	salt	2 mL
1¼ cups	granulated sugar	300 mL
14 tbsp	unsalted butter, softened (see tip)	205 mL
3	large eggs, at room temperature	3
2	large egg whites, at room temperature	2
1 cup	cream of coconut (see tip, page 94)	250 mL
1 tsp	coconut extract	5 mL
1 tsp	vanilla extract	5 mL
½ cup	buttermilk	125 mL
1 cup	lightly toasted sweetened shredded coconut	250 mL

SOAKING SYRUP

2 tbsp	granulated sugar	30 mL
¼ cup	full-fat coconut milk (see tip)	60 mL
1	recipe Coconut Glaze (page 272)	1
½ cup	lightly toasted unsweetened large-flake coconut (optional)	125 mL

1. *Cake:* In a medium bowl, whisk together flour, baking powder and salt.

2. In the stand mixer bowl, beat sugar and butter on medium speed for 5 minutes or until very light and fluffy.

3. In another medium bowl, whisk together eggs and egg whites. Whisk in cream of coconut, coconut extract and vanilla.

4. With the mixer on low speed, slowly add egg mixture to the butter mixture, stopping to scrape down the sides of the bowl as necessary, until fully incorporated. Beat for 1 minute.

5. With the mixer still on low speed, alternately beat in flour mixture and buttermilk, making three additions of flour and two of buttermilk, and beating until incorporated. Beat in coconut. Transfer batter to prepared pan and smooth the top.

6. Bake in preheated oven for 45 to 60 minutes or until puffed and golden and a tester inserted in the center comes out clean. Let cool in pan while preparing soaking syrup.

7. *Soaking Syrup:* In a small microwave-safe bowl, combine sugar and coconut milk. Microwave on High in 15-second increments, stirring between each, until sugar is dissolved.

Make Ahead

You can prepare this cake up to 3 days in advance. Store the cooled glazed cake in a cake container at room temperature or in the refrigerator.

8. Using a pastry brush, brush the warm cake evenly with half the syrup. Let cool for 10 minutes, then carefully invert cake onto a wire rack and brush the top with the remaining syrup. Let cool completely (see last tip, page 46).

9. Pour glaze over the cake, letting it drip down the sides. Garnish with large-flake coconut (if using) and let stand for at least 15 minutes before serving.

Variation

If you can't find unsweetened large-flake coconut flakes, use sweetened regular flaked or shredded coconut instead.

Blueberry-Glazed Maple Walnut Bundt

My husband grew up in Vermont, where his father continues to make his own maple syrup every spring, so we have an enviably ample supply for baking and breakfasts. The flavors of this Bundt were inspired by Sunday morning blueberry pancakes: a surprisingly simple fresh blueberry glaze makes a striking contrast to the lightly spiced maple walnut Bundt. This is the perfect excuse to have cake for breakfast — not that you need an excuse!

MAKES 12 TO 14 SERVINGS

Tips

Be sure to use pure maple syrup — not imitation pancake or table syrup. Look for Grade A syrup with a darker and stronger flavor, as it will have the most concentrated maple flavor.

For best results, wrap the cooled cake tightly in plastic wrap and store at room temperature or in the refrigerator overnight before glazing.

Make Ahead

You can prepare this cake up to 1 day in advance. Store the cooled glazed cake in a cake container at room temperature or in the refrigerator.

- Preheat oven to 350°F (180°C); dark pan, 325°F (160°C)
- Minimum 10-cup Bundt pan, sprayed

2¼ cups	cake flour, sifted	560 mL
1 tsp	baking powder	5 mL
½ tsp	baking soda	2 mL
½ tsp	salt	2 mL
½ tsp	ground cinnamon	2 mL
¾ cup	packed light brown sugar	175 mL
1 cup	unsalted butter, softened	250 mL
¾ cup	pure maple syrup (see tip)	175 mL
3	large eggs, at room temperature	3
½ tsp	maple extract	2 mL
½ tsp	vanilla extract	2 mL
1 cup	buttermilk	250 mL
1 cup	chopped walnuts	250 mL
1	recipe Blueberry Glaze (page 272)	1

1. In a medium bowl, whisk together flour, baking powder, baking soda, salt and cinnamon.

2. In the stand mixer bowl, beat brown sugar and butter on medium speed for 3 minutes or until light and fluffy. Beat in maple syrup. Beat in eggs, one at a time. Beat in maple extract and vanilla.

3. With the mixer on low speed, alternately beat in flour mixture and buttermilk, making three additions of flour and two of buttermilk, and beating until incorporated. Beat in walnuts. Transfer batter to prepared pan and smooth the top.

4. Bake in preheated oven for 45 to 55 minutes or until browned and a tester inserted in the center comes out clean. Let cool in pan for 15 minutes, then carefully invert cake onto a wire rack to cool completely (see tip).

5. Pour glaze over the cooled cake, letting it drip down the sides. Let glaze set for at least 20 minutes before serving.

Variation

Add up to 1 tsp (5 mL) maple extract for a more pronounced maple flavor, until the batter has your preferred level of "maple-ness."

Pistachio Bundt with Coconut Glaze

This Bundt boasts plenty of pistachios, despite having a color closer to white. Finely grinding most of the pistachios to a powder creates a fragrant and tender cake that, when topped with sweet coconut glaze, is a great choice for spring parties and celebrations.

MAKES 12 TO 14 SERVINGS

Tips

The lightly salted pistachios add a nice contrast to the sweetness of the cake, but unsalted pistachios can also be used if you are concerned about sodium levels or prefer a less salty-sweet flavor.

Use a clean, dry bowl in step 5 to ensure the egg whites firm up as they are beaten. For best results, use a stainless steel, copper or glass bowl, as plastic and wooden bowls can absorb oils and water, which can inhibit the whipping process. "Firm" peaks means that the whites stand up on their own and don't bend over when the beater is lifted from the bowl. Also make sure your beaters are clean and oil-free before whipping.

Make Ahead

You can prepare this cake up to 2 days in advance. Store the cooled glazed cake in a cake container at room temperature.

- Preheat oven to 350°F (180°C); dark pan, 325°F (160°C)
- Food processor
- Handheld electric mixer
- Minimum 10-cup Bundt pan, sprayed

1½ cups	lightly salted shelled pistachios, divided	375 mL
2¼ cups	cake flour, sifted	560 mL
2 tsp	baking powder	10 mL
½ tsp	baking soda	2 mL
½ tsp	salt	2 mL
1¾ cups	granulated sugar	425 mL
1 cup	unsalted butter, softened	250 mL
2 tsp	vanilla extract	10 mL
1¼ cups	buttermilk	300 mL
4	large egg whites, at room temperature	4
2 tbsp	granulated sugar	30 mL
1	recipe Coconut Glaze (page 272)	1
¼ cup	chopped pistachios (optional)	60 mL

1. In food processor, finely grind 1¼ cups (300 mL) pistachios. Using a knife, chop the remaining pistachios and set aside.
2. In a medium bowl, whisk together flour, baking powder, baking soda, salt and ground pistachios.
3. In the stand mixer bowl, beat 1¾ cups (425 mL) sugar and butter on medium speed for 3 minutes or until light and fluffy. Beat in vanilla.
4. With the mixer on low speed, alternately beat in flour mixture and buttermilk, making three additions of flour and two of buttermilk, and beating until incorporated.
5. In another medium bowl (see tip), using the handheld mixer, beat egg whites with 2 tbsp (30 mL) sugar on medium-low speed until foamy. Gradually increase to high speed and beat until firm peaks form.
6. Using a spatula, carefully fold egg whites into batter in three additions. Fold in chopped pistachios. Transfer batter to prepared pan and smooth the top.
7. Bake in preheated oven for 45 to 60 minutes or until puffed and browned and a tester inserted in the center comes out clean. Let cool in pan for 15 minutes, then carefully invert cake onto a wire rack to cool completely (see last tip, page 46).
8. Pour glaze over the cooled cake, letting it drip down the sides. Garnish with additional chopped pistachios, if desired. Let glaze set for at least 20 minutes before serving.

Peach Jam Buttermilk Bundt

I can't eat enough peaches while they are in season! I've been known to purchase several flats at a time, which usually disappear within the week. I blend peaches into breakfast smoothies, slice them on top of salads and even grill them for a simple dessert. I also make peach jam, which is one of the two ways that my favorite fruit is featured in this simple Southern-inspired cake — which just screams for a glass of sweet tea! The jam replaces some of the regular sugar and elevates the flavor of the diced ripe peaches. Garnish this cake with the thick vanilla glaze, or simply with a dusting of confectioners' sugar.

MAKES 12 TO 14 SERVINGS

Tips

Look for fragrant peaches that are only slightly soft so that they hold their shape during baking. Store peaches at room temperature, never in the refrigerator — as this gives them a mealy texture.

Use a clean, dry bowl in step 4 to ensure the egg whites firm up as they are beaten. For best results, use a stainless steel, copper or glass bowl, as plastic and wooden bowls can absorb oils and water, which can inhibit the whipping process. Also make sure your beaters are clean and oil-free before whipping.

Make Ahead

You can prepare this cake up to 2 days in advance. Store the cooled glazed cake in a cake container at room temperature or in the refrigerator.

- Preheat oven to 350°F (180°C); dark pan, 325°F (160°C)
- Handheld electric mixer
- Minimum 10-cup Bundt pan, sprayed

2¼ cups	all-purpose flour	560 mL
1 tsp	baking soda	5 mL
1 tsp	salt	5 mL
1 tsp	ground cinnamon	5 mL
1 cup	granulated sugar	250 mL
1 cup	unsalted butter, softened	250 mL
4	large eggs, at room temperature, separated	4
2 tbsp	granulated sugar	30 mL
¾ cup	buttermilk	175 mL
¾ cup	peach jam	175 mL
1½ cups	diced peeled peaches	375 mL
1	recipe Vanilla Glaze (page 271)	1

1. In a medium bowl, whisk together flour, baking soda, salt and cinnamon.
2. In the stand mixer bowl, beat 1 cup (250 mL) sugar and butter on medium speed for 3 to 4 minutes or until light and fluffy. Add egg yolks and beat until incorporated.
3. With the mixer on low speed, alternately beat in flour mixture and buttermilk, making three additions of flour and two of buttermilk, and beating until well incorporated. Beat in peach jam.
4. In another medium bowl (see tip), using the handheld mixer, beat egg whites with 2 tbsp (30 mL) sugar on medium-low speed until foamy. Gradually increase to high speed and beat until firm peaks form.
5. Using a spatula, carefully fold egg whites into batter in three additions. Fold in chopped peaches. Transfer batter to prepared pan and smooth the top.
6. Bake in preheated oven for 50 to 60 minutes or until puffed and golden and a tester inserted in the center comes out clean. Let cool in pan for 15 minutes, then carefully invert cake onto a wire rack to cool completely (see last tip, page 46).
7. Pour glaze over the cooled cake, letting it drip down the sides. Let glaze set for at least 20 minutes before serving.

Berries and Yogurt Parfait Bundt

I have my own line of granola products, so I have spent plenty of time thinking about granola's versatility and different ways that it can be used in baking. Of course, for this book, I had to incorporate granola into at least one Bundt! This colorful cake was inspired by the popular yogurt parfaits that I used to sell at my bakery — layers of creamy yogurt, fresh berries and vanilla-orange almond granola. Using rich Greek yogurt makes this cake extra moist. A generous 4 cups (1 L) of berries ensures there are some in every bite, along with a little crunchy sweetness from granola clusters.

MAKES 12 TO
14 SERVINGS

Tips

Use a chunky or clustered granola without too many bells and whistles (fruit and nuts, for example). A simple vanilla-almond or honey granola would work well.

The best berries for this recipe are a mixture of raspberries, blueberries and blackberries. Gently fold in berries to ensure that they don't break up too much and color the batter (a little bit is expected). Frozen fruit should not be used as a substitute for fresh.

For best results, wrap the cooled cake tightly in plastic wrap and store in the refrigerator overnight before dusting with confectioners' sugar.

Make Ahead

You can prepare this cake up to 3 days in advance. Store the dusted cake in a cake container in the refrigerator.

- Preheat oven to 350°F (180°C); dark pan, 325°F (160°C)
- Minimum 10-cup Bundt pan, sprayed

2½ cups	cake flour, sifted, divided	625 mL
2 tsp	baking powder	10 mL
½ tsp	salt	2 mL
2 cups	granulated sugar	500 mL
1 cup	unsalted butter, softened	250 mL
3	large eggs, at room temperature	3
½ tsp	almond extract	2 mL
¾ cup	plain whole milk Greek yogurt	175 mL
1 cup	granola	250 mL
4 cups	mixed fresh berries (see tip)	1 L
	Confectioners' (icing) sugar (optional)	

1. In a medium bowl, whisk together 2¼ cups (560 mL) flour, baking powder and salt.

2. In the stand mixer bowl, beat granulated sugar and butter on medium speed for 3 minutes or until light and fluffy. Beat in eggs, one at a time. Add almond extract and beat for 3 minutes.

3. With the mixer on low speed, alternately beat in flour mixture and yogurt, making three additions of flour and two of yogurt, and beating until incorporated. Beat in granola.

4. In another medium bowl, toss berries with the remaining flour. Using a spatula, carefully fold berries into batter (try not to let them break into smaller pieces). Transfer batter to prepared pan and smooth the top.

5. Bake in preheated oven for 45 to 65 minutes or until deep golden brown and a tester inserted in the center comes out clean. Let cool in pan for 15 minutes, then carefully invert it onto a wire rack to cool completely (see tip). If desired, dust with confectioners' sugar before serving.

Variation

You can replace the whole-milk Greek yogurt in this recipe with low-fat, but I don't recommend fat-free. If you can't find Greek yogurt, you can use plain or vanilla-flavored full-fat yogurt instead. Flavored yogurts usually contain added sugar, so the resulting cake will likely taste sweeter.

Carrot Cake Bundt with White Chocolate Cream Cheese Frosting

There are as many carrot cake recipes in cookbooks and online as there are carats at Cartier — and I think I've tried most of them (all in the name of research, of course). This recipe is a compilation of my favorite parts from several of my favorite recipes. To me, a good carrot cake needs spice, so there is plenty of that here. It also needs to be moist, so I've used oil instead of butter, a whopping 3 cups (750 mL) carrots, and some shredded coconut for good measure. Walnuts add crunch, and a luxurious white chocolate cream cheese glaze takes this cake over the top. This Bundt will have everyone eating their vegetables, without complaining!

MAKES 12 TO 14 SERVINGS

Tip

To make this cake look extra-festive, decorate it with candied carrot curls: Use a peeler to create thin lengthwise strips of carrot and simmer them in a small saucepan of equal parts granulated sugar and water for 15 minutes. Transfer drained strips to a baking sheet lined with parchment paper. Bake in a 250°F (120°C) oven for 25 minutes, until dry but flexible. Wind strips around a chopstick or skewer, slip them off and return to lined baking sheet. Bake for 20 to 30 minutes or until crisp. Let cool completely. Lightly press into top of cake before frosting is set.

Make Ahead

You can prepare this cake up to 2 days in advance. Store the frosted cake in a cake container in the refrigerator.

- Preheat oven to 350°F (180°C); dark pan, 325°F (160°C)
- Minimum 10-cup Bundt pan, sprayed

2¼ cups	all-purpose flour	560 mL
1½ tsp	baking powder	7 mL
1 tsp	salt	5 mL
½ tsp	baking soda	2 mL
2 tsp	ground cinnamon	10 mL
½ tsp	ground nutmeg	2 mL
¼ tsp	ground cloves	1 mL
1 cup	granulated sugar	250 mL
1 cup	packed light brown sugar	250 mL
1¼ cups	vegetable oil	300 mL
4	large eggs, at room temperature	4
3 cups	grated carrots	750 mL
1 cup	sweetened shredded coconut	250 mL
1 cup	chopped toasted walnuts (see tip, page 72)	250 mL
1	recipe White Chocolate Cream Cheese Frosting (page 278)	1

1. In a medium bowl, whisk together flour, baking powder, salt, baking soda, cinnamon, nutmeg and cloves.
2. In the stand mixer bowl, beat granulated sugar, brown sugar and oil on medium speed until combined. Beat in eggs, one at a time, then beat for 3 minutes.
3. With the mixer on low speed, beat in flour mixture in three additions until incorporated. Using a spatula, fold in carrots, coconut and walnuts. Transfer batter to prepared pan and smooth the top.
4. Bake in preheated oven for 45 to 60 minutes or until puffed and golden and a tester inserted in the center comes out clean. Let cool in pan for 15 minutes, then carefully invert cake onto a wire rack to cool completely (see last tip, page 58).
5. Pour frosting over the cooled cake, letting it drip down the sides. Let frosting set for at least 20 minutes before serving.

Pecan Praline Bundt

This Bundt, a tender buttermilk cake dotted with spiced bourbon pecans, is loosely based on Southern pecan pralines, drizzled with a decadent salted, spiked caramel glaze. (You should probably make a double batch of this, since you'll want extra to serve over ice cream.)

MAKES 12 TO 14 SERVINGS

Tips

Use a clean, dry bowl in step 6 to ensure the egg whites firm up as they are beaten. For best results, use a stainless steel, copper or glass bowl, as plastic and wooden bowls can absorb oils and water, which can inhibit the whipping process. "Firm" peaks means that the whites stand up on their own and don't bend over when the beater is lifted from the bowl. Also make sure your beaters are clean and oil-free before whipping.

Wider Bundt pans will bake the batter more quickly, while cakes in narrower, deeper pans will need more time to bake through.

- Preheat oven to 350°F (180°C); dark pan, 325°F (160°C)
- Baking sheet, lined with parchment paper or sprayed with nonstick baking spray
- Handheld electric mixer
- Minimum 10-cup Bundt pan, sprayed

SPICED PECANS

½ cup	packed dark brown sugar	125 mL
1 tbsp	ground cinnamon	15 mL
½ tsp	salt	2 mL
6 tbsp	unsalted butter, melted	90 mL
1 tbsp	bourbon	15 mL
2¼ cups	pecan halves	560 mL

CAKE

3 cups	cake flour, sifted	750 mL
2 tsp	baking powder	10 mL
1 tsp	salt	5 mL
½ tsp	baking soda	2 mL
1¾ cups	granulated sugar	425 mL
1 cup	unsalted butter, softened	250 mL
4	large eggs, at room temperature, separated	4
2 tbsp	granulated sugar	30 mL
1 tbsp	bourbon	15 mL
2 tsp	vanilla extract	10 mL
1¼ cups	buttermilk	300 mL
1	recipe Bourbon Caramel Glaze (variation, page 273)	1

1. *Spiced Pecans:* In a medium bowl, combine brown sugar, cinnamon, salt, butter and bourbon. Add pecans and toss to coat. Spread mixture evenly on prepared baking sheet.

2. Bake in preheated oven for 20 to 25 minutes, stirring halfway through, until fragrant and caramelized. Let pecans cool completely in pan, then chop (leave oven on).

3. *Cake:* In another medium bowl, whisk together flour, baking powder, salt and baking soda.

4. In the stand mixer bowl, beat 1¾ cups (425 mL) sugar and butter on medium speed for 3 minutes or until light and fluffy. Beat in eggs yolks, one at a time. Beat in bourbon and vanilla.

5. With the mixer on low speed, alternately beat in flour mixture and buttermilk, making three additions of flour and two of buttermilk, and beating until incorporated.

Make Ahead

You can prepare the spiced pecans up to 1 week in advance. Store in a resealable plastic storage bag or cookie tin at room temperature.

You can prepare the whole cake recipe up to 1 day in advance. Store the glazed cake in a cake container in the refrigerator.

6. In another medium bowl (see tip), using the handheld mixer, beat egg whites with 2 tbsp (30 mL) sugar on medium-low speed until foamy. Gradually increase speed to high and beat until firm peaks form.

7. Using a spatula, carefully fold egg whites into batter in three additions. Fold in 2 cups (500 mL) spiced pecans. Transfer batter to prepared pan and smooth the top.

8. Bake in preheated oven for 45 to 65 minutes or until a tester inserted in the center comes out clean. Let cool in pan for 15 minutes, then carefully invert cake onto a wire rack to cool completely (see last tip, page 58).

9. Pour glaze over the cooled cake, letting it drip down the sides. Garnish with the remaining spiced pecans. Let glaze set for at least 30 minutes before serving.

Variation

The bourbon in this recipe can be replaced with an equal amount of rum, whiskey or brandy.

Decadent Vegan Chocolate Bundt

After creating this recipe, I served this Bundt to my husband (definitely not a vegan!) without telling him it was vegan. As he polished off the last bite, I thought, "Success!" With its deep chocolate flavor and moist, fluffy texture, this cake is proof that just because a dessert falls into the "vegan" category, it doesn't mean that it can't also be in the "decadent" category. I love to chill this cake after glazing, which makes it taste extra-chocolaty, and serve slices with a scoop of coconut milk ice cream.

MAKES 12 TO 14 SERVINGS

Tips

The cider vinegar acts as an acid that reacts with the baking soda, to give the batter a lift as it bakes. You will not taste it in the finished product, I promise!

Whisk the can of coconut milk well before measuring to make sure you evenly blend the cream and the milk, which tend to separate in the can.

For best results, wrap the cooled cake tightly in plastic wrap and store at room temperature or in the refrigerator overnight before glazing.

Make Ahead

You can prepare this cake up to 2 days in advance. Store the glazed cake in a cake container at room temperature or in the refrigerator.

- Preheat oven to 350°F (180°C); dark pan, 325°F (160°C)
- Minimum 10-cup Bundt pan, sprayed

2½ cups	all-purpose flour	625 mL
1 cup	unsweetened cocoa powder, sifted	250 mL
1 tsp	baking powder	5 mL
1 tsp	baking soda	5 mL
½ tsp	salt	2 mL
2 cups	granulated sugar	500 mL
¾ cup	vegetable oil	175 mL
½ cup	strong brewed coffee, at room temperature	125 mL
2 tsp	vanilla extract	10 mL
2 tsp	cider vinegar	10 mL
1 cup	full-fat coconut milk	250 mL
1	recipe Vegan Chocolate Glaze (page 270)	1

1. In a medium bowl, whisk together flour, cocoa, baking powder, baking soda and salt.
2. In the stand mixer bowl, beat sugar and oil on medium speed until combined. Beat in coffee, vanilla and vinegar.
3. With the mixer on low speed, alternately beat in flour mixture and coconut milk, making three additions of flour and two of coconut milk, and beating until incorporated. Transfer batter to prepared pan and smooth the top.
4. Bake in preheated oven for 40 to 55 minutes or until a tester inserted in the center comes out clean. Let cool in pan for 15 minutes, then carefully invert cake onto a wire rack to cool completely (see tip).
5. Pour glaze over the cooled cake, letting it drip down the sides. Let glaze set for at least 20 minutes before serving.

Variation

You can replace the coconut milk with unsweetened plain almond milk, although the coconut milk provides a slightly richer, more moist texture due to its higher fat content.

Gluten-Free Banana Chocolate Bundt

I created this recipe for a friend of mine, whose husband follows a gluten-free diet. My standard gluten-free flour blend creates a dense, spiced cake with plenty of banana flavor in every bite. The rich ganache glaze is literally the icing on the cake, and it tastes just as great chilled as it does at room temperature.

MAKES 12 TO
14 SERVINGS

Tips

For best results, purée bananas in a food processor until smooth. Mashing bananas by hand often leaves several lumps, so the banana flavor isn't evenly distributed.

Most grocery stores now have a section of gluten-free foods, which is where you can find many of the ingredients in this recipe. Natural food stores are also a good place to look.

For best results, wrap the cooled cake tightly in plastic wrap and store at room temperature or in the refrigerator overnight before glazing.

Make Ahead

You can prepare this cake up to 2 days in advance. Store the glazed cake in a cake container at room temperature or in the refrigerator. (I prefer chilled, as it creates a fudgy texture for the glaze!)

- Preheat oven to 350°F (180°C); dark pan, 325°F (160°C)
- Minimum 12-cup Bundt pan, sprayed

1½ cups	brown rice flour	375 mL
⅔ cup	sweet white rice flour	150 mL
⅔ cup	potato starch	150 mL
½ cup	almond flour	125 mL
6 tbsp	tapioca starch	90 mL
1½ tsp	baking powder	7 mL
1 tsp	xanthan gum	5 mL
1 tsp	baking soda	5 mL
1 tsp	ground cinnamon	5 mL
½ tsp	ground cardamom	2 mL
½ tsp	ground ginger	2 mL
½ tsp	salt	2 mL
1 cup	granulated sugar	250 mL
½ cup	packed light brown sugar	125 mL
¾ cup	unsalted butter, softened	175 mL
3 tbsp	vegetable oil	45 mL
3	large eggs, at room temperature	3
1½ cups	puréed or mashed ripe bananas (see tip)	375 mL
2 tsp	vanilla extract	10 mL
½ cup	sour cream (not fat-free)	125 mL
1½ cups	semisweet or dark chocolate chunks	375 mL
1	recipe Chocolate Glaze (page 270)	1

1. In a large bowl, whisk brown rice flour, sweet white rice flour, potato starch, almond flour, tapioca starch, baking powder, xanthan gum, baking soda, cinnamon, cardamom, ginger and salt.

2. In the stand mixer bowl, beat granulated sugar, brown sugar, butter and oil on medium speed for 3 minutes or until light and fluffy. Beat in eggs, one at a time. Beat in bananas and vanilla.

3. With the mixer on low speed, alternately beat in flour mixture and sour cream, making three additions of flour and two of sour cream, and beating until incorporated. Beat in chocolate chunks. Transfer batter to prepared pan and smooth the top.

4. Bake in preheated oven for 60 to 70 minutes or until puffed and golden and a tester inserted in the center comes out clean. Let cool in pan for 15 minutes, then carefully invert cake onto a wire rack to cool completely (see tip).

5. Pour glaze over the cooled cake, letting it drip down the sides. Let glaze set for at least 20 minutes before serving.

Glazed Cinnamon-Raisin Roll Bundt

Breakfast and Brunch Bundts

Lemon-Glazed Blueberry Streusel

When I mentioned that I was developing recipes for a Bundt cookbook, a woman in my husband's office said, "Are you going to have a lemon-blueberry one in there? You *must* have a lemon-blueberry one in there!" Indeed, the popular flavor combination was near the top of my list and is featured in this almond-and-streusel-filled Bundt that fits in just as well at breakfast or brunch as it does for a not-too-sweet dessert. I love to drizzle a generous amount of the tart lemon glaze over the top, so that you get a taste of it in every bite.

MAKES 10 TO 12 SERVINGS

Tips

It's best to use fresh blueberries, not frozen, in this recipe. If you do use frozen blueberries, thaw and drain them before adding to the batter. Gently fold in blueberries to ensure that they don't break up too much and color the batter (a little bit is expected).

Don't use instant or quick-cooking oats in the streusel, as they will lose structure and become mushy during the baking process.

Wider Bundt pans will bake the batter more quickly, while cakes in narrower, deeper pans will need more time to bake through.

For best results, wrap the cooled cake tightly in plastic wrap and store overnight at room temperature before glazing.

- Preheat oven to 350°F (180°C); dark pan, 325°F (160°C)
- Minimum 10-cup Bundt pan, sprayed

CAKE

2¾ cups	all-purpose flour	675 mL
1½ tsp	baking powder	7 mL
1 tsp	salt	5 mL
½ tsp	baking soda	2 mL
1 cup	unsalted butter, melted	250 mL
1½ cups	granulated sugar	375 mL
4	large eggs, at room temperature	4
2 tsp	vanilla extract	10 mL
1 cup	sour cream (not fat-free)	250 mL
1½ cups	blueberries (see tip)	375 mL

STREUSEL

¼ cup	all-purpose flour	60 mL
¼ cup	large-flake (old-fashioned) rolled oats	60 mL
¼ cup	sliced almonds	60 mL
¼ cup	packed light brown sugar	60 mL
1 tsp	ground cinnamon	5 mL
¼ tsp	salt	1 mL
2 tbsp	unsalted butter, melted	30 mL
1	recipe Lemon Glaze (page 272)	1

1. *Cake:* In a medium bowl, whisk together flour, baking powder, salt and baking soda.
2. In the stand mixer bowl, beat sugar and butter on medium speed until combined. Beat in eggs, one at a time. Add vanilla and beat for 2 minutes.
3. With the mixer on low speed, alternately beat in flour mixture and sour cream, making three additions of flour and two of sour cream, and beating until incorporated.
4. Using a spatula, carefully fold in blueberries. Transfer half the batter to prepared pan and smooth the top.
5. *Streusel:* In another medium bowl, whisk together flour, oats, almonds, brown sugar, cinnamon and salt. Stir in butter until thoroughly blended.
6. Sprinkle streusel evenly over batter in pan and top with the remaining batter. Smooth the top.

Make Ahead

You can prepare this cake up to 3 days in advance. Store the cooled glazed cake in a cake container at room temperature or in the refrigerator.

7. Bake in preheated oven for 45 to 65 minutes or until puffed and golden and a tester inserted in the center comes out clean. Let cool in pan for 10 minutes, then carefully invert cake onto a wire rack to cool completely (see tip).

8. Pour glaze over the cooled cake, letting it drip down the sides. Let glaze set for at least 20 minutes before serving.

Spiced Applesauce Breakfast Bundt

This Bundt will make it smell (and taste) like fall in your kitchen, even if it's baked in the middle of July. Most applesauce cakes contain only unsweetened applesauce, but I've added grated fresh apple, which contributes more natural sweetness while keeping the texture extra-moist. Although this cake slices neatly when completely cooled, it's really hard to resist when still warm from the oven.

MAKES 10 TO 12 SERVINGS

Tips

I used a large Granny Smith apple for this recipe. Other good choices would be Gala, Braeburn or Crispin.

To remove liquid from apples, using your hands, gently squeeze sections of the grated apple over a bowl or sink.

For best results, serve warm or at room temperature the same day cake is baked.

Make Ahead

You can prepare this cake up to 3 days in advance. Store in a cake container at room temperature or in the refrigerator. To warm, heat for a few seconds in the microwave or wrapped in foil in a 300°F (150°C) oven.

- Preheat oven to 350°F (180°C); dark pan, 325°F (160°C)
- Minimum 10-cup Bundt pan, sprayed

CAKE

2 cups	all-purpose flour	500 mL
1 tsp	baking soda	5 mL
½ tsp	salt	2 mL
¼ tsp	baking powder	1 mL
1½ tsp	ground cinnamon	7 mL
1 tsp	ground ginger	5 mL
½ tsp	ground allspice	2 mL
¼ tsp	ground nutmeg	1 mL
1½ cups	packed light brown sugar	375 mL
¾ cup	unsalted butter, softened	175 mL
2	large eggs, at room temperature	2
1¼ cups	unsweetened applesauce	300 mL
1 cup	coarsely grated apple (unpeeled), liquid squeezed out	250 mL

TOPPING

2 tbsp	granulated sugar	30 mL
½ tsp	ground cinnamon	2 mL
¼ tsp	ground allspice	1 mL
¼ tsp	ground nutmeg	1 mL
3 tbsp	unsalted butter, melted	45 mL

1. *Cake:* In a medium bowl, whisk together flour, baking soda, salt, baking powder, cinnamon, ginger, allspice and nutmeg.
2. In the stand mixer bowl, beat brown sugar and butter on medium speed for 3 to 4 minutes or until very light and fluffy. Beat in eggs, one at a time. Beat in applesauce until blended.
3. With the mixer on low speed, gradually add flour mixture in three additions, beating until incorporated.
4. Using a spatula, fold in grated apples until evenly distributed. Transfer batter to prepared pan and smooth the top.
5. Bake in preheated oven for 40 to 55 minutes or until puffed and golden brown and a tester inserted in the center comes out clean. Let cool in pan for 10 minutes, then carefully invert cake onto a wire rack to cool for 5 minutes before adding topping.
6. *Topping:* In a small bowl, whisk together sugar, cinnamon, allspice and nutmeg. Using a pastry brush, brush melted butter over the warm cake and sprinkle with spiced sugar topping.

Cardamom-Streusel Brunch Bundt with Blood Orange Glaze

This beautiful, tender Bundt is a variation on a coffee cake I've made dozens of times. In order to avoid "coffee cake fatigue" (if there is such a thing), I try to change up the recipe based on the seasons or on what catches my eye at the grocery store. During the winter, I love working the color of blood orange juice into as many recipes as I can, and it creates a striking glaze for this cake, which pairs well with the spicy-sweet and aromatic cardamom streusel.

MAKES 10 TO 12 SERVINGS

Tip

Cardamom, made from ground cardamom seeds removed from the pods, is one of the most expensive spices, so you might experience a bit of sticker shock when you find it in your grocery store. That said, it tends to last for a long time, as small amounts go a long way in recipes.

Make Ahead

You can prepare this cake up to 2 days in advance. Store the glazed cake in a cake container at room temperature.

- Preheat oven to 350°F (180°C); dark pan, 325°F (160°C)
- Minimum 12-cup Bundt pan, sprayed

STREUSEL

2¼ cups	all-purpose flour	560 mL
1 cup	chopped pecans	250 mL
1 cup	packed light brown sugar	250 mL
1 tsp	ground cinnamon	5 mL
1 tsp	ground cardamom	5 mL
¼ tsp	salt	1 mL
1 cup	unsalted butter, melted	250 mL

CAKE

2¼ cups	all-purpose flour	560 mL
1½ tsp	baking powder	7 mL
½ tsp	baking soda	2 mL
½ tsp	salt	2 mL
1¼ cups	granulated sugar	300 mL
¾ cup	unsalted butter, softened	175 mL
¼ cup	vegetable oil	60 mL
3	large eggs, at room temperature	3
2 tsp	vanilla extract	10 mL
1 cup	sour cream	250 mL
1	recipe Blood Orange Glaze (variation, page 272)	1

1. *Streusel:* In a large bowl, whisk together flour, pecans, brown sugar, cinnamon, cardamom and salt. Stir in melted butter until thoroughly blended.
2. *Cake:* In a medium bowl, whisk together flour, baking powder, baking soda and salt.
3. In the stand mixer bowl, beat sugar, butter and oil on medium speed for 3 minutes or until fluffy. Beat in eggs, one at a time. Beat in vanilla.
4. With the mixer on low speed, alternately beat in flour mixture and sour cream, making two additions of flour and two of sour cream, and beating until incorporated.
5. Transfer half the batter to prepared pan and smooth the top. Top evenly with streusel. Spread the remaining batter over streusel and smooth the top.

Tip

For best results, wrap the cooled cake tightly in plastic wrap and store overnight at room temperature before glazing.

6. Bake in preheated oven for 50 to 60 minutes or until deep golden brown and a tester inserted in the center comes out clean. Let cool in pan for 15 minutes, then carefully invert cake onto a wire rack to cool completely (see tip).

7. Pour glaze over the cooled cake, letting it drip down the sides. Let glaze set for at least 20 minutes before serving.

Maple-Glazed Raspberry Ribbon Bundt

My mother loves raspberry-flavored *anything*, so whenever I brainstorm cookbook recipes, I make sure that I include at least a few with her in mind (she is my mother, after all). Slicing into this Bundt reveals a bright pink raspberry swirl, created by mixing vanilla-yogurt batter into a tart raspberry purée.

MAKES 10 TO 12 SERVINGS

Tips

If you don't have cake flour, you can make a substitute. See page 16 for more information.

When swirling a Bundt batter, drag the knife or skewer back and forth in a medium-width "S" motion several times around the Bundt. This helps to create a pretty swirl without mixing the colors completely together.

For best results, wrap the cooled cake tightly in plastic wrap and store in the refrigerator overnight before glazing.

- Preheat oven to 350°F (180°C); dark pan, 325°F (160°C)
- Minimum 10-cup Bundt pan, sprayed

RASPBERRY SWIRL

5 oz	frozen raspberries, thawed	150 g
¼ cup	granulated sugar	60 mL
1 tbsp	freshly squeezed lemon juice	15 mL

CAKE

2½ cups	cake flour, sifted	625 mL
2 tsp	baking powder	10 mL
1 tsp	salt	5 mL
¼ tsp	baking soda	1 mL
½ tsp	ground cinnamon	2 mL
2 cups	granulated sugar	500 mL
1 cup	unsalted butter, softened	250 mL
4	large eggs, at room temperature	4
2 tsp	vanilla extract	10 mL
1 cup	plain whole milk Greek yogurt	250 mL
1 to 2	drops red food coloring (optional)	1 to 2
1	recipe Maple Glaze (page 274)	1

1. *Raspberry Swirl:* In a medium saucepan, combine raspberries, sugar and lemon juice. Bring to a boil over medium heat, reduce heat to low and simmer, stirring occasionally, for 8 to 10 minutes or until mixture has reduced to about ½ cup (125 mL). Let cool completely.

2. *Cake:* In a medium bowl, whisk together flour, baking powder, salt, baking soda and cinnamon.

3. In the stand mixer bowl, beat sugar and butter on medium speed for 3 minutes or until light and fluffy. Beat in eggs, one at a time. Add vanilla and beat for 2 minutes.

4. With the mixer on low speed, alternately beat in flour mixture and yogurt, making three additions of flour and two of yogurt, and beating until incorporated.

5. Transfer 1½ cups (375 mL) batter to raspberry mixture, stirring to blend. If desired, stir in 1 to 2 drops red food coloring to boost color.

6. Transfer half the remaining vanilla batter to prepared pan and smooth the top. Top with half the raspberry batter and use a knife or skewer to marble the raspberry mixture through the batter several times (see tip). Repeat with remaining vanilla and raspberry batters. Smooth the top.

Make Ahead

You can prepare this cake up to 2 days in advance. Store the cooled glazed cake in a cake container at room temperature or in the refrigerator.

7. Bake in preheated oven for 45 to 55 minutes or until puffed and golden and a tester inserted in the center comes out clean. Let cool in pan for 10 minutes, then carefully invert cake onto a wire rack to cool completely (see tip).

8. Pour glaze over the cooled cake, letting it drip down the sides. Let glaze set for at least 20 minutes before serving.

Variation

I love using Greek yogurt in recipes because it is extra thick and rich. You can replace the whole-milk variety in this recipe with low-fat, but I don't recommend fat-free. If you can't find Greek yogurt, you can use plain or vanilla-flavored full-fat yogurt instead. Flavored yogurts usually contain added sugar, so the resulting cake will likely taste sweeter.

Healthy Start Bundt

When I first created this recipe for my bakery (in loaf form), I wasn't convinced it would resonate with customers, since it competed with decadent brownies, pound cakes and pies. But it became one of our top sellers. Chock-full of fruit, nuts, coconut, spice and yogurt, this Bundt features something for everyone, and it is still my favorite healthy and satisfying breakfast on-the-go.

MAKES 10 TO 12 SERVINGS

Tips

Wheat bran and wheat germ can be used interchangeably in this recipe. Wheat bran is the outer layer of the wheat kernel and is a better source of fiber, while wheat germ is the heart of the wheat berry.

To toast walnuts, spread in an even layer on a baking sheet and bake in a 350°F (180°C) oven, checking often, for 8 to 10 minutes, until fragrant and lightly browned.

Although this Bundt is delicious at room temperature, I love it toasted. Thin slices tend to break in an upright toaster, so use a toaster oven or conventional oven.

Make Ahead

Wrap the cooled cake tightly in plastic wrap and store in the refrigerator for up to 1 week. Alternatively, wrap it tightly in plastic wrap, then foil, and store in the freezer for up to 2 months.

- Preheat oven to 350°F (180°C); dark pan, 325°F (160°C)
- Minimum 10-cup Bundt pan, sprayed

1 cup	whole wheat flour	250 mL
1 cup	all-purpose flour	250 mL
1 cup	wheat bran or wheat germ	250 mL
2 tsp	baking soda	10 mL
¾ tsp	salt	3 mL
1½ tsp	ground cinnamon	7 mL
1 tsp	ground ginger	5 mL
½ tsp	ground nutmeg	2 mL
1 cup	grated tart apple (unpeeled), liquid squeezed out (see tip, page 66)	250 mL
3	large eggs	3
1¾ cups	plain Greek yogurt (see variation, page 71)	425 mL
½ cup	unsweetened applesauce	125 mL
½ cup	liquid honey	125 mL
1 tsp	vanilla extract	5 mL
1½ cups	sweetened shredded coconut	375 mL
¾ cup	dried cranberries	175 mL
¾ cup	chopped dried dates	175 mL
¾ cup	toasted chopped walnuts or pecans	175 mL

1. In a medium bowl, whisk together whole wheat flour, all-purpose flour, wheat bran, baking soda, salt, cinnamon, ginger and nutmeg.

2. In a large bowl, stir together grated apple, eggs, yogurt, applesauce, honey and vanilla.

3. Using a spatula, fold in flour mixture, followed by coconut, cranberries, dates and walnuts. Transfer batter to prepared pan and smooth the top.

4. Bake in preheated oven for 45 to 60 minutes or until puffed and golden and a tester inserted in the center comes out clean. Let cool in pan for 10 minutes, then carefully invert cake onto a wire rack to cool completely.

Variation

You can mix and match dried fruits and nuts in this recipe. Dark or golden raisins, figs, cherries, currants, apricots, hazelnuts and almonds would all work well.

Spiced Cranberry Orange Pecan Bundt

Because fresh cranberries are typically available during fall and winter, this Bundt has a holiday feel to it — although you could do as I do and stock up on fresh cranberries when available and freeze for year-round use (see tip). Because of the many flavors and textures featured in each slice — crunchy spiced pecans, orange and tart cranberries — you need nothing more than a dusting of snow-like confectioners' sugar for garnish.

MAKES 10 TO 12 SERVINGS

Tips

Store fresh cranberries in an airtight container in the refrigerator for up to 1 month or in the freezer for up to 1 year.

When swirling a Bundt batter, drag a knife or skewer back and forth in a medium-width "S" motion several times around the Bundt. This helps to create a pretty swirl without mixing the elements completely together.

For best results, wrap the cooled cake tightly in plastic wrap and store overnight at room temperature before dusting with confectioners' sugar.

Make Ahead

You can prepare this cake up to 3 days in advance. Wrap cooled cake tightly in plastic wrap and store at room temperature.

- Preheat oven to 350°F (180°C); dark pan, 325°F (160°C)
- Minimum 10-cup Bundt pan, sprayed

2½ cups	all-purpose flour	625 mL
1 tsp	baking powder	5 mL
1 tsp	salt	5 mL
½ tsp	baking soda	2 mL
1 cup	chopped pecans	250 mL
2 cups	granulated sugar, divided	500 mL
2 tsp	ground cinnamon	10 mL
1 cup	unsalted butter, softened	250 mL
3	large eggs, at room temperature	3
	Grated zest of 2 oranges	
½ cup	freshly squeezed orange juice	125 mL
2 tsp	vanilla extract	10 mL
½ cup	full-fat sour cream	125 mL
1½ cups	fresh cranberries	375 mL
	Confectioners' (icing) sugar	

1. In a medium bowl, whisk together flour, baking powder, salt and baking soda.

2. In a small bowl, stir together pecans, ½ cup (125 mL) granulated sugar and cinnamon.

3. In the stand mixer bowl, beat the remaining granulated sugar and butter on medium speed for 3 minutes or until light and fluffy. Beat in eggs, one at a time. Beat in orange zest, orange juice and vanilla. Beat for 2 minutes.

4. With the mixer on low speed, alternately beat in flour mixture and sour cream, making three additions of flour and two of sour cream, and beating until incorporated. Beat in cranberries.

5. Transfer half the batter to prepared pan and smooth the top. Sprinkle with half the pecan mixture. Repeat with the remaining batter and pecan mixture. Using a thin knife or skewer, marble the pecan mixture by swirling through the batter several times (see tip). Smooth the top.

6. Bake in preheated oven for 45 to 65 minutes or until deep golden brown and a tester inserted in the center comes out clean. Let cool in pan for 10 minutes, then carefully invert cake onto a wire rack to cool completely (see tip). Dust with confectioners' sugar before serving.

Glazed Cinnamon-Raisin Roll Bundt

Thanks to shopping mall food courts and airports, one of the most familiar — and enticing — aromas is that of cinnamon rolls baking. In this Bundt, pillowy buttermilk-based cinnamon-raisin rolls are arranged in layers so that the swirls show around the sides and on top.

MAKES 12 TO 16 SERVINGS

Tips

Water for proofing yeast should be about 100 to 110°F (38 to 40°C). If the water is too hot, it will kill the yeast, but it needs to be warm to activate the yeast. If your yeast mixture still doesn't foam after 10 minutes, your yeast could be too old or the water wasn't the right temperature.

Dried cranberries, dried cherries or a combination of dried fruits and nuts can replace the raisins.

A good, draft-free place for dough to rise is in your oven. Turn the oven on for 30 seconds, just to infuse a little bit of warmth, then turn it off before placing the bowl or pan of dough in the oven.

Cut baked ring of rolls into slices for a neater presentation, or sit around the Bundt with a group of friends and simply pull them apart (with a large stack of napkins nearby).

- Large bowl, lightly coated with oil
- Minimum 14-cup Bundt pan, sprayed

DOUGH

1	package (¼ oz/8 g) active dry yeast	1
1 tsp	granulated sugar	5 mL
¼ cup	warm water (see tip)	60 mL
⅓ cup	granulated sugar	75 mL
2	large egg yolks, at room temperature	2
1	large egg, at room temperature	1
1 cup	buttermilk, at room temperature	250 mL
½ cup	unsalted butter, melted	125 mL
4 to 4½ cups	all-purpose flour	1 to 1.125 L
1 tsp	salt	5 mL

FILLING

1 cup	packed light brown sugar, divided	250 mL
1½ tbsp	ground cinnamon	22 mL
¼ tsp	salt	1 mL
½ cup	unsalted butter, very soft but not melted	125 mL
¾ cup	raisins	175 mL
1	recipe Buttery Vanilla Glaze (variation, page 271)	1

1. *Dough:* In the stand mixer bowl, stir together yeast, 1 tsp (5 mL) sugar and water. Let stand for 5 to 10 minutes or until foamy.

2. Attach paddle to mixer. Beat in ⅓ cup (75 mL) sugar, egg yolks, egg, buttermilk and butter on medium speed until blended. Add 4 cups (1 L) flour and salt; beat on low speed for about 2 minutes or until combined.

3. Replace paddle with dough hook. Knead on medium speed for 5 to 7 minutes or until dough is smooth, soft and elastic, adding more flour if necessary for a dough that is only slightly sticky.

4. Transfer dough to prepared bowl, cover with plastic wrap and let rise in a warm, draft-free place for about 1 hour or until doubled in bulk.

5. *Filling:* In a small bowl, whisk together ¾ cup (175 mL) brown sugar, cinnamon and salt.

6. Turn dough out onto a lightly floured work surface and dust with flour. Using a rolling pin, roll dough out into a 20- by- 14 inch (50 by 35 cm) rectangle, with a long side facing you. Spread butter evenly over rectangle. Sprinkle evenly with brown sugar mixture, then with raisins, pressing lightly to adhere.

Make Ahead

For the first rising, in step 4, dough can instead be stored, covered, in the refrigerator overnight. Let dough come to room temperature for 1 hour before proceeding with step 5.

These rolls are best enjoyed the day they are baked, but you can prepare them up to 1 day in advance. Tightly wrap cooled rolls in plastic wrap and store at room temperature.

7. Starting at the long side closest to you, tightly roll dough into a cylinder, trimming ends to straighten or make neat. Using a very sharp knife, cut dough into 16 pieces.

8. Sprinkle the remaining brown sugar over prepared pan, shaking to coat as evenly as possible.

9. Arrange a layer of pieces, cut sides down, around the bottom of the prepared pan. Line the outer wall of the pan with a layer of pieces, so that they are standing on top of the bottom layer. Arrange a final layer of pieces around the center of the pan, so that they are standing next to the outer layer. Cover pan with plastic wrap and let rise in a warm, draft-free place for about 1 hour or until doubled in bulk (the rolls will expand in the pan, so don't worry if they look awkward before rising).

10. Preheat oven to 350°F (180°C), or 325°F (160°C) for a dark pan.

11. Uncover pan and bake for 30 to 40 minutes or until deep golden brown, puffed and firm. Let cool in pan for 10 minutes, then carefully invert Bundt onto a wire rack to cool for 10 minutes before glazing.

12. Spread glaze evenly over warm cake, letting it melt and drip down the sides. Let glaze set for a few minutes before serving. Serve warm (my preference!) or at room temperature.

Peanut Butter and Jelly Babka Bundt

There's a famous *Seinfeld* episode called "The Dinner Party" during which Jerry and his friends are unable to get their hands on the last chocolate babka at the bakery. As an alternative, they resort to buying a cinnamon babka, called "the lesser babka" by Elaine. Well, this peanut butter and jelly babka might not contain chocolate, but there is nothing "lesser" about it — unless you count the fact that there will be "lesser" and "lesser" of it as people quickly devour it!

MAKES 12 TO 16 SERVINGS

Tips

Milk for proofing yeast should be about 100°F to 110°F (38°C to 40°C). If the milk is too hot, it will kill the yeast, but it needs to be warm to activate the yeast. If your yeast mixture still doesn't foam after 10 minutes, your yeast could be too old or the milk wasn't the right temperature.

Use regular (not "natural") peanut butter for this recipe, as it is easier to spread and will give a better texture to the filling. Warm it in a microwave-safe bowl in the microwave in 30-second intervals, or transfer to a small saucepan and heat over medium-low heat, stirring occasionally, until heated through.

Don't worry if the twisting process of forming the babka rope is a bit messy. It's supposed to be messy — it's peanut butter and jelly!

- Large bowl, lightly coated with oil
- Minimum 14-cup Bundt pan, sprayed

BABKA DOUGH

1	package (¼ oz/8 g) active dry yeast	1
1 tsp	granulated sugar	5 mL
¾ cup	warm whole milk (see tip)	175 mL
½ cup	granulated sugar	125 mL
2	large eggs, at room temperature	2
2	large egg yolks, at room temperature	2
¾ cup	unsalted butter, melted	175 mL
4¼ cups	all-purpose flour	1.06 L
½ tsp	salt	2 mL

FILLING

4 tbsp	unsalted butter, melted, divided	60 mL
¾ cup	creamy peanut butter (see tip), warmed until spreadable	175 mL
½ cup	strawberry jelly	125 mL
½ cup	packed light brown sugar	125 mL
⅓ cup	chopped lightly salted peanuts	75 mL

EGG WASH

1	large egg	1
1 tbsp	heavy or whipping (35%) cream	15 mL
	Additional chopped salted peanuts	

1. *Babka Dough:* In the stand mixer bowl, stir together yeast, 1 tsp (5 mL) sugar and milk. Let stand for 5 to 10 minutes or until foamy.
2. Attach paddle to mixer. Beat in ½ cup (125 mL) sugar, eggs, egg yolks and butter on medium speed until blended. Add flour and salt; beat on low speed for 2 minutes or until combined.
3. Replace paddle with dough hook. Knead on medium speed for 5 minutes or until dough is very smooth, soft and elastic.
4. Transfer dough to prepared bowl, turning to coat. Cover with plastic wrap and let rise in a warm, draft-free place for about 1 hour or until doubled in bulk.
5. Turn babka dough out onto a lightly floured work surface and dust with flour. Using a rolling pin, roll dough out into a 24- by 12-inch (60 by 30 cm) rectangle, with a long side facing you.

Make Ahead

6. *Filling:* Using a pastry brush, brush dough with 2 tbsp (30 mL) melted butter. Spread peanut butter over dough, then spread with jelly. Top with brown sugar and peanuts, pressing ingredients lightly to adhere.

7. Starting at the long side closest to you, carefully roll dough into a tight cylinder; pinch the ends together to seal the filling inside. Using a sharp knife, slice the log lengthwise, so that you have two long strips of dough. Starting at one end, pinch ends of dough together, then twist the two strips around each other like a rope. Brush rope with the remaining butter.

8. Carefully transfer rope to prepared pan. You might need to shorten the rope a bit by pushing ends towards each other to make it fit (this will also increase the thickness of the rope). Overlap ends slightly in pan, pressing to seal. Cover pan with plastic wrap and let dough rise in a warm, draft-free place for 1 hour or until doubled in bulk.

9. Preheat oven to 350°F (180°C), or 325°F (160°C) for a dark pan.

10. *Egg Wash:* Whisk together egg and cream until blended. Brush top of babka with egg wash and sprinkle with additional chopped peanuts.

11. Bake for 25 minutes, reduce heat to 325°F (160°C) if necessary and bake for 15 to 20 minutes or until deep golden brown and firm on top. Let cool in pan for 15 minutes, carefully invert babka onto a wire rack, then carefully invert it a second time so that the rope design is facing up, to cool completely.

Orange, Fig and Pistachio Babka Bundt

A babka is a traditional Eastern European Jewish cake made with yeast-raised dough that has been filled and formed into a pretty twisted rope — or, in this case, a Bundt-shaped twisted rope! The most common fillings are chocolate or cinnamon, but this recipe — semi-inspired by Fig Newtons — contains a sweet, nutty and slightly tangy combination of dried figs, pistachios and orange.

MAKES 12 TO 16 SERVINGS

Tips

This recipe was tested using dried black Mission figs, but Calimyra figs would also work well.

A good, draft-free place for dough to rise is in your oven. Turn the oven on for 30 seconds, just to infuse a little bit of warmth, then turn it off before placing the pan of dough in the oven.

Make Ahead

This cake is best enjoyed the day it is baked, but you can prepare it up to 2 days in advance. Store glazed cake in a cake container at room temperature. Day-old babkas taste better warmed, either for a few seconds in the microwave or wrapped in foil in a 300°F (150°C) oven.

- Food processor
- Minimum 14-cup Bundt pan, sprayed and lightly coated with granulated sugar

1	recipe Babka Dough (page 78)	1
	Grated zest of 1 orange	

FILLING

1 cup	shelled pistachios	250 mL
7 oz	dried figs, coarsely chopped (1 cup/250 mL)	210 g
¾ cup	packed light brown sugar	175 mL
	Grated zest and juice of 1 orange	
½ cup	unsalted butter, softened	125 mL

EGG WASH

1	large egg	1
1 tbsp	water	15 mL
½	recipe Orange Glaze (variation, page 272)	½
	Chopped shelled pistachios	

1. Prepare babka dough through step 4 on page 78, beating in orange zest along with the eggs in step 2.
2. *Filling:* In food processor, pulse pistachios, figs, brown sugar, orange zest and orange juice until nuts and figs are finely chopped.
3. Turn babka dough out onto a lightly floured work surface and dust with flour. Using a rolling pin, roll dough out into a 24- by 12-inch (60 by 30 cm) rectangle, with a long side facing you. Spread butter evenly over dough. Top evenly with fig mixture, pressing lightly to adhere.
4. Starting at the long side closest to you, carefully roll dough into a tight cylinder; pinch the ends together to seal the filling inside. Using a sharp knife, slice the cylinder lengthwise, so that you have two long strips of dough. Starting at one end, pinch ends of dough together, then twist the two strips around each other like a rope.
5. Carefully transfer rope to prepared pan. You might need to shorten the rope a bit by pushing ends towards each other to make it fit (this will also increase the thickness of the rope). Overlap ends slightly in pan, pressing to seal.
6. *Egg Wash:* Whisk together egg and water until blended.

Tip

I like a thinner glaze for this cake, so keep that in mind when whisking in additional orange juice in the glaze recipe.

7. Using a pastry brush, brush top evenly with egg wash. Cover pan with plastic wrap and let dough rise in a warm, draft-free place for 1 hour or until doubled in bulk.

8. Preheat oven to 350°F (180°C), or 325°F (160°C) for a dark pan.

9. Uncover pan and bake for 25 minutes. Reduce heat to 325°F (160°C) if necessary and bake for 15 to 25 minutes or until deep golden brown and firm on top. Let cool in pan for 15 minutes, carefully invert babka onto a wire rack, then carefully invert it a second time so that the rope design is facing up, to cool completely.

10. Pour glaze over the cooled cake, letting it drip down the sides. Sprinkle with chopped pistachios. Let glaze set for at least 20 minutes before serving.

Banana Macadamia Nut French Toast

Whenever I'm on vacation, I take extra time to enjoy my breakfasts, since my at-home versions usually consist of smoothies or a power bar as I drive my daughter to school. One morning, on the island of Lanai, I had an outstanding island-kissed-banana-stuffed French toast. Instead of maple syrup, it was served with coconut syrup, which I learned is customary in Hawaii. I've recreated the flavors of that breakfast in this Bundt. If you close your eyes while eating, you can almost hear the ocean!

MAKES 10 TO 12 SERVINGS

Tip

Challah bread is a fluffy, sweet, braided egg bread that you can find in the bakery section of most well-stocked grocery stores. It is frequently used for French toast or for bread pudding (page 212). Day-old bread is drier and absorbs the custard better.

Make Ahead

This Bundt is best enjoyed the day it is baked, but you can prepare it up to 2 days in advance. Tightly wrap the cooled Bundt in plastic wrap or store in a cake container and store in the refrigerator. If desired, warm a slice in the microwave on High for 30 to 45 seconds or wrapped in foil in a 300°F (150°C) oven.

• **Minimum 12-cup Bundt pan, sprayed and lightly coated with granulated sugar**

FRENCH TOAST

½ cup	unsalted butter	125 mL
1 cup	packed dark brown sugar	250 mL
3 tbsp	dark rum	45 mL
1 tbsp	vanilla extract	15 mL
3	bananas, halved lengthwise and sliced into ¼-inch (0.5 cm) slices	3
¾ cup	chopped macadamia nuts	175 mL
½ cup	sweetened shredded coconut	125 mL
½ tsp	ground cinnamon	2 mL
¼ tsp	ground nutmeg	1 mL
¼ tsp	ground allspice	1 mL
¼ tsp	salt	1 mL
8	large eggs	8
2½ cups	half-and-half (10%) cream	625 mL
1 lb	day-old challah bread, cut into ½-inch (1 cm) cubes	500 g

STREUSEL

½ cup	all-purpose flour	125 mL
½ cup	packed light brown sugar	125 mL
¼ cup	chopped macadamia nuts	60 mL
½ tsp	ground cinnamon	2 mL
⅛ tsp	salt	0.5 mL
6 tbsp	unsalted butter, melted	90 mL
	Pure maple syrup or coconut syrup	

1. *French Toast:* In a large skillet, melt butter over medium heat. Stir in brown sugar, rum and vanilla until smooth. Add bananas, stirring to coat; remove from heat. Stir in macadamia nuts and coconut. Let cool.

2. In a medium bowl, whisk together cinnamon, nutmeg, allspice, salt and eggs until blended. Whisk in cream.

3. Place challah cubes in a large bowl. Add egg mixture and banana mixture. Using your hands, toss gently to combine (see tip).

4. Transfer challah mixture to prepared pan. Tap the pan lightly on the counter to evenly distribute. Cover pan with plastic wrap and refrigerate for 6 hours or overnight.

5. Preheat oven to 375°F (190°C).

Tip

I've found that it's best to use clean hands — rather than a spoon or spatula — to toss together the ingredients in step 3. This helps prevent the bread cubes from breaking up too much.

6. *Streusel:* In a small bowl, stir together flour, brown sugar, macadamia nuts, cinnamon, salt and butter. Remove pan from refrigerator and sprinkle with streusel, pressing to adhere.

7. Bake for 45 to 50 minutes or until puffed, deep golden brown and firm and a tester inserted in the center comes out clean. Let cool in pan for 10 minutes, then carefully invert Bundt onto a plate to firm up and cool for 10 minutes more. Serve warm or at room temperature, drizzled with maple syrup.

Variations

Use cashews instead of macadamia nuts.

The cream can be replaced with whole milk or, if you want really rich results, heavy or whipping (35%) cream.

Savory Caprese Strata Brunch Bundt

Every Thanksgiving, in addition to some sort of sweet treat, my mom prepares a savory egg casserole for breakfast — something that satisfies both taste buds and stomachs until dinner. Our tradition served as inspiration for this strata, named because the ingredients are layered before they soak up the egg custard. Featuring the popular flavor combination of mozzarella, tomato and basil, this Bundt-shaped version is a great way to serve brunch to a crowd.

MAKES 10 TO 12 SERVINGS

Tips

To cut basil leaves chiffonade style, stack about 10 leaves at a time on top of each other. Roll them lengthwise into a fairly tight cigar shape. Cut across in thin slices to get long, uniform strips.

If desired, buy your bread a day in advance so that it has a chance to dry out a bit.

Make Ahead

This strata is best enjoyed the day it is baked, but you can prepare it up to 3 days in advance. Tightly wrap the cooled strata in plastic wrap and store at room temperature. If desired, warm a slice in the microwave for a few seconds, or wrap in foil, heat in a 300°F (150°C) oven, and sandwich between two pieces of buttered whole-grain toast for an extra-special breakfast on-the-go!

- **Minimum 12-cup Bundt pan, sprayed**

1 lb	Italian turkey sausage (bulk or casings removed)	500 g
3	cloves garlic, minced	3
½	red onion, finely chopped	½
⅔ cup	chopped drained oil-packed sun-dried tomatoes	150 mL
¼ cup	basil chiffonade (see tip)	60 mL
9	large eggs	9
3 cups	half-and-half (10%) cream	750 mL
1 tsp	salt	5 mL
½ tsp	freshly ground black pepper	2 mL
1 lb	crusty Italian or French bread, cut into 1-inch (2.5 cm) cubes (see tip)	500 g
2 cups	shredded mozzarella cheese	500 mL

1. In a large nonstick skillet, cook sausage over medium-high heat, breaking it up with a fork or rubber spatula, for 8 to 10 minutes or until no longer pink. Add garlic and onion; cook, stirring, for 2 minutes. Add tomatoes and basil; cook, stirring, for 1 to 2 minutes or until heated through. Let cool.

2. In a large bowl, whisk together eggs, cream, salt and pepper.

3. Arrange one-third of the bread cubes in the bottom of prepared pan. Top with half the sausage mixture, then half the mozzarella. Repeat with another third of the bread cubes and the remaining sausage mixture and mozzarella. Arrange the remaining bread cubes on top, pressing down gently.

4. Pour egg mixture evenly over the layers. Cover the pan with plastic wrap and refrigerate for 8 hours or overnight to allow bread to absorb egg mixture.

5. Preheat oven to 375°F (190°C).

6. Bake for 45 to 50 minutes or until puffed, golden brown and bubbling around the edges. Let cool in pan for 15 minutes, then carefully invert strata onto a plate. Serve warm or at room temperature.

Variations

To make this recipe a bit lighter, substitute whole milk for the cream.

Use a loaf of bakery sourdough instead of Italian or French bread.

Peanut Butter Cup Bundt

Filled Bundts

Filling a Bundt Cake

1 After baking the cake and letting it cool completely, place the clean, dry pan over the cake on the rack and invert them together so that the bottom of the cake is facing up inside the pan.

2 Using a paring knife, cut a circle around the cake, straight down, about 1 inch (2.5 cm) from the outer edge and reaching about two-thirds deep in the pan (don't cut all the way through the cake.)

3 Cut a second circle parallel to the first, about 1 inch (2.5 cm) from the inner edge of the cake, also reaching about two-thirds deep, forming a ring inside the cake.

4 Cut lines across the inner ring until you have 8 to 10 equal sections.

5 Working with one section at a time, carefully cut and lift out the inner ring of the cake, keeping the top of each section intact (you will return the pieces to the pan to cover up the filling).

6 Use a spoon to dig out excess cake, if necessary, creating a "moat" that extends evenly around the inside of the cake, about two-thirds deep.

7 Give the filling a quick stir to loosen it, if necessary.

8 Carefully spoon the filling into the moat, filling it to about ½ inch (1 cm) from the top.

9 Trim the bottoms of the cut-out cake sections so that they will fit snugly back together on top of the filling, even with the top of the cake.

10 Piece the cake sections back together inside the moat, pressing them to adhere to the filling and completely covering up the filling.

11 Carefully invert the Bundt back onto a serving plate.

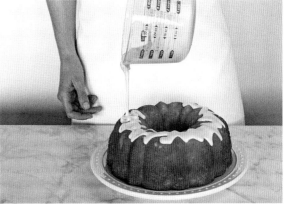

12 If desired, pour glaze over the cake, letting it drip down the sides. Let glaze set for at least 15 minutes before serving.

Peanut Butter Cup Bundt

Every Halloween, my husband insists that we pass out peanut butter cups in addition to other treats. His goal? To have plenty of leftovers that he can enjoy and take to work. Much to his dismay, the peanut butter cups are (always!) also popular with the neighborhood kids, and they are the first to disappear from our cauldron-shaped bowl. As the old commercial used to say, peanut butter and chocolate are "two great tastes that taste great together" — and they translate just as well into this double-glazed and filled Bundt.

MAKES 12 TO 14 SERVINGS

Tips

It's important to sift cocoa powder before adding to dry ingredients, to avoid bitter-tasting clumps.

You can make your own version of buttermilk by stirring together 1¼ cups (300 mL) milk (not fat-free) and 4 tsp (20 mL) white or apple cider vinegar; let stand at room temperature for 15 minutes before using.

Use regular name-brand creamy peanut butter rather than the "natural" variety for the filling. Natural varieties tend to separate into the oil and peanut components, whereas regular peanut butters stay blended.

- Preheat oven to 350°F (180°C); dark pan, 325°F (160°C)
- Handheld electric mixer
- Minimum 10-cup Bundt pan, sprayed

CAKE

1 tsp	espresso powder	5 mL
3 tbsp	hot water	45 mL
2 cups	all-purpose flour	500 mL
1 cup	unsweetened cocoa powder, sifted	250 mL
½ tsp	baking powder	2 mL
½ tsp	baking soda	2 mL
½ tsp	salt	2 mL
2¼ cups	granulated sugar	560 mL
¾ cup	vegetable oil	175 mL
3	large eggs, at room temperature	3
1 tsp	vanilla extract	5 mL
1¼ cups	buttermilk	300 mL

PEANUT BUTTER FILLING

½ cup	creamy peanut butter, softened (see tip)	125 mL
¼ cup	unsalted butter, softened	60 mL
½ cup	packed light brown sugar	125 mL
¼ tsp	salt	1 mL
1	large egg	1
¼ cup	whole milk	60 mL
1 tsp	vanilla extract	5 mL
¼ cup	all-purpose flour	60 mL

PEANUT BUTTER GANACHE

1 cup	peanut butter chips (6 oz/175 g)	250 mL
6 tbsp	heavy or whipping (35%) cream	90 mL

DECORATIVE CHOCOLATE GLAZE

⅔ cup	chocolate chips (4 oz/125 g)	150 mL
¼ cup	heavy or whipping (35%) cream	60 mL
1 tbsp	light (white or golden) corn syrup	15 mL
	Chopped peanuts	

For best results, wrap the cooled cake tightly in plastic wrap and store at room temperature or in the refrigerator overnight before glazing.

If you add the chocolate glaze too soon, the ganache and glaze will swirl together.

Make Ahead

You can prepare this cake up to 3 days in advance. Store the cooled glazed filled cake in a cake container at room temperature or in the refrigerator. If necessary, let chilled cake stand at room temperature for 1 hour before serving.

See a photograph of this cake on page 86.

1. *Cake:* In a small bowl, combine espresso powder and hot water.
2. In a medium bowl, whisk together flour, cocoa, baking powder, baking soda and salt.
3. In the stand mixer bowl, beat sugar and oil on medium speed for 2 minutes or until combined. Beat in eggs, one at a time. Add vanilla and espresso mixture and beat for 2 minutes.
4. With the mixer on low speed, alternately beat in flour mixture and buttermilk, making three additions of flour and two of buttermilk, and beating until incorporated.
5. *Filling:* In another medium bowl, using the handheld mixer, beat peanut butter and butter on medium speed for 2 to 3 minutes or until light. Beat in brown sugar and salt. Beat in egg until incorporated, then milk and vanilla. Reduce speed to low. Add flour and beat until well incorporated.
6. Transfer half the batter to prepared pan and smooth the top. Carefully spoon filling in a ring on top of batter, leaving a border on both sides. Top with the remaining batter, covering filling completely. Smooth the top.
7. Bake in preheated oven for 45 to 60 minutes or until a tester inserted in the center comes out with a few moist crumbs attached and the top springs back and retains its shape when lightly pressed. Let cool in pan for 10 minutes, then carefully invert cake onto a wire rack to cool completely (see tip).
8. *Ganache:* In a small saucepan, combine peanut butter chips and cream over medium-low heat, stirring often, until melted and smooth.
9. Pour ganache over the cooled cake, letting it drip down the sides. Refrigerate cake for 15 minutes to help the ganache set (see tip).
10. *Glaze:* In clean small saucepan, combine chocolate chips, cream and corn syrup over medium-low heat, stirring often, until melted and smooth.
11. Using the tines of a fork or a spoon, drizzle chocolate glaze over peanut butter glaze in a contrasting pattern. Sprinkle with peanuts. Let glaze set for at least 20 minutes before serving.

German Chocolate Bundt

Although this Bundt looks pretty irresistible to begin with, just wait until you cut into it and reveal the nutty, gooey coconut filling! A triple-punch of flavor and texture makes this dessert a true showstopper for any occasion. And the "surprise" inside gives its traditional layer-cake counterpart a run for its money.

MAKES 12 TO 14 SERVINGS

Tips

It's important to sift cocoa powder before adding to dry ingredients, to avoid bitter-tasting clumps.

When testing this recipe for doneness, the "toothpick test" is not a good indicator, as the gooey center filling prevents a clean result. Lightly pressing the top of the cake to see if it springs back is a good alternative.

For best results, wrap the cooled cake tightly in plastic wrap and store at room temperature or in the refrigerator overnight before glazing.

- **Minimum 10-cup Bundt pan, sprayed**

FILLING

½ cup	sweetened condensed milk	125 mL
¼ cup	unsalted butter	60 mL
2	large egg yolks	2
1 cup	sweetened shredded coconut	250 mL
⅔ cup	chopped pecans	150 mL

CAKE

2 cups	all-purpose flour	500 mL
1 cup	unsweetened cocoa powder, sifted	250 mL
¾ tsp	baking powder	3 mL
½ tsp	baking soda	2 mL
½ tsp	salt	2 mL
2 cups	granulated sugar	500 mL
¾ cup	vegetable oil	175 mL
3	large eggs, at room temperature	3
2 tsp	vanilla extract	10 mL
¾ cup	half-and-half (10%) cream	175 mL
1	recipe Salted Caramel Glaze (page 273)	1
	Toasted unsweetened large-flake coconut (optional)	
	Toasted chopped pecans (optional)	

1. *Filling:* In a medium saucepan, stir condensed milk and butter over medium heat until butter has melted and mixture is combined.

2. In a medium bowl, whisk together egg yolks. Slowly add hot milk mixture, whisking constantly. Return to saucepan and cook, stirring, for about 5 minutes or until thickened enough to coat the back of a spoon. Remove from heat. Stir in coconut and pecans. Cover and refrigerate for several hours or until chilled.

3. Meanwhile, preheat oven to 350°F (180°C), or 325°F (160°C) for a dark pan.

4. *Cake:* In a large bowl, whisk together together flour, cocoa, baking powder, baking soda and salt.

5. In the stand mixer bowl, beat sugar and oil on medium speed for 2 minutes or until light. Beat in eggs, one at a time. Beat in vanilla.

6. With the mixer on low speed, alternately beat in flour mixture and cream, making three additions of flour and two of cream, and beating until incorporated.

Make Ahead

You can prepare this cake up to 1 day in advance. Store the cooled glazed cake in a cake container at room temperature or in the refrigerator.

7. Transfer half the batter to prepared pan and smooth the top. Carefully spoon chilled filling in a ring on top of batter, leaving a border on both sides. Top with the remaining batter, covering filling completely. Smooth the top.

8. Bake for 45 to 55 minutes or until cake is puffed and springs back when lightly touched (see tip). Let cool in pan for 15 minutes, then carefully invert cake onto a wire rack to cool completely (see tip).

9. Pour glaze over the cooled cake, letting it drip down the sides. If desired, sprinkle with coconut and pecans. Let toppings set for at least 15 minutes before serving.

Lemon-Filled Coconut Snowball Bundt

Featuring the popular flavor combination of tart lemon and sweet coconut, this pretty Bundt was named for the way it looks after being iced and completely coated in shredded coconut. Once sliced, a bright yellow center is revealed, a beautiful contrast to the snow-white cake. Because lemon curd thins as it warms, I like to serve this slightly chilled so that the filling stays intact in each sweet tooth–satisfying slice.

MAKES 12 TO 14 SERVINGS

Tips

Don't confuse cream of coconut with coconut milk! The former is a thick, sweet liquid made from fresh coconut, commonly used in mixed drinks and baking. Look for it in the cocktail condiments section of your grocery store or in liquor stores. Coconut milk is typically found in cans in the Asian foods section of many supermarkets.

Use a clean, dry bowl in step 9 to ensure egg whites firm up as they are beaten. "Firm" peaks means that the whites stand up on their own and don't bend over when the beater is lifted from the bowl.

- Handheld electric mixer
- Minimum 12-cup Bundt pan, sprayed

LEMON CURD FILLING

3	large eggs	3
3	large egg yolks	3
1½ cups	granulated sugar	375 mL
¼ cup	cornstarch	60 mL
Pinch	salt	Pinch
	Grated zest of 2 large lemons	
¾ cup	freshly squeezed lemon juice (about 3 large lemons)	175 mL
¼ cup	water	60 mL
½ cup	unsalted butter	125 mL

CAKE

2¾ cups	all-purpose flour	675 mL
¾ tsp	baking powder	3 mL
½ tsp	baking soda	2 mL
½ tsp	salt	2 mL
1½ cups	granulated sugar	375 mL
1 cup	unsalted butter, softened	250 mL
3	large eggs, at room temperature, separated	3
1 cup	cream of coconut (see tip)	250 mL
1 tsp	coconut extract	5 mL
½ tsp	vanilla extract	2 mL
1 cup + 2 tbsp	buttermilk	280 mL

COCONUT FROSTING

2 cups	confectioners' (icing) sugar, sifted	500 mL
½ cup	unsalted butter, softened	125 mL
1	jar (7 oz/198 g) marshmallow creme	1
3 to 5 tbsp	heavy or whipping (35%) cream	45 to 75 mL
1 tsp	coconut extract	5 mL
1½ cups	sweetened shredded coconut	375 mL

1. *Filling:* In a medium heatproof bowl, whisk eggs and egg yolks until blended.

continued on page 97

Tips

For best results, wrap the cooled cake tightly in plastic wrap and store at room temperature or in the refrigerator overnight before filling.

After filling cake, it's best to invert it onto a serving plate instead of a wire rack. Because sections of the cake have been removed and replaced, the cake should be moved as little as possible.

Don't worry if the frosting isn't perfectly even when covering the cake. The coconut will cover it up, giving it the pretty "snowball effect"!

Make Ahead

You can prepare the lemon curd filling up to 5 days in advance. Store in an airtight container in the refrigerator.

This cake is best enjoyed the day it is filled and frosted, but you can prepare it up to 3 days in advance. Store frosted filled cake in a cake container in the refrigerator.

2. In a medium saucepan, whisk sugar, cornstarch, salt, lemon zest, lemon juice and water over medium heat. Cook, stirring, until sugar dissolves and mixture boils and thickens.

3. Gradually add lemon mixture to eggs, whisking constantly until blended. Return to saucepan and cook over medium heat, whisking often, for 2 minutes. Add butter, 1 tbsp (15 mL) at a time, whisking to incorporate. Reduce heat to low and cook, whisking constantly, for 5 to 6 minutes or until thickened.

4. Transfer curd to a clean heatproof bowl and cover with plastic wrap, pressing it directly onto surface of curd. Refrigerate for 3 hours or overnight.

5. *Cake:* Preheat oven to 350°F (180°C), or 325°F (160°C) for a dark pan.

6. In a medium bowl, whisk together flour, baking powder, baking soda and salt.

7. In the stand mixer bowl, beat sugar and butter on medium speed for 4 minutes or until light and fluffy. Add egg yolks, one at a time. Beat in cream of coconut, coconut extract and vanilla.

8. With the mixer on low speed, alternately beat in flour mixture and buttermilk, making three additions of flour and two of buttermilk, and beating until incorporated.

9. In another medium bowl (see tip), using the handheld mixer, beat egg whites on medium speed until stiff peaks form.

10. Using a spatula, carefully fold egg whites into batter in two additions. Transfer batter to prepared pan and smooth the top.

11. Bake for 45 to 55 minutes or until a tester inserted in the center comes out clean. Let cool in pan for 10 minutes, then carefully invert cake onto a wire rack to cool completely (see tip).

12. Return cooled cake to its cleaned and dried pan. Stir chilled curd to loosen and fill cake with lemon curd as described on page 88. Carefully invert cake onto a serving plate.

13. *Frosting:* In the stand mixer bowl, beat sugar and butter on medium-low speed until smooth. Beat in marshmallow creme, 3 tbsp (45 mL) cream and coconut extract. Increase speed to medium-high and beat until frosting is light, fluffy and very spreadable. Beat in more cream if necessary, 1 tbsp (15 mL) at a time, until frosting reaches desired consistency.

14. Spread frosting all over the cake, covering it completely (see tip). Sprinkle coconut over frosting, lightly pressing it into sides and interior of Bundt to cover. Serve chilled.

Cream-Filled Vanilla Snack Cake Bundt

When the lunch bell rang at school, it was always a surprise to open my lunchbox and discover that my mom had snuck a Twinkie inside. My mom was a great baker, and we rarely had store-bought sweets like that at home, so the classic cream-filled vanilla snack cake that I always saw in my friends' lunches was a treat — whereas they coveted my homemade desserts! This Bundt is my from-scratch version of the famous spongy vanilla snack cakes, complete with the signature cream filling.

MAKES 12 TO 14 SERVINGS

Tips

Use a clean, dry bowl in step 4 to ensure egg whites firm up as they are beaten. "Firm" peaks means that the whites stand up on their own and don't bend over when the beater is lifted from the bowl.

Look for marshmallow creme (also known as fluff) in the baking section or peanut butter section of your grocery store.

For best results, wrap the cooled cake tightly in plastic wrap and store at room temperature or in the refrigerator overnight before filling.

After filling cake, it's best to invert it onto a serving plate instead of a wire rack. Because sections of the cake have been removed and replaced, the cake should be moved as little as possible.

- Preheat oven to 325°F (160°C)
- Handheld electric mixer
- Minimum 12-cup Bundt pan, sprayed

CAKE

2 cups	cake flour, sifted	500 mL
½ cup	all-purpose flour	125 mL
2 tsp	baking powder	10 mL
½ tsp	salt	2 mL
1¾ cups	granulated sugar	425 mL
½ cup	unsalted butter, softened	125 mL
6 tbsp	vegetable oil	90 mL
6	large eggs, at room temperature, separated	6
2 tsp	vanilla extract	10 mL
¾ cup	whole milk	175 mL
Pinch	cream of tartar	Pinch

FILLING

1 cup	confectioners' (icing) sugar, sifted	250 mL
¼ tsp	salt	1 mL
1	jar (7 oz/198 g) marshmallow creme	1
6 tbsp	unsalted butter, softened	90 mL
3 tbsp	heavy or whipping (35%) cream	45 mL
1 tsp	vanilla extract	5 mL

1. *Cake:* In a medium bowl, whisk together cake flour, all-purpose flour, baking powder and salt.
2. In the stand mixer bowl, beat sugar, butter and oil on medium speed for 4 minutes or until light and fluffy. Beat in egg yolks, one at a time. Beat in vanilla.
3. With the mixer on low speed, alternately beat in flour mixture and milk, making three additions of flour and two of milk, and beating until incorporated.
4. In another medium bowl (see tip), using the handheld mixer, beat egg whites and cream of tartar on medium speed until foamy. Increase speed to high and beat until stiff peaks form.
5. Using a spatula, carefully fold egg white mixture into batter in three additions. Transfer batter to prepared pan and smooth the top.

Make Ahead

This cake is best enjoyed the day it is filled, but you can prepare it up to 3 days in advance. Store filled cake in a cake container in the refrigerator.

6. Bake in preheated oven for 50 to 60 minutes or until golden brown on top and a tester inserted in the center comes out clean. Let cool in pan for 10 minutes, then carefully invert cake onto a wire rack to cool completely (see tip).

7. *Filling:* In the stand mixer bowl, beat sugar, salt, marshmallow creme and butter on medium speed until blended. Beat in cream and vanilla until mixture is smooth, light and fluffy.

8. Return cooled cake to its cleaned and dried pan and fill with cream filling as described on page 88. Carefully invert cake onto a serving plate.

Boston Cream Bundt

It is said that the Boston cream pie got its name because it originated in Boston, at the Parker House Hotel (yes, the same place as the famous rolls!). Called the Parker House Chocolate Pie when first invented, this non-traditional "pie" consists of white cake, vanilla pastry cream filling and chocolate glaze. One of the most flattering compliments I received from taste-testers for this book was from a Boston native who said, "This Bundt took me right back home!"

MAKES 12 TO 14 SERVINGS

Tips

Look for a vanilla bean that is plump, glossy and pliable. To split it, slice down its length using a paring knife.

Use a clean, dry bowl in step 10 to ensure egg whites firm up as they are beaten. "Firm" peaks means that the whites stand up on their own and don't bend over when the beater is lifted from the bowl.

For best results, wrap the cooled cake tightly in plastic wrap and store at room temperature or in the refrigerator overnight before filling.

After filling cake, it's best to invert it onto a serving plate instead of a wire rack. Because sections of the cake have been removed and replaced, the cake should be moved as little as possible.

- Handheld electric mixer
- Minimum 12-cup Bundt pan, sprayed

VANILLA PASTRY CREAM FILLING

½	vanilla bean, split	½
1½ cups	whole milk	375 mL
½ cup	granulated sugar	125 mL
¼ cup	cornstarch	60 mL
4	large egg yolks	4
¼ tsp	salt	1 mL
½ cup	heavy or whipping (35%) cream	125 mL
2 tbsp	unsalted butter	30 mL

CAKE

2½ cups	all-purpose flour	625 mL
2 tsp	baking powder	10 mL
1 tsp	salt	5 mL
1¾ cups	granulated sugar	425 mL
½ cup	unsalted butter, softened	125 mL
¼ cup	vegetable oil	60 mL
5	large eggs, at room temperature, separated	5
1 tbsp	vanilla extract	15 mL
1 cup	whole milk	250 mL
Pinch	cream of tartar	Pinch
1	recipe Chocolate Glaze (page 270)	1

1. *Filling:* Press tip of the bean against a cutting board. Use the dull side of knife to scrape seeds from pod, moving from the tip down the length, flattening the bean as you go.

2. In a medium saucepan, stir together vanilla seeds and milk. Let steep for 10 minutes.

3. Meanwhile, in a large heatproof bowl, whisk together sugar, cornstarch, egg yolks and salt. Gradually whisk in cream.

4. Bring milk mixture to a simmer over medium heat. Gradually pour hot milk mixture into egg mixture, whisking constantly, until blended. Return to saucepan. Cook over medium heat, whisking constantly, for 4 to 5 minutes or until mixture almost comes to a boil and is thick enough to coat the back of a spoon. Remove from heat and whisk in butter until melted and smooth.

5. Transfer pastry cream to a clean heatproof bowl and cover with plastic wrap, pressing it directly onto surface of pastry cream. Refrigerate for 3 hours or overnight.

Make Ahead

You can prepare the pastry cream up to 3 days in advance. Store in an airtight container in the refrigerator.

This cake is best enjoyed the day it is filled and glazed, but you can prepare it up to 3 days in advance. Store glazed filled cake in a cake container in the refrigerator. Let chilled cake stand at room temperature for 1 hour before serving.

6. *Cake:* Preheat oven to 325°F (160°C).

7. In a medium bowl, whisk together flour, baking powder and salt.

8. In the stand mixer bowl, beat sugar, butter and oil on medium speed for 4 minutes or until light and fluffy. Beat in egg yolks, one at a time. Beat in vanilla.

9. With the mixer on low speed, alternately beat in flour mixture and milk, making three additions of flour and two of milk, and beating until incorporated.

10. In another medium bowl (see tip), using the handheld mixer, beat egg whites and cream of tartar on medium speed until foamy. Increase speed to high and beat until stiff peaks form.

11. Using a spatula, carefully fold egg white mixture into batter in three additions. Transfer batter to prepared pan and smooth the top.

12. Bake for 50 to 60 minutes or until golden brown and a tester inserted in the center comes out clean. Let cool in pan for 10 minutes, then carefully invert cake onto a wire rack to cool completely (see tip).

13. Return cooled cake to its cleaned and dried pan. Stir chilled pastry cream to loosen and fill cake with pastry cream as described on page 88. Carefully invert cake onto a serving plate.

14. Pour glaze over the cake, letting it drip down the sides. Let glaze set for at least 20 minutes before serving.

S'mores Bundt Cake

When you can't get to the campfire to make this classic dessert, turning it into a Bundt is the next best thing. I put a great deal of thought into translating the components of a s'more — graham cracker, chocolate and marshmallow — successfully into a cake. I finally decided that a cake consisting of two swirled batters, one chocolate and one graham cracker, and filled and glazed with sweet fluffy marshmallow, allowed all three flavors to shine in every bite.

MAKES 12 TO 14 SERVINGS

Tips

To make graham cracker crumbs, break whole crackers into pieces and process in food processor until finely ground.

You will need two 7-oz (198 g) jars of marshmallow creme for this recipe. Because it is so sticky, the best way to measure it is to spray or oil the liquid measuring cup with nonstick spray beforehand.

Look for marshmallow creme (also known as fluff) in the baking section or peanut butter section of your grocery store.

After filling cake, it's best to invert it onto a serving plate instead of a wire rack. Because sections of the cake have been removed and replaced, the cake should be moved as little as possible.

- Preheat oven to 350°F (180°C); dark pan 325°F (160°C)
- Minimum 10-cup Bundt pan, sprayed

CAKE

2¼ cups	all-purpose flour	560 mL
1 tsp	baking powder	5 mL
1 tsp	baking soda	5 mL
½ tsp	salt	2 mL
1 cup	granulated sugar	250 mL
1 cup	packed light brown sugar	250 mL
½ cup	unsalted butter, softened	125 mL
6 tbsp	vegetable oil	90 mL
3	large eggs, at room temperature	3
1 tsp	vanilla extract	5 mL
1¼ cups	buttermilk	300 mL
½ cup	finely ground graham cracker crumbs	125 mL
½ tsp	ground cinnamon	2 mL
2 tbsp	liquid honey	30 mL
½ cup	unsweetened cocoa powder, sifted	125 mL

MARSHMALLOW FILLING

1½ cups	confectioners' (icing) sugar, sifted	375 mL
¼ tsp	salt	1 mL
1½ cups	marshmallow creme (see tips)	375 mL
6 tbsp	unsalted butter, softened	90 mL
3 tbsp	heavy or whipping (35%) cream	45 mL
1 tsp	vanilla extract	5 mL
1	recipe Marshmallow Glaze (page 276)	1
	Coarsely crushed graham crackers	
	Chopped chocolate	

1. *Cake:* In a medium bowl, whisk together flour, baking powder, baking soda and salt.
2. In the stand mixer bowl, beat granulated sugar, brown sugar, butter and oil on medium speed for 4 minutes or until light and fluffy. Beat in eggs, one at a time. Beat in vanilla.
3. With the mixer on low speed, alternately beat in flour mixture and buttermilk, making three additions of flour and two of buttermilk, and beating until incorporated.
4. Transfer half the batter to another medium bowl; stir in graham cracker crumbs, cinnamon and honey. Add cocoa to the remaining batter and beat until blended.

Tip

For best results, wrap the cooled cake tightly in plastic wrap and store at room temperature or in the refrigerator overnight before filling.

Make Ahead

You can prepare this cake up to 3 days in advance. Store the cooled glazed filled cake in a cake container in the refrigerator.

5. Using a ¼-cup (60 mL) measure, transfer dollops of alternating batters into prepared pan, layering until all the batter is used. Using a thin knife or skewer, drag the knife or skewer back and forth in a medium-width "S" motion several times around the Bundt.

6. Bake in preheated oven for 45 to 60 minutes or until a tester inserted in the center comes out clean. Let cool in pan for 10 minutes, then carefully invert cake onto a wire rack to cool completely (see tip).

7. *Filling:* In clean stand mixer bowl, beat sugar, salt, marshmallow creme and butter on medium speed for 2 minutes or until blended. Add cream and vanilla; beat for 2 minutes or until smooth, light and fluffy.

8. Return cooled cake to its cleaned and dried pan and fill with marshmallow filling as described on page 88. Carefully invert cake onto a serving plate.

9. Pour glaze over the cake, letting it drip down the sides. Sprinkle with crushed graham crackers and chopped chocolate. Let glaze set for at least 15 minutes before serving.

Banana Pudding Bundt

Like the Cinnamon-Swirl Caramel Bundt (page 122), this recipe is based on a classic Southern dessert and, for me, a nostalgic comfort food. I once created mini banana puddings layered in parfait glasses for a party. They went over so well that they inspired this pudding-filled banana Bundt topped with salted caramel glaze and crushed vanilla wafers.

MAKES 12 TO 14 SERVINGS

Tips

For best results, purée bananas in a food processor or using an immersion blender until smooth. Mashing bananas by hand often leaves several lumps, so the banana flavor isn't evenly distributed.

For best results, wrap the cooled cake tightly in plastic wrap and store at room temperature or in the refrigerator overnight before filling.

After filling cake, it's best to invert it onto a serving plate instead of a wire rack. Because sections of the cake have been removed and replaced, the cake should be moved as little as possible.

For the batter, vanilla wafer cookies should be finely ground, but use coarsely crushed for the decorative garnish.

- **Minimum 12-cup Bundt pan, sprayed**

BANANA PUDDING FILLING

¾ cup	granulated sugar	175 mL
¼ cup	cornstarch	60 mL
⅛ tsp	salt	0.5 mL
2	large eggs	2
2	large egg yolks	2
2 cups	whole milk	500 mL
¼ cup	banana liqueur	60 mL
1 tsp	vanilla extract	5 mL
2 tbsp	unsalted butter	30 mL

CAKE

2¼ cups	all-purpose flour	560 mL
1 tsp	baking powder	5 mL
1 tsp	baking soda	5 mL
1 tsp	ground cinnamon	5 mL
½ tsp	salt	2 mL
½ cup	granulated sugar	125 mL
½ cup	packed light brown sugar	125 mL
⅔ cup	vegetable oil	150 mL
3	large eggs, at room temperature	3
1½ cups	banana purée (about 3 medium bananas)	375 mL
2 tsp	vanilla extract	10 mL
¾ cup	full-fat sour cream	175 mL
1 cup	finely ground vanilla wafer cookie crumbs (see tip)	250 mL
1	ripe but firm banana, thinly sliced	1
1	recipe Salted Caramel Glaze (page 273)	1
	Coarsely crushed vanilla wafer cookies	

1. *Filling:* In a medium heatproof bowl, whisk together sugar, cornstarch, salt, eggs and egg yolks.

2. In a medium saucepan, bring milk to a simmer over medium heat. Remove from heat and gradually pour milk into egg mixture, whisking constantly, until blended. Return to saucepan. Whisk in liqueur and vanilla; cook over medium-low heat, whisking often, for 4 to 5 minutes or until thickened and glossy. Remove from heat and whisk in butter until melted and smooth.

3. Transfer pudding to a clean heatproof bowl and cover with plastic wrap, pressing it directly onto surface of pudding. Refrigerate for 3 hours or overnight.

Make Ahead

You can prepare the banana pudding filling up to 3 days in advance. Store in an airtight container in the refrigerator.

You can prepare this cake up to 3 days in advance. Store the cooled glazed filled cake in a cake container in the refrigerator. Let chilled cake stand at room temperature for 1 hour before serving.

4. *Cake:* Preheat oven to 350°F (180°C), or 325°F (160°C) for a dark pan.

5. In a medium bowl, whisk together flour, baking powder, baking soda, cinnamon and salt.

6. In the stand mixer bowl, beat granulated sugar, brown sugar and oil on medium speed for 1 minute or until blended. Beat in eggs, one at a time. Add banana purée and vanilla; beat for 2 minutes.

7. With the mixer on low speed, alternately beat in flour mixture and sour cream, making three additions of flour and two of sour cream, and beating until incorporated.

8. Using a spatula, fold in finely ground vanilla wafers. Transfer batter to prepared pan and smooth the top.

9. Bake for about 40 to 50 minutes or until a tester inserted in the center comes out clean. Let cool in pan for 10 minutes, then carefully invert cake onto a wire rack to cool completely (see tip).

10. Return cooled cake to its cleaned and dried pan. Stir chilled pudding to loosen and fill cake with pudding as described on page 88. Carefully invert cake onto a serving plate.

11. Pour glaze over the cake, letting it drip down the sides. Sprinkle with crushed vanilla wafers. Let glaze set for at least 15 minutes before serving.

Key Lime Bundt

My husband doesn't have much of a sweet tooth, but it's a rare occasion that he passes up Key lime pie when we go out to eat. Naturally, of all the Bundts in this book, this was the recipe that made him sit up and take notice. Fortunately, this lime curd–filled graham cracker cake with lime glaze received his nod of approval (as he polished off his second piece).

MAKES 12 TO 14 SERVINGS

Tips

Fresh Key limes are not always easy to find (unless you live in Florida), but definitely use them if possible. Key limes tend to have more acidity and lime "bouquet" than their larger counterparts. You will need about 9 or 10 Key limes for this recipe. If you can't find Key limes, in this recipe, you can use 4 to 5 regular limes for the zest and 6 to 8 regular limes for the juice.

Bottled Key lime juice is often easier to find than fresh Key limes, and you can use it as a substitute.

To make graham cracker crumbs, break whole crackers into pieces and process in food processor until finely ground.

- **Minimum 12-cup Bundt pan, sprayed**

KEY LIME FILLING

3	large eggs	3
3	large egg yolks	3
1½ cups	granulated sugar	375 mL
3 tbsp	cornstarch	45 mL
Pinch	salt	Pinch
1½ tbsp	grated Key lime zest (see tip)	22 mL
⅔ cup	freshly squeezed Key lime juice	150 mL
⅓ cup	water	75 mL
½ cup	unsalted butter	125 mL

CAKE

2½ cups	all-purpose flour	560 mL
1 tsp	baking powder	5 mL
1 tsp	baking soda	5 mL
1 tsp	salt	5 mL
1½ cups	granulated sugar	375 mL
1 cup	unsalted butter, softened	250 mL
4	large eggs, at room temperature	4
2 tbsp	grated Key lime zest	30 mL
¼ cup	freshly squeezed Key lime juice	60 mL
1 tsp	vanilla extract	5 mL
1 cup	buttermilk	250 mL
1 cup	finely ground graham cracker crumbs	250 mL
1	recipe Key Lime Glaze (variation, page 272)	1
	Crushed graham cracker crumbs	

1. *Filling:* In a medium heatproof bowl, whisk eggs and eggs yolks until blended.

2. In a medium saucepan, whisk together sugar, cornstarch, salt, lime zest, lime juice and water. Cook over medium heat, stirring constantly, for 4 to 5 minutes or until mixture boils and thickens.

3. Gradually add lime mixture to eggs, whisking constantly until blended. Return to saucepan and cook over medium heat, whisking often, for 2 minutes. Add butter, 1 tbsp (15 mL) at a time, whisking to incorporate. Reduce heat to low and cook for 5 to 6 minutes or until thickened.

4. Transfer filling to a clean heatproof bowl and cover with plastic wrap, pressing it directly onto surface of filling. Refrigerate for 3 hours or overnight.

Make Ahead

You can prepare the Key lime filling up to 5 days in advance. Store in an airtight container in the refrigerator.

You can prepare this cake up to 3 days in advance. Store the cooled glazed filled cake in a cake container in the refrigerator. If necessary, let chilled cake stand at room temperature for 1 hour before serving.

5. *Cake:* Preheat oven to 350°F (180°C), or 325°F (160°C) for a dark pan.

6. In a medium bowl, whisk together flour, baking powder, baking soda and salt.

7. In the stand mixer bowl, beat sugar and butter on medium speed for 4 minutes or until light and fluffy. Beat in eggs, one at a time. Add lime zest, lime juice and vanilla; beat for 2 minutes.

8. With the mixer on low speed, alternately beat in flour mixture and buttermilk, making three additions of flour and two of buttermilk, and beating until incorporated.

9. Using a spatula, fold in graham cracker crumbs. Transfer batter to prepared pan and smooth the top.

10. Bake for 40 to 50 minutes or until golden brown and a tester inserted in the center comes out clean. Let cool in pan for 10 minutes, then carefully invert cake onto a wire rack to cool completely (see second tip, page 104).

11. Return cooled cake to its cleaned and dried pan. Stir chilled filling to loosen and fill cake with Key lime filling as described on page 88. Carefully invert cake onto a serving plate.

12. Pour glaze over the cake, letting it drip down the sides. Sprinkle top of cake with crushed graham cracker crumbs. Let glaze set for at least 20 minutes before serving.

Mini Chocolate Lava Bundts

The chocolate lava cake, also called molten chocolate cake, became all the rage in the 1980s after it made its debut on a high-end restaurant's dessert menu in New York City. According to "lava cake legend," the chef pulled a chocolate cake from the oven before it was done, discovering that the center was still unbaked, but warm, and it had a decadent taste and the texture of a thick chocolate sauce. Individual versions of this cake are usually baked in muffin tins or soufflé cups, but I've created a version perfect for your mini Bundts. These "filled" cakes do part of the work for you by creating their own rich and gooey filling while baking!

MAKES 8 TO 10 MINI BUNDTS

Tips

If you are working with one mini Bundt pan, halve the recipe or prepare the cakes in two batches. Cover and chill the remaining batter until ready to use.

You'll want to keep an eye on these Bundts as they bake. At such a high temperature, the centers of the Bundts can go from "lava" to fully baked in just a few minutes.

After baking, invert Bundts onto something with a solid surface (not a wire rack), as the warm filling will seep through the bottoms and onto the counter.

Make Ahead

These cakes are best enjoyed immediately after baking, while "lava" centers are still warm.

- **Preheat oven to 425°F (220°C)**
- **Two 6-cake mini Bundt pans, sprayed**

1¾ cups	confectioners' (icing) sugar, sifted	425 mL
¾ cup	all-purpose flour	175 mL
¼ tsp	salt	1 mL
4	large eggs, at room temperature	4
4	large egg yolks, at room temperature	4
8 oz	dark or semisweet chocolate, chopped	250 g
¾ cup	unsalted butter	175 mL
	Fresh berries	
	Lightly sweetened whipped cream or ice cream	

1. In a medium bowl, whisk together confectioners' sugar, flour and salt.

2. In another medium bowl, whisk eggs and egg yolks until blended.

3. In a medium saucepan, melt chocolate and butter over medium-low heat, stirring often, until smooth. Remove from heat.

4. Slowly add eggs to chocolate mixture, whisking constantly, until smooth and glossy. Slowly add flour mixture, whisking until smooth.

5. Pour or spoon batter into prepared pans, filling each about halfway full. Smooth the tops.

6. Bake in preheated oven for 8 to 10 minutes or until tops are puffed and just set but still soft (see tip) and a tester inserted in the centers still appears wet. Let cool in pan for 2 to 3 minutes, then carefully invert cakes onto a platter or large plate (see tip). Serve warm alongside fresh berries and/or whipped cream or ice cream.

Variation

Add more flavor to your Bundts by beating in 1 tsp (5 mL) extract (such as almond, coconut, raspberry or peppermint) at the end of step 4.

Cherry, Vanilla and Chocolate Chunk Swirl Bundt

Layered and Swirled Bundts

Chocolate and Vanilla Marbled Bundt

I'm a very indecisive person when it comes to dessert. At the frozen yogurt shop, I never choose just one flavor; I get at least two flavors swirled — but I often try to fit three or four flavors in the cup. Asked if I prefer chocolate or vanilla, my answer is always "Both, please." When we were growing up, my brother would always request chocolate cake on his birthday (with chocolate frosting), but on my special day, I wanted a marbled cake, like this one. Half chocolate. Half vanilla. The best of both cake worlds in every bite.

MAKES 12 TO 14 SERVINGS

Tips

When swirling a Bundt batter, drag the knife or skewer back and forth in a medium-width "S" motion several times around the Bundt. This helps to create a pretty swirl without mixing the colors completely together.

For best results, wrap the cooled cake tightly in plastic wrap and store at room temperature or in the refrigerator overnight before glazing.

If the glaze needs "coaxing" down the sides of the Bundt, tap the plate or wire rack a few times on the counter.

Make Ahead

You can prepare this cake up to 3 days in advance. Store the cooled glazed cake in a cake container at room temperature or in the refrigerator (the chocolate glaze becomes dense and fudgy when chilled).

- Preheat oven to 350°F (180°C); dark pan, 325°F (160°C)
- Minimum 10-cup Bundt pan, sprayed

2½ cups	all-purpose flour	625 mL
2 tsp	baking powder	10 mL
¾ tsp	salt	3 mL
¼ tsp	baking soda	1 mL
1⅔ cups	granulated sugar	400 mL
½ cup	unsalted butter, softened	125 mL
⅓ cup	vegetable oil	75 mL
5	large eggs, at room temperature	5
2 tsp	vanilla extract	10 mL
1 cup	buttermilk	250 mL
½ cup	unsweetened cocoa powder, sifted	125 mL
1	recipe Chocolate Glaze (page 270)	1

1. In a medium bowl, whisk together flour, baking powder, salt and baking soda.

2. In the stand mixer bowl, beat sugar, butter and oil on medium speed for 3 minutes or until light and fluffy. Beat in eggs, one at a time. Add vanilla and beat for 2 minutes.

3. With the mixer on low speed, alternately beat in flour mixture and buttermilk, making three additions of flour and two of buttermilk, and beating until just incorporated.

4. Transfer half the batter to another medium bowl and stir in cocoa.

5. Spoon large dollops (about ¼ cup/60 mL each) of both batters into prepared pan, alternating vanilla and chocolate, until you have used all of the batter. Use a knife or skewer to marble the batters (see tip). Smooth the top.

6. Bake in preheated oven for 45 to 55 minutes or until puffed and golden brown and a tester inserted in the center comes out clean. Let cool in pan for 10 minutes, then carefully invert cake onto a wire rack to cool completely (see tip).

7. Pour glaze over the cooled cake, letting it drip down the sides (see tip). Let glaze set for at least 20 minutes before serving.

Strawberries and Cream Bundt

This summery, pretty swirled Bundt with subtle strawberry accents would be right at home during a "proper" garden tea — or during a not-so-proper one on a blanket on the floor, like the ones I attend with my daughter! If strawberries are the stars of the cake, then the vanilla bean is the best supporting role. Featured in both the cake and glaze, the vanilla bean infuses an intensely warm, rich and creamy flavor throughout each slice. Store scraped-out pods in jars of sugar to make vanilla-scented sugar!

MAKES 12 TO 14 SERVINGS

Tips

If you don't have cake flour, you can make a substitute. See page 16 for more information.

When swirling a Bundt batter, drag the knife or skewer back and forth in a medium-width "S" motion several times around the Bundt. This helps to create a pretty swirl without mixing the colors completely together.

For best results, wrap the cooled cake tightly in plastic wrap and store at room temperature or in the refrigerator overnight before glazing.

- Preheat oven to 350°F (180°C); dark pan, 325°F (160°C)
- Minimum 10-cup Bundt pan, sprayed

1 cup	finely chopped strawberries	250 mL
6 tbsp	granulated sugar	90 mL
2 tbsp	freshly squeezed lemon juice	30 mL
2½ cups	cake flour, sifted	625 mL
1 tsp	baking powder	5 mL
1 tsp	salt	5 mL
2½ cups	granulated sugar	625 mL
1 cup	unsalted butter, softened	250 mL
6	large eggs, at room temperature	6
½	vanilla bean, split	½
1 cup	heavy or whipping (35%) cream	250 mL
2 to 3	drops red food coloring (optional)	2 to 3
1	recipe Vanilla Bean Glaze (page 271)	1

1. In a small saucepan, bring strawberries, 6 tbsp (90 mL) sugar and lemon juice to a simmer over medium heat, stirring often. Reduce heat and simmer, stirring occasionally, for 10 minutes or until strawberries have broken down and mixture has thickened to a jam-like consistency. Let cool completely.
2. In a medium bowl, whisk together flour, baking powder and salt.
3. In the stand mixer bowl, beat 2½ cups (625 mL) sugar and butter on medium speed for 4 minutes or until very light and fluffy. Beat in eggs, one at a time.
4. Using a paring knife, scrape seeds from vanilla bean (see box, page 18). Add seeds to batter and beat for 2 minutes.
5. With the mixer on low speed, alternately beat in flour mixture and cream, making three additions of flour and two of cream, and beating until incorporated.
6. Transfer half the batter to another medium bowl. Stir in reserved strawberry mixture. Add 2 to 3 drops of red food coloring, if desired, to boost color.
7. Transfer half the vanilla batter to prepared pan and smooth the top. Top with half the strawberry batter and smooth the top. Repeat layering with the remaining batters. Use a knife or skewer to marble the batters (see tip).

Make Ahead

You can prepare this cake up to 3 days in advance. Store the cooled glazed cake in a cake container in the refrigerator. Let chilled cake stand at room temperature for 1 hour before serving.

8. Bake in preheated oven for 45 to 60 minutes or until puffed and golden brown and a tester inserted in the center comes out clean. Let cool in pan for 10 minutes, then carefully invert cake onto a wire rack to cool completely (see tip).

9. Pour glaze over the cooled cake, letting it drip down the sides. Let glaze set for at least 15 minutes before serving.

Variations

One cup (250 mL) drained thawed frozen strawberries may be used in place of fresh.

Ground vanilla bean (also called vanilla bean powder) is available in jars in specialty baking and spice shops and makes a good substitute for whole vanilla beans; use ¾ tsp (3 mL) ground in both the cake and the glaze. Or you can substitute 1½ tsp (7 mL) vanilla extract for the vanilla bean in both the cake and glaze (added at the same times as the vanilla bean), although I prefer the pretty black specks and the deep vanilla flavor that result from using beans.

Triple Butterscotch Swirl Bundt

I love the salty-sweet-buttery flavor profile of butterscotch, which is why I've featured it not once, not twice, but three times in this Bundt.

MAKES 12 TO
14 SERVINGS

Tips

This cake is best prepared using full-fat sour cream, as it helps to keep it moist, but you can also use a lower-fat version (not fat-free).

For best results, wrap the cooled cake tightly in plastic wrap and store at room temperature or in the refrigerator overnight before glazing.

Make Ahead

You can prepare this cake up to 3 days in advance. Store the cooled glazed cake in a cake container at room temperature or in the refrigerator.

- Preheat oven to 350°F (180°C); dark pan, 325°F (160°C)
- Food processor
- Minimum 12-cup Bundt pan, sprayed

BUTTERSCOTCH SWIRL

⅔ cup	butterscotch chips	150 mL
⅔ cup	chopped pecans	150 mL
⅓ cup	packed dark brown sugar	75 mL
2 tsp	ground cinnamon	10 mL
½ tsp	salt	2 mL
¼ cup	unsalted butter, softened	60 mL

CAKE

3 cups	all-purpose flour	750 mL
1½ tsp	baking powder	7 mL
1 tsp	salt	5 mL
¾ tsp	baking soda	3 mL
1½ cups	packed dark brown sugar	375 mL
¾ cup	unsalted butter, softened	175 mL
¼ cup	vegetable oil	60 mL
3	large eggs, at room temperature	3
2 tbsp	Scotch or whiskey	30 mL
1¼ cups	sour cream (not fat-free)	300 mL
1	recipe Butterscotch Glaze (page 274)	1

1. *Swirl:* In food processor, pulse butterscotch chips, pecans, brown sugar, cinnamon, salt and butter until mixture is very finely chopped and moist clumps form.

2. *Cake:* In a medium bowl, whisk together flour, baking powder, salt and baking soda.

3. In the stand mixer bowl, beat brown sugar, butter and oil on medium speed for 4 minutes or until light and fluffy. Beat in eggs, one at a time. Add scotch and beat for 2 minutes.

4. With the mixer on low speed, alternately beat in flour mixture and sour cream, making three additions of flour and two of sour cream, and beating until incorporated.

5. Transfer half the batter to prepared pan and smooth the top. Sprinkle butterscotch mixture evenly over batter and top with the remaining batter. Smooth the top.

6. Bake in preheated oven for 60 to 70 minutes or until puffed and golden brown and a tester inserted in the center comes out clean. Let cool in pan for 10 minutes, then carefully invert cake onto a wire rack to cool completely (see tip).

7. Pour glaze over the cooled cake, letting it drip down the sides. Let glaze set for at least 20 minutes before serving.

Neapolitan Bundt

Most people are familiar with Neapolitan ice cream, which displays three flavors side-by-side. Originating in Naples, Italy, early recipes used flavors that resembled the Italian flag (for example, green pistachio instead of chocolate), but as the concept was introduced to the United States in the late 1800s, chocolate, vanilla and strawberry were substituted due to their popularity. In this Bundt, the three flavored batters layered in the pan magically swirl on their own during baking.

MAKES 12 TO 14 SERVINGS

Tips

Use a clean, dry bowl in step 4 to ensure the egg whites firm up as they are beaten. For best results, use a stainless steel, copper or glass bowl, as plastic and wooden bowls can absorb oils and water, which can inhibit the whipping process. Also make sure your beaters are clean and oil-free before whipping.

The batter for the chocolate cake can be stirred by hand instead of using an electric or stand mixer. If you're not using the mixer, you need to transfer only half the batter in step 6 to a separate bowl.

It's okay if the layers of batter aren't perfectly even in the pan. This cake requires no "swirling," since the batters will magically swirl on their own during the baking process.

- Preheat oven to 350°F (180°C); dark pan, 325°F (160°C)
- Handheld electric mixer
- Minimum 10-cup Bundt pan, sprayed

STRAWBERRY AND VANILLA BATTERS

1¾ cups	all-purpose flour	425 mL
1½ tsp	baking powder	7 mL
½ tsp	salt	2 mL
1 cup	granulated sugar	250 mL
¾ cup	unsalted butter, softened	175 mL
1 tsp	vanilla extract	5 mL
⅔ cup	whole milk	150 mL
3	large egg whites, at room temperature	3
¼ cup	strawberry jam	60 mL
1 tsp	strawberry-flavored gelatin powder	5 mL

CHOCOLATE BATTER

¾ cup + 2 tbsp	all-purpose flour	205 mL
⅓ cup	unsweetened cocoa powder, sifted	75 mL
¼ tsp	baking powder	1 mL
¼ tsp	baking soda	1 mL
¼ tsp	salt	1 mL
¾ cup	granulated sugar	175 mL
⅓ cup	vegetable oil	75 mL
1	large egg, at room temperature	1
½ cup	buttermilk	125 mL
	Confectioners' (icing) sugar, sifted	

1. *Strawberry and Vanilla Batters:* In a medium bowl, whisk together flour, baking powder and salt.
2. In the stand mixer bowl, beat sugar and butter on medium speed for 4 minutes or until light and fluffy. Beat in vanilla.
3. With the mixer on low speed, alternately beat in flour mixture and milk, making three additions of flour and two of milk, and beating until incorporated.
4. In another medium bowl (see tip), using the handheld mixer, beat egg whites on medium-low speed until foamy. Gradually increase to high speed and beat until firm peaks form.
5. Using a spatula, carefully fold egg whites into batter in two additions.

Tip

For best results, wrap the cooled cake tightly in plastic wrap and store at room temperature or in the refrigerator overnight before dusting with confectioners' sugar.

Make Ahead

You can prepare this cake up to 3 days in advance. Store the cooled cake in a cake container at room temperature.

6. Divide batter evenly between two bowls. Stir jam and strawberry gelatin into one of the bowls until blended.

7. *Chocolate Batter:* In another medium bowl, whisk together flour, cocoa, baking powder, baking soda and salt.

8. In clean mixer bowl, beat sugar and oil on medium speed for 4 minutes or until light and fluffy. Add egg and beat for 2 minutes.

9. With the mixer on low speed, alternately beat in flour mixture and buttermilk, making three additions of flour and two of buttermilk, and beating until incorporated.

10. Transfer vanilla batter to prepared pan and smooth the top. Pour strawberry batter over vanilla batter and smooth the top, then pour on chocolate batter and smooth the top.

11. Bake in preheated oven for 45 to 55 minutes until puffed and golden brown and a tester inserted in the center comes out clean. Let cool in pan for 10 minutes, then carefully invert cake onto a wire rack to cool completely (see tip). Dust with confectioners' sugar before serving.

Après-Ski Bundt (Irish Cream and Chocolate Swirl Cake)

My husband and I go skiing in Wyoming every year. He grew up skiing competitively in Vermont, so he conquers those double–black diamond slopes as if they were beginner-level hills. We usually split up so we can ski at our respective levels — to be honest, I prefer relatively flat cross-country skiing! After a few runs, he is ready to head back up the mountain for more, while I am ready to head into a lodge, take off my boots and enjoy a rich, warming Irish cream coffee by the fire, topped with whipped cream and chocolate shavings. This swirled Bundt mimics the flavors of my favorite après-ski ritual.

MAKES 10 TO 12 SERVINGS

Tips

It's important to sift cocoa before adding to batter, to avoid bitter-tasting clumps.

When swirling a Bundt batter, drag the knife or skewer back and forth in a medium-width "S" motion several times around the Bundt. This helps to create a pretty swirl without mixing the colors completely together.

For best results, wrap the cooled cake tightly in plastic wrap and store at room temperature or in the refrigerator overnight before glazing.

Make Ahead

You can prepare this cake up to 3 days in advance. Store the cooled glazed cake in a cake container at room temperature or in the refrigerator.

- Preheat oven to 350°F (180°C); dark pan, 325°F (160°C)
- Minimum 10-cup Bundt pan, sprayed

2 cups	all-purpose flour	500 mL
1 tsp	baking soda	5 mL
½ tsp	salt	2 mL
2 cups	granulated sugar	500 mL
¾ cup	vegetable oil	175 mL
4	large eggs, at room temperature	4
1 tsp	vanilla extract	5 mL
1 cup	buttermilk	250 mL
½ cup	unsweetened cocoa powder, sifted	125 mL
½ tsp	ground cinnamon	2 mL
⅓ cup	Irish cream liqueur	75 mL
1	recipe Irish Cream Glaze (page 275)	1

1. In a medium bowl, whisk together flour, baking soda and salt.
2. In the stand mixer bowl, beat sugar and oil on medium speed for 2 minutes or until light and fluffy. Beat in eggs, one at a time. Add vanilla and beat for 2 minutes.
3. With the mixer on low speed, alternately beat in flour mixture and buttermilk, making three additions of flour and two of buttermilk, and beating until incorporated.
4. Transfer half the batter to another medium bowl. Stir in cocoa and cinnamon.
5. Stir Irish cream into the remaining batter.
6. Spoon large dollops (about ¼ cup/60 mL each) of alternating batters into prepared pan until you have used all of the batter. Use a knife or skewer to marble the batters (see tip). Smooth the top.
7. Bake in preheated oven for 50 to 60 minutes or until puffed and golden brown and a tester inserted in the center comes out clean. Let cool in pan for 10 minutes, then carefully invert cake onto a wire rack to cool completely (see tip).
8. Pour glaze over the cooled cake, letting it drip down the sides. Let glaze set for at least 15 minutes before serving.

Cinnamon-Swirl Caramel Bundt

Caramel cake, with its signature thick, candy-like frosting, has been a Southern staple for generations. The traditional cake is a moist yellow cake covered in a thick caramel frosting that is slow-cooked for up to 2 hours in some recipes. In my version, I've thinned out the frosting slightly in order to make it Bundt-friendly, but it still maintains the texture and taste of the classic recipes. I've also added a cinnamon-sugar swirl, which creates a pretty presentation when sliced.

MAKES 12 TO 14 SERVINGS

Tips

If you don't have cake flour, you can make a substitute. See page 16 for more information.

For best results, wrap the cooled cake tightly in plastic wrap and store at room temperature or in the refrigerator overnight before glazing.

Make Ahead

You can prepare this cake up to 3 days in advance. Store the cooled glazed cake in a cake container at room temperature or in the refrigerator.

- Preheat oven to 350°F (180°C); dark pan, 325°F (160°C)
- Minimum 12-cup Bundt pan, sprayed

CINNAMON SWIRL

1 cup	packed light brown sugar	250 mL
1½ tsp	ground cinnamon	7 mL
¼ tsp	salt	1 mL
¼ cup	full-fat sour cream	60 mL

CAKE

3 cups	cake flour, sifted	750 mL
1 tsp	salt	5 mL
½ tsp	baking powder	2 mL
½ tsp	baking soda	2 mL
1½ cups	granulated sugar	375 mL
1 cup	unsalted butter, softened	250 mL
½ cup	vegetable oil	125 mL
5	large eggs, at room temperature	5
1 tbsp	vanilla extract	15 mL
1 cup	full-fat sour cream	250 mL
1	recipe Thick Caramel Glaze (page 273)	1

1. *Swirl:* In a small bowl, stir together brown sugar, cinnamon, salt and sour cream until blended.

2. *Cake:* In a medium bowl, whisk together flour, salt, baking powder and baking soda.

3. In the stand mixer bowl, beat sugar, butter and oil on medium speed for 4 minutes or until light and fluffy. Beat in eggs, one at a time. Add vanilla and beat for 2 minutes.

4. With the mixer on low speed, alternately beat in flour mixture and sour cream, making three additions of flour and two of sour cream, and beating until incorporated.

5. Transfer half the batter to prepared pan and smooth the top. Sprinkle cinnamon mixture evenly over batter and top with the remaining batter. Smooth the top.

6. Bake in preheated oven for 55 to 65 minutes or until puffed and golden brown and a tester inserted in the center comes out clean. Let cool in pan for 10 minutes, then carefully invert cake onto a wire rack to cool completely (see tip).

7. Pour glaze over the cooled cake, letting it drip down the sides. Let glaze set for at least 20 minutes before serving.

Rainbow Swirl Bundt

For anyone who believes that cake can't make you happy, try to not smile when presented with a slice of this stunningly bright and colorful Bundt. I'll be honest: When I came up with this concept, I wasn't sure if it would work — would the flavors blend and create one big mess? But, after waiting impatiently for it to cool, I breathed a sigh of relief when I saw the magically swirled rainbow layers in every slice (similar to Neapolitan Bundt, page 118). Topped with a tart, "sunny" lemon glaze, this vanilla-flavored cake is perfect for kids and kids at heart!

MAKES 12 TO 14 SERVINGS

Tips

The most accurate way to evenly divide batter is to weigh it. Using a kitchen scale, weigh an empty bowl, add all the batter and subtract the original weight of the bowl. Divide this number by 6 to see how much batter should be placed in each small bowl.

I prefer gel-based food coloring (rather than liquid), because it produces the most vivid colors. Colors vary in intensity, so you may need to use fewer or more drops to achieve your desired color.

This cake requires no "swirling," since the batters will magically swirl on their own during the baking process.

Make Ahead

You can prepare this cake up to 3 days in advance. Store the cooled glazed cake in a cake container at room temperature or in the refrigerator.

- Preheat oven to 350°F (180°C); dark pan, 325°F (160°C)
- Minimum 12-cup Bundt pan, sprayed

3 cups	all-purpose flour	750 mL
2 tsp	baking powder	10 mL
1 tsp	salt	5 mL
½ tsp	baking soda	2 mL
2¼ cups	granulated sugar	560 mL
1 cup	unsalted butter, softened	250 mL
¼ cup	vegetable oil	60 mL
4	large eggs, at room temperature	4
1 tbsp	vanilla extract	15 mL
1⅓ cups	buttermilk	325 mL
	Red, orange, yellow, green, blue and purple food coloring	
⅔	recipe Lemon Glaze (page 272)	⅔

1. In a medium bowl, whisk together flour, baking powder, salt and baking soda.

2. In the stand mixer bowl, beat sugar, butter and oil on medium speed for 4 minutes or until light and fluffy. Beat in eggs, one at a time. Add vanilla and beat for 2 minutes.

3. With the mixer on low speed, alternately beat in flour mixture and buttermilk, making three additions of flour and two of buttermilk, and beating until incorporated.

4. Divide batter equally among 6 small bowls (see tip), about 1⅓ cups (325 mL) in each (you can leave one portion in the mixer bowl). Stir 4 to 8 drops red food coloring into one bowl and stir until thoroughly blended and color is even. Repeat with other food coloring and batters (see tip).

5. Transfer red batter to prepared pan, spreading evenly using a spoon or an offset spatula. Repeat process with the remaining batters in the following order: orange, yellow, green, blue and purple. Do your best to layer each color evenly without swirling into other colors, but expect some imperfections.

6. Bake in preheated oven for 55 to 65 minutes or until puffed and golden brown and a tester inserted in the center comes out clean. Let cool in pan for 10 minutes, then carefully invert cake onto a wire rack to cool completely (see tip, page 122).

7. Pour glaze over the cooled cake, letting it drip down the sides. Let glaze set for at least 15 minutes before serving.

Red Velvet Bundt with Cream Cheese Swirl

Red velvet pancakes. Red velvet cake balls. Red velvet cocktails — yes, I've seen them! I think we can all agree that red velvet is *everywhere*. And it almost always comes with a side of cream cheese, whether it's a frosting, syrup, glaze, filling or drizzle. I couldn't get away without including a red velvet Bundt in this book, so I doubled up on the cream cheese, using it in both in the filling and the smooth glaze, which contrasts beautifully with the deep red color of the cake.

MAKES 10 TO 12 SERVINGS

Tips

If you don't have cake flour, you can make a substitute. See page 16 for more information.

The apple cider vinegar acts as an acid that reacts with the baking soda, to give the batter a lift as it bakes. You will not taste it in the finished product, I promise!

When swirling a Bundt batter, drag the knife or skewer back and forth in a medium-width "S" motion several times around the Bundt. This helps to create a pretty swirl without mixing the cake completely.

For best results, wrap the cooled cake tightly in plastic wrap and store at room temperature or in the refrigerator overnight before glazing.

- Preheat oven to 350°F (180°C); dark pan, 325°F (160°C)
- Minimum 10-cup Bundt pan, sprayed

CAKE

2¼ cups	cake flour, sifted	560 mL
3 tbsp	unsweetened cocoa powder, sifted	45 mL
½ tsp	salt	2 mL
2 cups	granulated sugar	500 mL
½ cup	unsalted butter, softened	125 mL
½ cup	vegetable oil	125 mL
4	large eggs, at room temperature	4
2 tsp	vanilla extract	10 mL
¾ tsp	baking soda	3 mL
1½ tsp	apple cider vinegar	7 mL
3 tbsp	liquid red food coloring	45 mL
1 cup	buttermilk	250 mL

FILLING

⅓ cup	granulated sugar	75 mL
2 tbsp	all-purpose flour	30 mL
1	large egg, at room temperature	1
8 oz	brick-style cream cheese, softened	250 g
2 tsp	vanilla extract	10 mL
1	recipe Cream Cheese Glaze (page 276)	1

1. *Cake:* In a medium bowl, whisk together flour, cocoa and salt.
2. In the stand mixer bowl, beat sugar, butter and oil on medium speed for 3 minutes or until light. Beat in eggs, one at a time. Beat in vanilla.
3. In a small bowl, stir together baking soda and vinegar until dissolved. Beat into batter.
4. Add food coloring to batter and beat for 1 minute or until color is even.
5. With the mixer on low speed, alternately beat in flour mixture and buttermilk, making three additions of flour and two of buttermilk, and beating until incorporated.
6. *Filling:* In another medium bowl, stir together sugar, flour, egg, cream cheese and vanilla until well blended.

Make Ahead

You can prepare this cake up to 3 days in advance. Store the cooled glazed cake in a cake container at room temperature or in the refrigerator.

7. Transfer half the batter to prepared pan and smooth the top. Drop filling in dollops on top of batter, spreading evenly around pan. Top filling with the remaining batter. Use a knife or skewer to marble the cake (see tip). Smooth the top.

8. Bake in preheated oven for 45 to 55 minutes or until a tester inserted in the center comes out with only a few moist crumbs attached. Let cool in pan for 10 minutes, then carefully invert cake onto a wire rack to cool completely (see tip).

9. Pour glaze over the cooled cake, letting it drip down the sides. Let glaze set for at least 20 minutes before serving.

Peanut Butter Banana Swirl Bundt

I almost named this recipe the Peanut Butter Banana "Invisible Swirl" Bundt because, compared to the other cakes in this chapter, the swirled pattern is not as detectable. (But I promise, one bite and you'll know it's there.) I could have also named it "The Elvis," based on The King's notorious fondness of these two flavors. For that matter, I suppose I could have also named it "The Julie." No matter what the name, topped with a sweet peanut-y glaze, this Bundt certainly qualifies as comfort food and will be a hit with any peanut-butter lover in your life.

MAKES 12 TO 14 SERVINGS

Tips

For best results, purée bananas in a food processor or an immersion blender until smooth. Mashing bananas by hand often leaves several lumps, so the banana flavor isn't evenly distributed.

Use regular (not "natural") peanut butter for this recipe.

Look for dried banana chips in the bulk or natural foods section of your grocery store.

When swirling a Bundt batter, drag the knife or skewer back and forth in a medium-width "S" motion several times around the Bundt. This helps to create a pretty swirl without mixing the colors completely together.

For best results, wrap the cooled cake tightly in plastic wrap and store at room temperature or in the refrigerator overnight before glazing.

- Preheat oven to 325°F (160°C)
- Minimum 12-cup Bundt pan, sprayed

3 cups	all-purpose flour	750 mL
1½ tsp	baking powder	7 mL
1 tsp	baking soda	5 mL
½ tsp	salt	2 mL
¾ cup	granulated sugar	175 mL
¾ cup	packed light brown sugar	175 mL
1 cup	vegetable oil	250 mL
4	large eggs, at room temperature	4
1 tsp	vanilla extract	5 mL
1 cup	buttermilk	250 mL
½ tsp	ground ginger	2 mL
¾ cup	banana purée (see tip)	175 mL
1 tsp	ground cinnamon	5 mL
¾ cup	smooth peanut butter	175 mL
1	recipe Peanut Butter Glaze (page 276)	1
	Chopped peanuts (optional)	
	Coarsely chopped dried banana chips (optional)	

1. In a medium bowl, whisk together flour, baking powder, baking soda and salt.
2. In the stand mixer bowl, beat granulated sugar, brown sugar and oil on medium speed for 2 minutes or until light and fluffy. Beat in eggs, one at a time. Add vanilla and beat for 2 minutes.
3. With the mixer on low speed, alternately beat in flour mixture and buttermilk, making three additions of flour and two of buttermilk, and beating until incorporated.
4. Transfer 2½ cups (625 mL) batter (about half) to another medium bowl. Stir in ginger and banana purée.
5. Stir cinnamon and peanut butter into the remaining batter until blended and smooth.
6. Transfer half the peanut butter batter to prepared pan and smooth the top. Pour over half the banana batter (banana batter will be thinner than peanut butter batter). Repeat layering with the remaining batters. Use a knife or skewer to marble the batters (see tip). Smooth the top.

Make Ahead

You can prepare this cake up to 4 days in advance. Store the cooled glazed cake in a cake container at room temperature or in the refrigerator.

7. Bake in preheated oven for 55 to 65 minutes or until puffed and golden brown and a tester inserted in the center comes out clean. Let cool in pan for 10 minutes, then carefully invert cake onto a wire rack to cool completely (see tip).

8. Pour glaze over the cooled cake, letting it drip down the sides. If desired, garnish with peanuts and banana chips. Let glaze set for at least 15 minutes before serving.

Cookies-and-Cream Bundt

I'm in danger of dating myself, but I remember very clearly when cookies-and-cream ice cream first started showing up in grocery stores and ice cream shops around town. Before long, cookies-and-cream was the *only* flavor my friends and I wanted to eat, especially when they started selling it as ice cream sandwiches and ice cream bars. It's still one of the most popular flavors, ranking right up there with vanilla, chocolate and strawberry. In this sweet, white cake, chocolate wafer sandwich cookies are not only mixed into the batter, but they are also layered in the center to create a swirl upon baking and sprinkled atop the creamy vanilla glaze for garnish.

MAKES 12 TO 14 SERVINGS

Tip

For ground sandwich cookies, use a food processor to process sandwich cookies to the texture of coarse sand. You will need 15 to 20 cookies to yield 1 cup (250 mL). For coarsely chopped cookies, use either a sharp knife to chop, or pulse 4 to 6 times for 1 second in the food processor.

Make Ahead

You can prepare this cake up to 3 days in advance. Store the cooled glazed cake in a cake container at room temperature or in the refrigerator (I prefer chilling cakes that have a cream-based glaze, but it's not necessary). If desired, let chilled cake stand at room temperature for 1 hour before serving.

- Preheat oven to 350°F (180°C); dark pan, 325°F (160°C)
- Handheld electric mixer
- Minimum 10-cup Bundt pan, sprayed

2½ cups	cake flour, sifted	625 mL
2 tsp	baking powder	10 mL
½ tsp	salt	2 mL
1¼ cups	granulated sugar	300 mL
½ cup	unsalted butter, softened	125 mL
½ cup	vegetable shortening, softened	125 mL
1 tsp	vanilla extract	5 mL
1 cup	half-and-half (10%) cream	250 mL
5	large egg whites, at room temperature	5
1 tbsp	granulated sugar	15 mL
1 cup	coarsely crushed cream-filled chocolate sandwich cookies (such as Oreos)	250 mL
1 cup	ground cream-filled chocolate sandwich cookies (see tip)	250 mL
1	recipe Vanilla Glaze (page 271)	1
	Additional crushed cream-filled chocolate sandwich cookies (optional)	

1. In a medium bowl, whisk together flour, baking powder and salt.
2. In the stand mixer bowl, beat 1¼ cups (300 mL) sugar, butter and shortening on medium speed for 4 minutes or until light and fluffy. Beat in vanilla.
3. With the mixer on low speed, alternately beat in flour mixture and cream, making three additions of flour and two of cream, and beating until incorporated.
4. In another medium bowl (see tip, page 118), using the handheld mixer, beat egg whites with 1 tbsp (15 mL) sugar on medium-low speed until foamy. Gradually increase to high speed and beat until firm peaks form.
5. Using a spatula, carefully fold egg whites into batter in three additions until fully incorporated. Fold in coarsely crushed sandwich cookies.
6. Transfer half the batter to prepared pan and smooth the top. Sprinkle ground sandwich cookies evenly over batter and top with the remaining batter. Smooth the top.

Tip

This Bundt is on the
sweeter side, so smaller
slices will still be very
satisfying! Have lots of
ice-cold milk on hand
to serve alongside
the cake.

7. Bake in preheated oven for 45 to 60 minutes or until a tester inserted in the center comes out clean (there may be a few cookie crumbs attached). Let cool in pan for 10 minutes, then carefully invert cake onto a wire rack to cool completely (see last tip, page 132).

8. Pour glaze over the cooled cake, letting it drip down the sides. If desired, garnish with more crushed sandwich cookies. Let glaze set for at least 15 minutes before serving.

Variation

Substitute Cream Cheese Glaze (page 276) for the Vanilla Glaze.

Cherry, Vanilla and Chocolate Chunk Swirl Bundt

This Bundt looks like one big sundae: a chocolate-studded, cherry-swirled vanilla cake covered in vanilla bean glaze and garnished with cherries. That said, it never hurts to serve it with a scoop of ice cream. Just grab a spoon and dig in! I love the tart-rich flavor combination of chocolate and cherry (see Chocolate Malt and Sour Cherry Bundts with Cherry Vanilla Bean Glaze, page 222). Together, they steal the show in this recipe, contrasting not only in taste but also in appearance throughout each beautiful slice.

MAKES 12 TO 14 SERVINGS

Tips

Pitted fresh cherries can be used in place of frozen.

An easy way to soften butter is to cut it into 1 to 2 tbsp (15 to 30 mL) chunks and microwave it on Low (10%) in 15-second intervals until it reaches the desired consistency.

When swirling a Bundt batter, drag the knife or skewer back and forth in a medium-width "S" motion several times around the Bundt. This helps to create a pretty swirl without mixing the colors completely together.

Wider Bundt pans will bake the batter more quickly, while cakes in narrower, deeper pans will need more time to bake through.

For best results, wrap the cooled cake tightly in plastic wrap and store at room temperature or in the refrigerator overnight before glazing.

- Preheat oven to 350°F (180°C); dark pan, 325°F (160°C)
- Food processor
- Minimum 10-cup Bundt pan, sprayed

1 cup	frozen pitted cherries	250 mL
2½ cups	granulated sugar, divided	625 mL
1 tbsp	freshly squeezed lemon juice	15 mL
2½ cups	all-purpose flour	625 mL
1 tsp	baking powder	5 mL
½ tsp	baking soda	2 mL
½ tsp	salt	2 mL
1 cup	unsalted butter, softened	250 mL
4	large eggs, at room temperature	4
2 tsp	vanilla extract	10 mL
1 cup	full-fat sour cream	250 mL
¼ tsp	almond extract	1 mL
¾ cup	chopped dark or semisweet chocolate (4½ oz/135 g)	175 mL
1	recipe Vanilla Bean Glaze (page 271)	1

1. In food processor, pulse frozen cherries several times, until finely chopped.
2. In a small saucepan, bring cherries, ¼ cup (60 mL) sugar and lemon juice to a simmer, stirring, over medium heat. Reduce heat and simmer, stirring occasionally, for 10 minutes or until mixture has broken down and thickened to a jam-like consistency and has reduced to about ⅔ cup (150 mL). Let cool completely.
3. In a medium bowl, whisk together flour, baking powder, baking soda and salt.
4. In the stand mixer bowl, beat the remaining sugar and butter on medium speed for 4 minutes or until light and fluffy. Beat in eggs, one at a time. Add vanilla and beat for 2 minutes.
5. With the mixer on low speed, alternately beat in flour mixture and sour cream, making three additions of flour and two of sour cream, and beating until incorporated.
6. Transfer 1½ cups (375 mL) batter (about one-third) to another medium bowl. Stir in cherry mixture and almond extract.

Make Ahead

You can prepare this cake up to 3 days in advance. Store the cooled glazed cake in a cake container in the refrigerator. Let chilled cake stand at room temperature for 1 hour before serving.

7. Stir chocolate into the remaining vanilla batter.

8. Spoon large dollops of batters into prepared pan, alternating flavors, making two chocolate dollops for every cherry dollop, until you have used all the batter. Use a knife or skewer to marble the batters (see tip). Smooth the top.

9. Bake in preheated oven for 45 to 65 minutes or until puffed and golden brown and a tester inserted in the center comes out clean. Let cool in pan for 10 minutes, then carefully invert cake onto a wire rack to cool completely (see tip).

10. Pour glaze over the cooled cake, letting it drip down the sides. Let glaze set for at least 15 minutes before serving.

Chocolate Hazelnut Latte Bundt

The first time I tried the chocolate hazelnut spread Nutella was during French class in high school. My teacher, Madame Miller, would often bring in French foods for the class to try. At that point, Nutella wasn't widely available in the United States, so tasting the smooth chocolate-hazelnut spread was a deliciously memorable treat — no wonder French was my favorite class! Today, of course, Nutella is everywhere, sitting right next to the peanut butter on grocery store shelves. There is even a coffee house in my town that is famous for their decadent Nutella-swirled lattes, a favorite indulgence of mine and the inspiration for this recipe.

MAKES 12 TO 14 SERVINGS

Tips

If you can't find espresso powder, replace the powder and water with ¼ cup (60 mL) strong brewed coffee.

Chocolate hazelnut spread is quite thick and will be difficult to spread over the batter at room temperature. Warm it in its packaging (if in glass) or in a microwave-safe bowl in the microwave in 15-second intervals, or transfer to a small saucepan and heat over medium-low heat, stirring occasionally, until heated through.

Make Ahead

You can prepare this cake up to 3 days in advance. Store the cooled glazed cake in a cake container at room temperature or in the refrigerator — chilling the cake results in a denser, fudgier glaze, which I love!

- Preheat oven to 350°F (180°C); dark pan, 325°F (160°C)
- Minimum 10-cup Bundt pan, sprayed

1½ tsp	espresso powder	7 mL
¼ cup	hot water	60 mL
2½ cups	all-purpose flour	625 mL
2 tsp	baking powder	10 mL
½ tsp	salt	2 mL
1¾ cups	granulated sugar	425 mL
1 cup	unsalted butter, softened	250 mL
4	large eggs, at room temperature	4
1 cup	whole milk	250 mL
¾ cup	chocolate hazelnut spread (such as Nutella), warmed	1/5 mL
1	Chocolate Hazelnut Glaze (page 270) Chopped hazelnuts (optional)	1

1. In a small bowl, stir together espresso powder and hot water.
2. In a medium bowl, whisk together flour, baking powder and salt.
3. In the stand mixer bowl, beat sugar and butter on medium speed for 4 minutes or until light and fluffy. Beat in eggs, one at a time.
4. With the mixer on low speed, alternately beat in flour mixture, espresso mixture and milk, making three additions of flour and one each of espresso and milk, and beating until incorporated.
5. Transfer half the batter to prepared pan and smooth the top. Drizzle with chocolate hazelnut spread. Using the back of a spoon or an offset spatula, spread as evenly as possible. Top with the remaining batter and smooth the top.
6. Bake in preheated oven for 50 to 60 minutes or until puffed and golden brown and a tester inserted in the center comes out clean. Let cool in pan for 10 minutes, then carefully invert cake onto a wire rack to cool completely (see last tip, page 132).
7. Pour glaze over the cooled cake, letting it drip down the sides. If desired, garnish with chopped hazelnuts. Let glaze set for at least 15 minutes before serving.

Pretzel Pull-Apart Bundt with Smoky-Spicy Cheese Sauce

Pull-Apart Bundts

How to Make Monkey Bread

1 Turn prepared monkey bread dough (see page 142) out onto a lightly floured work surface and dust it with flour, punching it down to deflate.

2 Using a rolling pin, roll the dough out into an 8- by 6-inch (20 by 15 cm) rectangle.

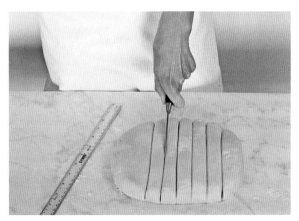

3 Cut the rectangle crosswise into 8 equal strips, each about 1 inch (2.5 cm) wide.

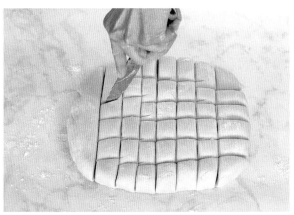

4 Cut each strip into six 1-inch (2.5 cm) pieces, so that you have 48 pieces total.

5 If using a filling, sprinkle or arrange one-third of the filling ingredients in the bottom of the prepared Bundt pan.

6 Using your hands, roll one piece of dough into a ball.

7 Dip the ball in melted butter, turning to coat.

8 Roll the ball in the prepared coating, covering it evenly. Place the coated ball on top of the filling in the pan (or in the bottom of the pan, if you're not using a filling).

9 Repeat steps 6 to 8 until you have created one full layer of dough balls in the pan. If applicable, sprinkle or arrange another third of the filling ingredients on top.

10 Create another layer of dough balls above the first, then (if applicable) sprinkle or arrange the remaining filling ingredients on top.

11 Finish with a third layer of dough balls, using them all up (you may have less than a full layer, or may even add a fourth layer, depending on pan size).

12 Combine any remaining coating and butter, and drizzle over the final layer. Cover and let rise as directed in the recipe, then bake as directed.

How to Make Accordion-Style Bundts

1 Turn prepared dough (see recipes, pages 148–154) out onto an evenly floured work surface and dust it with flour, punching it lightly to deflate.

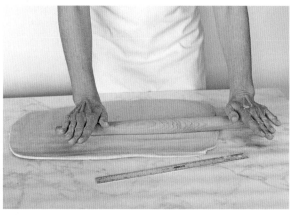

2 Using a rolling pin, roll the dough out into a 22- by 16-inch (55 by 40 cm) rectangle.

3 Spread or sprinkle the prepared filling evenly over the top of the dough, pressing lightly to adhere if sprinkling.

4 Cut the rectangle lengthwise into 6 even strips.

5 Cut each strip into 5 even pieces, so that you have 30 pieces total.

6 Stack 3 pieces, filling side up. (This part can be messy — that's expected!)

7 Repeat step 6 until you have 10 stacks of 3 pieces each.

8 Turn one stack on its edge and place it in the prepared Bundt pan so that the layers are against the side of the pan, with the filled and plain sides perpendicular to the side of the pan.

9 Continue adding stacks to the pan in the same direction, one after another, squeezing to fit if necessary (it's okay if the stacks aren't evenly spaced and there are gaps in between them).

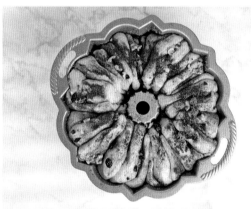

10 Sprinkle any filling that has fallen out over the top of the dough. Cover loosely with plastic wrap and let rise in a warm, draft-free place for 1 to 2 hours or until doubled in bulk.

11 Bake as directed in the recipe and let cool for 10 minutes, then carefully invert the Bundt onto a plate.

12 Carefully invert the Bundt a second time so that the textured side is facing up. Let cool to warm.

Spiced Apple Hazelnut Monkey Bread

Monkey bread is a sweet, sticky Bundt composed of dozens of dough balls, meant to be pulled from the loaf and enjoyed one at a time. The balls are rolled in sweet or savory ingredients before being pieced together, and other components — in this case, spiced apples and toasted hazelnuts — are sprinkled between the layers of dough before baking. It is officially impossible to eat only one piece of this treat, which is best served warm, while the dough is still soft.

MAKES 12 TO 16 SERVINGS

Tips

In step 3, dough is the right consistency if it springs back when poked with your finger; if it doesn't, keep kneading.

Granny Smith, Braeburn and Honeycrisp apples would all be good choices for this recipe.

To toast hazelnuts, arrange in a single layer on a baking sheet and bake in a 350°F (180°C) oven for 8 to 10 minutes, checking often, until fragrant and lightly browned.

Bundt pans and dough piece sizes may vary slightly, which may result in fewer or more than three layers of dough.

When testing pull-apart Bundts for doneness, the "toothpick test" is not a good indicator, as raw dough can result in a clean tester. When pressing dough as a test, it should spring back and feel firm, but not hard. Dough that is too soft or squishy is likely still raw.

- Large bowl, lightly coated with oil
- Minimum 15-cup Bundt pan, sprayed and lightly coated with granulated sugar

MONKEY BREAD DOUGH

1	package (¼ oz/8 g) active dry yeast	1
1 tsp	granulated sugar	5 mL
¼ cup	warm water (see box, page 25)	60 mL
⅓ cup	granulated sugar	75 mL
1	large egg, at room temperature	1
2	large egg yolks, at room temperature	2
1 cup	whole milk, at room temperature	250 mL
½ cup	unsalted butter, melted	125 mL
4¼ cups	all-purpose flour	1.06 L
1 tsp	salt	5 mL

COATING/FILLING

1½ cups	granulated sugar	375 mL
2 tsp	ground cinnamon	10 mL
½ tsp	ground allspice	2 mL
¼ tsp	ground nutmeg	1 mL
¾ cup	unsalted butter, melted	175 mL
2	large tart cooking apples, peeled and chopped	2
¾ cup	chopped lightly toasted blanched hazelnuts	175 mL

1. *Dough:* In a small bowl, stir together yeast, 1 tsp (5 mL) sugar and water. Let stand for 5 to 10 minutes or until foamy.
2. In the stand mixer bowl with paddle attachment, beat ⅓ cup (75 mL) sugar, egg, egg yolks, milk and butter on medium-low speed until blended. Beat in yeast mixture. On low speed, beat in flour and salt until a soft dough forms.
3. Replace paddle with dough hook. Knead on medium speed for 5 to 7 minutes or until dough is smooth, soft and elastic (see tip).
4. Gather dough into a ball and transfer to prepared bowl, turning to coat. Cover with plastic wrap and let rise in a warm, draft-free place for 1½ to 2 hours or until doubled in bulk.
5. Turn dough out onto a lightly floured work surface and dust with flour, punching down to deflate. Using a rolling pin, roll dough out into an 8- by 6-inch (20 by 15 cm) rectangle. Using a sharp knife, cut rectangle crosswise into eight equal slices, each about 1 inch (2.5 cm) wide. Cut each slice into six 1-inch (2.5 cm) pieces, so that you have 48 pieces.

Make Ahead

In step 4, the dough can instead rise in the refrigerator overnight.

For best results, serve monkey bread the day it is baked, but you can prepare it up to 2 days in advance. Wrap the cooled Bundt tightly in plastic wrap and store at room temperature. Warm pieces in the microwave for a few seconds or wrapped in foil in a 300°F (150°C) oven.

6. *Coating/Filling:* In a small, shallow bowl, whisk together sugar, cinnamon, allspice and nutmeg. Place melted butter in a second small, shallow bowl.

7. Arrange one-third of the apples in prepared pan. Top with one-third of the hazelnuts. Using your hands, roll one piece of dough into a ball. Dip ball in melted butter, turning to coat, then roll ball in sugar mixture to coat. Place ball on top of hazelnuts in pan.

8. Repeat process with the remaining dough pieces, melted butter and sugar mixture until you have created one full layer in the pan (see tip). Create two other similar layers, using apples, hazelnuts, dough, melted butter and sugar mixture.

9. Combine any remaining sugar mixture and butter and drizzle over dough. Cover Bundt loosely with plastic wrap and let dough rise in a warm, draft-free place for 45 to 60 minutes or until dough has reached the top of the pan.

10. Preheat oven to 350°F (180°C), or 325°F (160°C) for a dark pan.

11. Bake for 35 to 45 minutes or until top of dough is puffed, golden brown and feels firm when pressed (see tip). Let cool in pan for 10 minutes, then carefully invert cake onto a serving plate. Serve warm or at room temperature.

Maple Bacon Monkey Bread

This monkey bread will elevate your family breakfast to an entirely new level! Once baked and inverted, the smoky-sweet maple bacon filling creates a glossy coat over each piece of cinnamon sugar dough. In each bite, you get saltiness from the bacon, toasty crunch from the pecans and richness from the maple glaze. Start preparing this recipe the night before, and bake it the next morning. The heavenly aroma created is guaranteed to get the entire household out of bed and to the breakfast table in minutes.

MAKES 12 TO 16 SERVINGS

Tips

Be sure to use pure maple syrup — not imitation pancake or table syrup. Look for Grade A syrup with a darker and stronger flavor, as it will have the most concentrated maple flavor.

Bundt pans and dough piece sizes may vary slightly, which may result in fewer or more than 3 layers of dough.

Make Ahead

For best results, serve monkey bread the same day it is baked, but you can prepare it up to 2 days in advance. Wrap the cooled cake tightly in plastic wrap and store at room temperature. Warm pieces in the microwave for a few seconds or wrapped in foil in a 300°F (150°C) oven.

- Minimum 15-cup Bundt pan, sprayed and lightly coated with granulated sugar

MAPLE BACON FILLING

½ cup	unsalted butter	125 mL
¾ cup	packed dark brown sugar	175 mL
¾ cup	pure maple syrup	175 mL
½ tsp	ground cinnamon	2 mL
½ tsp	salt	2 mL
1 tsp	vanilla extract	5 mL
1 lb	sliced smoked bacon, cooked crisp and crumbled	500 g
1 cup	finely chopped pecans	250 mL

COATING

1 cup	packed dark brown sugar	250 mL
2 tsp	ground cinnamon	10 mL
¼ tsp	salt	1 mL
½ cup	unsalted butter, melted	125 mL
1	recipe Monkey Bread Dough (see page 142), prepared through step 5	1

1. *Filling:* In a medium saucepan, melt butter over medium heat. Stir in brown sugar, maple syrup, cinnamon and salt and bring to a gentle boil, stirring often. Boil, stirring constantly, for 2 minutes. Remove from heat and stir in vanilla. Let cool slightly.

2. *Coating:* In a small, shallow bowl, whisk together brown sugar, cinnamon and salt. Place melted butter in a second small, shallow bowl.

3. Arrange one-third of the bacon in prepared pan. Top with one-third of the pecans. Drizzle with one-quarter of maple mixture. Using your hands, roll one piece of dough into a ball. Dip ball in melted butter, turning to coat, then roll ball in sugar mixture to coat. Place ball on top of pecans.

4. Repeat process with the remaining dough pieces, melted butter and sugar mixture until you have created one full layer in the pan (see tip). Create two other similar layers, using bacon, pecans, maple mixture, dough, melted butter and sugar mixture. Drizzle the remaining maple mixture over top.

5. Combine any remaining sugar mixture and butter and drizzle over dough. Cover loosely with plastic wrap and let dough rise in a warm, draft-free place for 45 to 60 minutes or until dough has reached the top of the pan.

6. Meanwhile, line bottom of oven with foil or place a large baking sheet on the lowest rack to catch any bubbling-over maple topping. Preheat oven to 350°F (180°C), or 325°F (160°C) for a dark pan.

7. Bake for 35 to 45 minutes or until top of dough is puffed, crisp, golden brown and feels firm when pressed (see tip). If top starts to get too dark, tent with foil. Let cool in pan for 10 minutes, then carefully invert cake onto a serving plate. Serve warm.

Savory Cheese and Herb Monkey Bread Bundt

I'm a self-proclaimed bread-basket connoisseur. When out to dinner with my husband, I must try at least a little bit of every variety of bread on offer before choosing the piece (or two) I want to eat. Fortunately, I never embarrass him by doing this when we are out to dinner with friends! This savory version of monkey bread would solve that dilemma, featuring two varieties in one Bundt: a spicy herb and cheese version, and a garlicky onion and herb version. Instead of making a few recipes for your next holiday gathering or dinner party, make this one and place the Bundt in the center for all to enjoy.

MAKES 12 TO 16 SERVINGS

Tip

A good warm, draft-free place for dough to rise is in your oven. Turn the oven on for 30 seconds, just to infuse a little bit of warmth, then turn it off before placing the pan of dough in the oven.

Make Ahead

For best results, serve monkey bread the day it is baked, but you can prepare it up to 2 days in advance. Wrap the cooled Bundt tightly in plastic wrap and store at room temperature. Warm pieces in the microwave for a few seconds or wrapped in foil in a 300°F (150°C) oven.

- **Minimum 15-cup Bundt pan, sprayed**

FIRST TOPPING

4	green onions, trimmed and minced	4
½ cup	finely chopped flat-leaf (Italian) parsley	125 mL
1 tbsp	minced garlic	15 mL
½ tsp	salt	2 mL
¼ tsp	freshly ground black pepper	1 mL

SECOND TOPPING

1½ cups	finely shredded sharp (old) Cheddar cheese	375 mL
1 tbsp	finely chopped fresh rosemary	15 mL
¼ to ½ tsp	cayenne pepper	1 to 2 mL
½ tsp	salt	2 mL
1	recipe Monkey Bread Dough (see page 142), prepared through step 5	1
1 cup	unsalted butter, melted and cooled	250 mL

1. *First Topping:* In a small, shallow bowl, mix together green onions, parsley, garlic, salt and pepper.
2. *Second Topping:* In a second small, shallow bowl, mix together cheese, rosemary, cayenne and salt.
3. Place melted butter in a third small bowl.
4. Using your hands, roll one piece of dough into a ball. Dip ball into melted butter, turning to coat, then roll ball in first topping. Place ball in bottom of prepared pan.
5. Roll a second piece of dough into a ball. Dip ball into melted butter, turning to coat, then roll ball in second topping. Place second ball next to the first.
6. Repeat process with the remaining dough pieces and toppings, alternating between toppings and arranging balls accordingly in pan. Drizzle any remaining butter over top of dough. Cover loosely with plastic wrap and let dough rise in a warm, draft-free place for 45 to 60 minutes or until dough has reached the top of the pan.

Tip

When testing pull-apart Bundts for doneness, the "toothpick test" is not a good indicator, as raw dough can result in a clean tester. When pressing dough as a test, it should spring back and feel firm, but not hard. Dough that is too soft or squishy is likely still raw.

7. Preheat oven to 350°F (180°C), or 325°F (160°C) for a dark pan.

8. Bake for 35 to 45 minutes or until top of dough is puffed, deep golden brown and firm to the touch. Let cool in pan for 10 minutes, carefully invert Bundt onto a plate, then carefully invert it a second time so that the textured side is facing up. Serve warm.

Variation

Substitute other fresh herbs and cheeses in equal amounts for the ones used in this recipe. Monterey Jack, mozzarella, Parmesan and fontina are all good choices for cheese, and thyme is a good substitute for rosemary. If using dried herbs instead of fresh, use 1 tsp (5 mL) dried for every 1 tbsp (15 mL) fresh.

Pumpkin Spice Pull-Apart Bundt

A pumpkin spice phenomenon has swept across North America. What started out as a holiday-flavored latte has turned into seasonal bagels, cookies, marshmallows — you name it. And yes, now all of you pumpkin-spice fanatics can have a pumpkin spice–flavored pull-apart Bundt too. The pull-apart Bundt is made up of several rectangles of dough, positioned "accordion-style" around the circumference of the pan, and separated by filling. You can cut it into neat, larger slices or tear it apart into individual slices, which is much more fun!

MAKES 12 TO 16 SERVINGS

Tips

In step 3, dough is the right consistency if it springs back when poked with your finger.

Because this dough can be messy and sticky, make sure the work surface is evenly floured so that the pieces don't stick and stretch.

Make Ahead

Dough can be prepared up through step 3, then placed in a lightly oiled large bowl, covered with plastic wrap and refrigerated overnight for a "slow rise." Proceed with step 5.

For best results, serve Bundt the day it is baked, but you can prepare this recipe up to 3 days in advance. Wrap the cooled Bundt tightly in plastic wrap and store at room temperature. Rewarm pieces in microwave for a few seconds or wrapped in foil in a 300°F (150°C) oven.

- Large bowl, lightly coated with oil
- Minimum 15-cup Bundt pan, sprayed and lightly coated with granulated sugar

PUMPKIN PULL-APART DOUGH

1	package (¼ oz/8 g) active dry yeast	1
1 tsp	granulated sugar	5 mL
¼ cup	warm water (see box, page 25)	60 mL
⅓ cup	granulated sugar	75 mL
1	large egg, at room temperature	1
2	large egg yolks, at room temperature	2
½ cup	whole milk, at room temperature	125 mL
6 tbsp	unsalted butter, melted	90 mL
1 cup	pumpkin purée (not pie filling)	250 mL
4¼ cups	all-purpose flour	1.06 L
1 tsp	salt	5 mL

FILLING

¼ cup	unsalted butter, melted and cooled	60 mL
½ cup	packed light brown sugar	125 mL
2 tsp	ground cinnamon	10 mL
1 tsp	ground ginger	5 mL
½ tsp	ground nutmeg	2 mL
1 cup	pumpkin purée (not pie filling)	250 mL
1	recipe Cinnamon Glaze (variation, page 271)	1

1. *Dough:* In a small bowl, stir together yeast, 1 tsp (5 mL) sugar and water. Let stand for 5 to 10 minutes or until foamy.

2. In the stand mixer bowl with paddle attachment, beat ⅓ cup (75 mL) sugar, egg, egg yolks, milk and butter on medium-low speed until blended. Beat in yeast mixture, then beat in pumpkin. On low speed, add flour and salt and beat until a soft dough forms.

3. Replace paddle with dough hook. Knead on medium speed for 5 to 7 minutes or until dough is smooth, soft and elastic (see tip).

4. Gather dough into a ball and transfer to prepared large bowl, turning to coat. Cover bowl with plastic wrap and let rise in a warm, draft-free place for 1½ to 2 hours or until doubled in bulk.

5. Turn dough out onto an evenly floured work surface and dust with flour, punching lightly to deflate. Using a rolling pin, roll dough out into a 22- by 16-inch (55 by 40 cm) rectangle.

Tip

When testing pull-apart Bundts for doneness, the "toothpick test" is not a good indicator, as raw dough can result in a clean tester. When pressing dough as a test, it should spring back and feel firm, but not hard. Dough that is too soft or squishy is likely still raw.

6. *Filling:* Using a pastry brush, brush dough with melted butter.

7. In a small bowl, stir together brown sugar, cinnamon, ginger, nutmeg and pumpkin. Using an offset spatula or a knife, spread pumpkin mixture evenly over buttered dough, leaving no border.

8. Cut dough into pieces and arrange stacks in prepared pan as described on pages 140–141. Cover loosely with plastic wrap and let rise in a warm, draft-free place for 1 to 2 hours or until doubled in bulk.

9. Preheat oven to 350°F (180°C), or 325°F (160°C) for a dark pan.

10. Bake for 35 to 45 minutes or until top of dough is puffed, deep golden brown and firm to the touch. Let cool in pan for 10 minutes, carefully invert cake onto a plate, then carefully invert it a second time so that the textured side is facing up. Let cool to warm.

11. Pour glaze over warm cake, letting it drip down the sides. Let glaze set for at least 15 minutes. Serve warm or at room temperature.

PULL-APART BUNDTS | **149**

Cranberry Nut Pull-Apart Bundt

When I finished glazing this pull-apart Bundt, my friend said, "This could easily replace a coffee cake at any holiday brunch, housewarming or office party." True, but it's much more eye-catching and unique. In this recipe, which almost reminds me of the decadent baked cinnamon toast that my dad used to make, flaky pieces of dough are separated by buttery, spiced brown sugar filling, walnuts and dried cranberries, which peek out of the top and sides after baking, creating festive little bits of red over the Bundt.

MAKES 12 TO 16 SERVINGS

Tips

A good warm, draft-free place for dough to rise is in your oven. Turn the oven on for 30 seconds, just to infuse a little bit of warmth, then turn it off before placing the pan of dough in the oven.

Because this dough can be messy and sticky during the rolling and cutting process, make sure the work surface is always evenly dusted with flour so that the pieces don't stick and stretch.

Make Ahead

For best results, serve Bundt the day it is baked, but you can prepare this recipe up to 3 days in advance. Wrap the cooled Bundt tightly in plastic wrap and store at room temperature. Warm pieces in microwave for a few seconds or wrapped in foil in a 300°F (150°C) oven.

- Minimum 15-cup Bundt pan, sprayed and lightly coated with light brown sugar
- Handheld electric mixer

1	recipe Monkey Bread Dough (see page 142), prepared through step 4, adding 1 tsp (5 mL) ground cinnamon with the flour	1
½ cup	unsalted butter, softened	125 mL
1 cup	packed light brown sugar	250 mL
1 tbsp	ground cinnamon	15 mL
¼ tsp	salt	1 mL
1 cup	dried cranberries, coarsely chopped	250 mL
1 cup	walnuts, coarsely chopped	250 mL
1	recipe Buttery Vanilla Glaze (variation, page 271)	1

1. Turn dough out onto an evenly floured work surface and dust with flour, punching lightly to deflate. Using a rolling pin, roll dough out into a 22- by 16-inch (55 by 40 cm) rectangle. Spread evenly with butter.

2. In a small bowl, whisk together brown sugar, cinnamon and salt. Sprinkle evenly over buttered dough, pressing lightly to adhere. Sprinkle cranberries and walnuts evenly over top, pressing lightly to adhere.

3. Cut dough into pieces and arrange stacks in prepared pan as described on pages 140–141. Sprinkle any filling that has fallen out over top of dough. Cover loosely with plastic wrap and let rise in a warm, draft-free place for 1 to 2 hours or until doubled in bulk.

4. Preheat oven to 350°F (180°C), or 325°F (160°C) for a dark pan.

5. Bake for 35 to 45 minutes or until top of dough is puffed, deep golden brown and firm to the touch. Let cool in pan for 10 minutes, carefully invert cake onto a plate, then carefully invert it a second time so that the textured side is facing up. Let cool to warm.

6. Pour glaze over the warm cake, letting it drip down the sides. Let glaze set for at least 15 minutes. Serve warm or at room temperature.

Pepperoni Pizza Pull-Apart Bundt

My husband doesn't have a sweet tooth, which means I have to look beyond our home when I need taste testers for most of my recipes. He always says, "Now, if you write a pizza cookbook, I'm your guy!" I'm not sure if a pizza cookbook is in my future, so I turned pizza into a pull-apart Bundt. Spicy pepperoni, basil, mozzarella and Parmesan divide seasoned layers of dough, making this Bundt a fun idea for a kid's birthday party or a game night.

MAKES 12 TO 16 SERVINGS

Tips

To cut basil leaves chiffonade style, stack about 10 leaves at a time on top of each other. Roll them lengthwise into a fairly tight cigar shape. Cut across in thin slices to get long, uniform strips.

In step 3, dough is the right consistency if it springs back when poked with your finger.

When testing pull-apart Bundts for doneness, the "toothpick test" is not a good indicator, as raw dough can result in a clean tester. When pressing dough as a test, it should spring back and feel firm, but not hard. Dough that is too soft or squishy is likely still raw.

- Large bowl, lightly coated with oil
- Minimum 15-cup Bundt pan, sprayed

DOUGH

1	package (¼ oz/8 g) active dry yeast	1
1 tsp	granulated sugar	5 mL
¼ cup	warm water (see box, page 25)	60 mL
2 tbsp	granulated sugar	30 mL
1	large egg, at room temperature	1
2	large egg yolks, at room temperature	2
¾ cup	whole milk, at room temperature	175 mL
½ cup	unsalted butter, melted	125 mL
4¼ cups	all-purpose flour	1.06 L
2 tsp	dried oregano	10 mL
1 tsp	garlic salt	5 mL

FILLING

¼ cup	unsalted butter, softened	60 mL
1 tbsp	minced garlic	15 mL
½ tsp	salt	2 mL
¼ tsp	freshly ground black pepper	1 mL
¾ cup	pizza sauce	175 mL
¾ cup	coarsely chopped pepperoni	175 mL
2 cups	finely shredded mozzarella cheese	500 mL
½ cup	grated Parmesan cheese	125 mL
3 tbsp	fresh basil chiffonade (see tip)	45 mL

Pizza or marinara sauce, warmed

1. *Dough:* In a small bowl, stir together yeast, 1 tsp (5 mL) sugar and water. Let stand for 5 to 10 minutes or until foamy.

2. In the stand mixer bowl with paddle attachment, beat 2 tbsp (30 mL) sugar, egg, egg yolks, milk and butter on medium-low speed until blended. Beat in yeast mixture. On low speed, add flour, oregano and garlic salt and beat until a soft dough forms.

3. Replace paddle with dough hook. Knead on medium speed for 5 to 7 minutes or until dough is smooth, soft and elastic (see tip).

4. Gather dough into a ball and transfer to prepared large bowl, turning to coat. Cover bowl with plastic wrap and let rise in a warm, draft-free place for 1½ to 2 hours or until doubled in bulk.

5. Turn dough out onto an evenly floured work surface, dust with flour and punch down lightly to deflate. Using a rolling pin, roll dough out into a 22- by 16-inch (55 by 40 cm) rectangle.

Make Ahead

In step 4, the dough can instead rise in the refrigerator overnight.

For best results, serve this Bundt the day it is baked, but you can prepare it up to 3 days in advance. Wrap the cooled Bundt tightly in plastic wrap and store at room temperature. Warm pieces in the microwave for a few seconds or wrapped in foil in a 300°F (150°C) oven.

6. *Filling:* In another small bowl, mix together butter, garlic, salt and pepper. Spread butter mixture evenly over dough, reaching to the edges. Spread pizza sauce over butter mixture. Sprinkle pepperoni evenly over top, followed by mozzarella, Parmesan and basil, pressing lightly to adhere.

7. Cut dough into pieces and arrange stacks in prepared pan as described on pages 140–141. Sprinkle any filling that has fallen out over top of dough. Cover loosely with plastic wrap and let rise in a warm, draft-free place for 1 to 2 hours or until doubled in bulk.

8. Preheat oven to 350°F (180°C), or 325°F (160°C) for a dark pan.

9. Bake for 35 to 45 minutes or until top of dough is puffed, deep golden brown and firm to the touch. Let cool in pan for 10 minutes, carefully invert Bundt onto a plate, then carefully invert it a second time so that the textured side is facing up. Serve warm, alongside pizza or marinara sauce for dipping.

Variation

Substitute your favorite pizza toppings. Use marinara sauce or pesto in place of pizza sauce, cooked Italian sausage instead of pepperoni, and fontina cheese in place of mozzarella.

French Onion Soup Pull-Apart Bundt

French onion soup became popular in the United States in the 1960s due to a greater interest in French cuisine. Now you can find it on restaurant menus from casual chains to fine dining establishments. Ironically, when I took a trip to Paris with my mom a few years ago, I don't recall seeing French onion soup *anywhere*! I do, however, remember tasting some of the best cheeses that I've ever tried, such as an aged nutty Comté, which I had specially packaged so that I could carry it home and use it in my own soup recipe. I've used Gruyère in this French onion–inspired Bundt, because it is similar to Comté and is generally easier to find.

MAKES 12 TO 16 SERVINGS

Tips

Choose a wine you have on hand that is not too sweet. Incorporating red wine will result in darker onions.

Gruyère is a nutty-flavored Swiss cheese, commonly used in fondue. Look for it in the specialty cheeses section of your grocery store. Good substitutes for Gruyère are French Comté or Swiss Emmentaler.

Make Ahead

For best results, serve this Bundt the day it is baked, but you can prepare it up to 2 days in advance. Wrap the cooled Bundt tightly in plastic wrap and store at room temperature. Warm pieces in the microwave for a few seconds or wrapped in foil in a 300°F (150°C) oven.

- **Minimum 15-cup Bundt pan, sprayed**

½ cup	unsalted butter, softened, divided	125 mL
3	cloves garlic, minced	3
2	medium sweet onions, quartered, peeled and thinly sliced	2
1 tbsp	chopped fresh thyme	15 mL
¾ tsp	salt	3 mL
¼ tsp	freshly ground black pepper	1 mL
⅓ cup	red or white wine (see tip)	75 mL
2 cups	finely shredded Gruyère cheese (see tip)	500 mL
1	recipe Monkey Bread Dough (see page 142), prepared through step 4	1

1. In a large skillet, melt ¼ cup (60 mL) butter over medium heat. Add garlic, onions, thyme, salt and pepper; cook for 5 minutes or until onions soften. Reduce heat to medium-low and cook, stirring often, for 30 to 40 minutes or until onions are soft and caramelized. Pour in wine and cook, stirring, until liquid has evaporated and onions are dry. Let cool completely.

2. Turn dough out onto an evenly floured work surface, dust with flour and punch down lightly to deflate. Using a rolling pin, roll dough out into a 22- by 16-inch (55 by 40 cm) rectangle.

3. Spread the remaining butter evenly over dough, reaching to the edges. Spread cooled onion mixture evenly over butter. Sprinkle Gruyère evenly over top, pressing lightly to adhere.

4. Cut dough into pieces and arrange stacks in prepared pan as described on pages 140–141. Sprinkle any filling that has fallen out over top of dough. Cover loosely with plastic wrap and let rise in a warm, draft-free place for 1 to 2 hours or until doubled in bulk.

5. Preheat oven to 350°F (180°C), or 325°F (160°C) for a dark pan.

6. Bake for 35 to 45 minutes or until top of dough is puffed, deep golden brown and firm to the touch. Let cool in pan for 10 minutes, carefully invert Bundt onto a plate, then carefully invert it a second time so that the textured side is facing up. Serve warm.

Garlic Knot Pull-Apart Bundt

There is a restaurant in Las Vegas, where I live now, called the Bootlegger. It's a classic Italian restaurant, featuring plush red booths, a pianist singing 1950s standards, and the most incredible garlic knots, called *panetti*, served with house-made tomato basil dipping sauce. I've been promising my husband for years that I would try to create these garlicky, buttery bites of heaven, so I decided to deliver on that promise in this book, in the form of a pull-apart Bundt.

MAKES 12 TO 16 SERVINGS

Tips

Bread flour has a higher level of protein than all-purpose flour, which aids in the formation of gluten in the dough and adds "springiness" and chew to the texture.

I like to use pecorino-Romano cheese in this recipe for its sharp, salty tang. Feel free to replace it with more traditional grated Parmesan cheese.

When testing pull-apart Bundts for doneness, the "toothpick test" is not a good indicator, as raw dough can result in a clean tester. When pressing dough as a test, it should spring back and feel firm, but not hard. Dough that is too soft or squishy is likely still raw.

Make Ahead

Dough can be prepared up through step 3, then placed in a lightly oiled large bowl, covered with plastic wrap and refrigerated overnight for a "slow rise." Proceed with step 5.

- Large bowl, lightly coated with oil
- Minimum 15-cup Bundt pan, sprayed

DOUGH

1	package (¼ oz/8 g) active dry yeast	1
1½ cups	warm water (see box, page 25)	375 mL
2 tbsp	liquid honey	30 mL
2 tbsp	extra virgin olive oil	30 mL
¾ cup	whole milk, at room temperature	175 mL
½ cup	unsalted butter, melted	125 mL
3½ cups	bread flour (see tip)	875 mL
¼ cup	grated pecorino-Romano cheese	60 mL
2 tsp	dried Italian seasoning	10 mL
1 tsp	garlic salt	5 mL

FILLING

¾ cup	unsalted butter	175 mL
6	cloves garlic, minced	6
½ tsp	garlic salt	2 mL
¾ cup	grated pecorino-Romano cheese, divided	175 mL
	Marinara sauce, warmed	

1. *Dough:* In the stand mixer bowl, stir together yeast, water, honey and 2 tbsp (30 mL) olive oil until blended. Let stand for about 10 minutes or until foamy.

2. Add milk and butter, attach paddle and beat on medium-low speed until blended. On low speed, add flour, cheese, Italian seasoning and garlic salt and beat until a soft dough forms.

3. Replace paddle with dough hook. Knead on medium speed for 3 to 5 minutes or until dough is smooth, soft and slightly sticky.

4. Gather dough into a ball and transfer to prepared large bowl, turning to coat. Cover bowl with plastic wrap and let rise in a warm, draft-free place for 1½ to 2 hours or until doubled in bulk.

5. *Filling:* In a small saucepan, stir together butter and garlic until butter is melted and mixture is fragrant. Remove from heat and keep warm.

6. Turn dough out onto a lightly floured work surface, dust with flour and punch down lightly to deflate. Using a rolling pin, roll dough out into an 18- by 12-inch (45 by 30 cm) rectangle. Using a knife, cut rectangle down the center so you have two 12- by 9-inch (30 by 23 cm) pieces. Cut each piece into twelve 9- by 1-inch (23 by 2.5 cm) strips.

Make Ahead

For best results, serve this Bundt the day it is baked, but you can prepare it up to 2 days in advance. Wrap the cooled Bundt tightly in plastic wrap and store at room temperature. Warm pieces in the microwave for a few seconds or wrapped in foil in a 300°F (150°C) oven.

7. Tie one strip into a loose knot. Using a pastry brush, brush knot on both sides with garlic butter and place it in the bottom of prepared pan. Continue with the remaining strips and garlic butter, placing knots in bottom of pan until you have 1 layer. Sprinkle layer with ¼ cup (60 mL) cheese.

8. Continue process until you have buttered and arranged all of the strips. Sprinkle with ¼ cup (60 mL) cheese. (Reserve the remaining garlic butter for step 11.)

9. Cover Bundt loosely with plastic wrap and let rise in a warm, draft-free place for 1 to 1½ hours or until doubled in bulk.

10. Preheat oven to 375°F (190°C).

11. Bake for 30 minutes, then brush top with the remaining garlic butter and sprinkle with the remaining cheese. Bake for 10 to 15 minutes or until top is puffed and golden brown (see tip). Let cool in pan for 10 minutes, then carefully invert Bundt onto a plate or wire rack. Serve warm alongside marinara sauce for dipping.

Pretzel Pull-Apart Bundt with Smoky-Spicy Cheese Sauce

Whenever I go to a live professional sporting event, I don't get a hot dog. I don't get nachos. I always get the big pretzel, topped with plenty of coarse salt and drizzled with yellow mustard or dipped into cheese sauce. When brainstorming ideas for this book, I thought, "Wouldn't it be fun to create one big pull-apart soft pretzel recipe — something you could serve at a Super Bowl party for everyone to share?" Thankfully, my hunger-generated idea turned out even better than I had hoped, especially when each piece is dipped into a smoky, spicy and tangy cheese sauce.

MAKES 12 TO 16 SERVINGS

Tips

Water for proofing yeast should be about 100°F to 110°F (38°C to 43°C). If the water is too hot, it will kill the yeast, but it needs to be warm to activate the yeast. If your yeast mixture still doesn't foam after 10 minutes, your yeast could be too old or the water wasn't the right temperature.

To warm milk, in a small saucepan, heat milk over medium-low heat, stirring, until steaming and bubbles form around the edge (do no let boil).

Bread flour has a higher level of protein than all-purpose flour, which aids in the formation of gluten in the dough and adds "springiness" and chew to the texture.

When adding cheese to the sauce, it's important to add it gradually so that it melts to a smooth, velvety consistency and doesn't form clumps.

- Large bowl, lightly coated with oil
- Baking sheet, lined with parchment paper
- Minimum 15-cup Bundt pan, sprayed

PRETZEL DOUGH

1	package (¼ oz/8 g) active dry yeast	1
1¼ cups	warm water (see tip)	300 mL
1 tbsp	liquid honey	15 mL
4¼ cups	bread flour	1.06 L
2 tsp	salt	10 mL
¼ cup	whole milk, at room temperature	60 mL
3 tbsp	unsalted butter, softened	45 mL

WATER BATH

12 cups	water	3 L
½ cup	baking soda	125 mL
1 tbsp	salt	15 mL

TOPPING

1	large egg	1
1 tbsp	water	15 mL
	Coarse or pretzel salt	

CHEESE SAUCE

¼ cup	unsalted butter	60 mL
3 tbsp	all-purpose flour	45 mL
1 cup	whole milk, warmed	250 mL
1½ cups	shredded sharp (old) Cheddar cheese	375 mL
1 tsp	smoked paprika (see tip)	5 mL
½ tsp	salt	2 mL
¼ tsp	cayenne pepper	1 mL
¼ tsp	freshly ground black pepper	1 mL

1. *Dough:* In the stand mixer bowl, stir together yeast, water and honey until blended. Let stand for 5 to 10 minutes or until foamy.
2. Attach paddle to mixer. Add flour, salt, milk and butter and beat on medium-low speed until a soft dough forms.
3. Replace paddle with dough hook. Knead on medium speed for 3 to 5 minutes or until dough is soft and smooth.

Tips

The easiest way to roll dough into a smooth ball is to place it between the palm of your hand and a lightly floured work surface. Cup the ball slightly and roll in circles, pressing down lightly as you roll.

When testing pull-apart Bundts for doneness, the "toothpick test" is not a good indicator, as raw dough can result in a clean tester. When pressing dough as a test, it should spring back and feel firm, but not hard. Dough that is too soft or squishy is likely still raw.

Make Ahead

In step 4, the dough can instead rise in the refrigerator overnight.

For best results, serve this Bundt the day it is baked, but you can prepare it up to 2 days in advance. Wrap the cooled Bundt tightly in plastic wrap and store at room temperature. Rewarm pieces in microwave for a few seconds or wrapped in foil in a 300°F (150°C) oven.

See a photograph of this Bundt on page 136.

4. Gather dough into a ball and transfer to prepared large bowl, turning to coat. Cover bowl with plastic wrap and let rise in a warm, draft-free place for 1 to 2 hours or until doubled in bulk.

5. Turn dough out onto a lightly floured work surface, dust with flour and punch down lightly to deflate. Using a rolling pin, roll dough out into a 16- by 8-inch (40 by 20 cm) rectangle. Cut dough into 24 even pieces. Using your hands, roll each piece into a ball (see tip) and place on prepared baking sheet, spacing apart. Cover baking sheet with plastic wrap and let dough rise in a warm, draft-free place for 15 minutes.

6. *Water Bath:* Meanwhile, in a large saucepan, bring water, baking soda and salt to a boil over high heat, stirring to dissolve baking soda and salt.

7. Working with 3 or 4 balls at a time, gently drop dough into water bath, letting them "bathe" for 30 seconds. Using a slotted spoon, return balls to prepared baking sheet while you repeat process with the remaining dough and water bath.

8. *Topping:* In a small bowl, whisk together egg and water until blended. Using a pastry brush, brush tops and sides of balls with egg wash. Sprinkle with coarse salt. Place balls of dough in two layers in prepared Bundt pan, so that the egg side is facing out.

9. Cover pan loosely with plastic wrap and let dough rise in a warm place for 15 minutes.

10. Preheat oven to 400°F (200°C).

11. Brush top of Bundt with egg wash and sprinkle with salt. Bake for 20 to 25 minutes or until top is puffed and deep golden brown (see tip).

12. *Sauce:* Meanwhile, in a medium saucepan, melt butter over medium heat. Add flour and cook, whisking constantly, for 2 minutes to form a paste. Gradually pour in milk, whisking constantly. Cook, whisking often, for 5 minutes or until mixture simmers and thickens. Remove from heat.

13. Add cheese, $\frac{1}{4}$ cup (60 mL) at a time (see tip), whisking constantly and making sure cheese is incorporated before adding more. Whisk in paprika, salt, cayenne and pepper.

14. Let Bundt cool in pan for 10 minutes, carefully invert Bundt onto a plate, then carefully invert it a second time so that the salted side is facing up.

15. Transfer sauce to a bowl. Serve warm with Pretzel Bundt for dipping.

Variation

Replace coarse salt with jarred "everything bagel topping." To make your own version (a little more than $\frac{1}{2}$ cup/125 mL topping), mix 1 tbsp (15 mL) coarse salt with 2 tbsp (30 mL) each poppy seeds, sesame seeds, dried garlic flakes and dried onion flakes.

King Cake Bundt

Holiday Bundts

King Cake Bundt

King cake is a brioche-like cake decorated with purple, green and yellow sanding sugars, thousands upon thousands of which are devoured in New Orleans (and around the world) during Mardi Gras season. After baking, it's traditional to hide a small plastic or porcelain baby in the cake, which symbolizes prosperity and luck for the person who finds it in his or her slice. It also means that lucky and prosperous person is responsible for bringing the king cake to the next party.

MAKES 12 TO 16 SERVINGS

Tips

If you don't have a dough hook, you can knead dough by hand on a lightly floured surface for 10 to 12 minutes.

If dough starts to "climb" up the dough hook while kneading, stop the mixer and scrape it off before continuing.

A good, draft-free place for dough to rise is in your oven. Turn the oven on for 30 seconds, just to infuse a little bit of warmth, then turn it off before placing the bowl or pan of dough in the oven.

When testing yeast Bundts for doneness, the "toothpick test" is not a good indicator, as raw dough can result in a clean tester. When pressing dough as a test, it should spring back and feel firm, but not hard. Dough that is too soft or squishy is likely still raw.

- Large bowl, lightly coated with oil
- Minimum 15-cup Bundt pan, sprayed

CAKE

1	package (¼ oz/8 g) active dry yeast	1
1 tsp	granulated sugar	5 mL
⅔ cup	whole milk, warmed (see box, page 25)	150 mL
4 cups	all-purpose flour	1 L
½ tsp	salt	2 mL
1 tsp	ground cinnamon	5 mL
½ tsp	ground cardamom	2 mL
½ cup	granulated sugar	125 mL
¾ cup	unsalted butter, softened	175 mL
3	large eggs, at room temperature	3
1	large egg yolk, at room temperature	1
	Grated zest of 1 lemon	

FILLING

¾ cup	packed light brown sugar	175 mL
1 tbsp	ground cinnamon	15 mL
	Grated zest of 1 orange	
½ cup	unsalted butter, melted, divided	125 mL
2 tbsp	bourbon (optional)	30 mL
½ cup	chopped pecans	125 mL
1	whole almond	1

GLAZE

2 cups	confectioners' (icing) sugar, sifted	500 mL
1	large egg white (see tip)	1
1 tbsp	light (white or golden) corn syrup	15 mL
2 to 3 tbsp	freshly squeezed lemon juice	30 to 45 mL

Green, purple and yellow sanding sugars

1. *Cake:* In a small bowl, stir together yeast, 1 tsp (5 mL) sugar and milk. Let stand for 10 minutes or until foamy.

2. In a medium bowl, whisk together flour, salt, cinnamon and cardamom.

If you can find a small, clean plastic or porcelain baby to hide in the cake after it is baked and cooled, by all means, use it. A whole almond is a common substitute.

The glaze contains a raw egg white. If you are concerned about the food safety of raw eggs, substitute pasteurized eggs in the shell or 2 tbsp (30 mL) pasteurized liquid egg whites.

Make Ahead

A king cake is best served the day it is baked, but you can prepare it up to 3 days in advance. Store glazed cooled cake in a cake container at room temperature. Warm slices in the microwave for a few seconds or wrapped in foil in a 300°F (150°C) oven for 10 to 15 minutes.

See a photograph of this cake on page 160.

3. In the stand mixer bowl with paddle attachment, beat ½ cup (125 mL) sugar and butter at medium speed for 3 minutes or until light and fluffy. Add yeast mixture and beat for 1 minute. Beat in eggs and egg yolk, one at a time. Beat in lemon zest.

4. With the mixer on low speed, beat in flour mixture in three additions until all ingredients are well incorporated.

5. Replace paddle with dough hook. Knead on medium-low speed for 8 minutes or until dough is smooth, soft, elastic and starts to pull away from sides of bowl (see tip).

6. Gather dough into a ball and transfer to prepared large bowl, turning to coat. Cover bowl with plastic wrap and let rise in a warm, draft-free place for 1 hour or until doubled in bulk.

7. Turn dough out onto work surface, punch it down and knead it a few times before forming it back into a ball. Return dough to bowl, cover with plastic wrap and refrigerate for 2 hours.

8. *Filling:* In a medium bowl, stir together brown sugar, cinnamon, orange zest, ¼ cup (60 mL) butter, bourbon (if using) and pecans.

9. On a lightly floured work surface, using a rolling pin, roll dough out into a 24- by 12-inch (60 by 30 cm) rectangle. Cut dough lengthwise into three 24- by 4-inch (50 by 10 cm) strips. Using a pastry brush, brush each strip with some of the remaining melted butter. Sprinkle strips with the filling, leaving a ½-inch (1 cm) border on all sides.

10. Fold each strip over lengthwise to enclose filling, pinching seams along the length and at the ends to seal. Braid three pieces together as snugly as possible. Brush top of braid with the remaining melted butter. Bring ends of braid together to create a loop, overlapping slightly and scrunching together as necessary to fit into prepared pan. Cover pan with plastic wrap and let rise in a warm, draft-free place for 45 minutes.

11. Preheat oven to 350°F (180°C), or 325°F (160°C) for a dark pan.

12. Uncover pan and bake for 35 to 40 minutes or until top is golden brown, firm and springs back when pressed (see tip). Let cool in pan for 10 minutes, carefully invert cake onto a plate, then carefully invert it a second time so that the puffed braided side is facing up. Let cool completely.

13. After cake has cooled, carefully tuck almond into cake through bottom or side (see tip).

14. *Glaze:* In clean mixer bowl, beat sugar and egg white on low speed until combined. Beat in corn syrup and 2 tbsp (30 mL) lemon juice. Beat in more lemon juice if necessary, 1 tsp (5 mL) at a time, until glaze is smooth and glossy but pourable.

15. Pour glaze over the cake, letting it drip down the sides. Sprinkle top with green, purple and yellow sanding sugars in alternating wide stripes across the top. Let glaze set for at least 15 minutes before serving.

"Surprise Inside" Valentine's Day Bundt

I've started calling this Bundt the "Magic Bundt." Everyone who has enjoyed a slice has asked me, "How did you do that?" My answer? "Magic!" Surprise Inside cakes are ones that have a special design baked into their centers, revealed only when sliced. The secret is to bake and cut out shapes (in this case, hearts) in advance and place them in the middle of the batter before baking the cake or Bundt. Impress your sweetheart, your kids or your coworkers with this "magically delicious" Valentine's Day Bundt. It's not a requirement to yell "Ta-da!" when you serve the first slice, but I think it adds a nice touch.

MAKES 12 TO 14 SERVINGS

Tips

You can make your own version of buttermilk by stirring together 1 cup (250 mL) milk (not fat-free) and 1 tbsp (15 mL) white or apple cider vinegar; let stand at room temperature for 15 minutes before using.

I prefer gel-based food coloring (rather than liquid), because it produces the most vivid colors.

If you see air bubbles in the batter, firmly tap the baking sheet a few times on the counter before baking.

Use a cookie cutter that is at least ½ inch (1 cm) narrower than the interior of your Bundt pan. This will give the batter room to cover both sides so that you won't catch glimpses of the surprise shapes inside.

- Preheat oven to 350°F (180°C); dark pan, 325°F (160°C)
- 18- by 13-inch (45 by 33 cm) rimmed baking sheet, sprayed and lined with parchment paper
- Heart-shaped cookie cutter (see tip)
- Minimum 12-cup Bundt pan (classic shape), sprayed

VANILLA CAKE FOR CUT-OUTS

2¼ cups	all-purpose flour	560 mL
2 tsp	baking powder	10 mL
1 tsp	salt	5 mL
1¾ cups	granulated sugar	425 mL
½ cup	unsalted butter, softened	125 mL
6 tbsp	vegetable oil	90 mL
4	large eggs, at room temperature	4
2 tsp	vanilla extract	10 mL
1 cup	buttermilk	250 mL
	Red food coloring (see tip)	

CHOCOLATE CAKE

2½ cups	all-purpose flour	625 mL
1¼ cups	unsweetened cocoa powder, sifted	300 mL
1 tbsp	baking powder	15 mL
1 tsp	salt	5 mL
2¼ cups	granulated sugar	560 mL
½ cup	unsalted butter, softened	125 mL
½ cup	vegetable oil	125 mL
3	large eggs, at room temperature	3
1 tsp	vanilla extract	5 mL
1½ cups	buttermilk	375 mL
1	recipe Vanilla Glaze (page 271)	1

1. *Vanilla Cake:* In a medium bowl, whisk together flour, baking powder and salt.
2. In the stand mixer bowl, beat sugar, butter and oil at medium speed for 4 minutes or until light and fluffy. Beat in eggs, one at a time. Beat in vanilla.

continued on page 167

It's important to sift cocoa before adding to batter, to avoid bitter-tasting clumps.

For best results, wrap the cooled cake tightly in plastic wrap and store overnight at room temperature or in the refrigerator before glazing.

Make Ahead

You can prepare this cake up to 2 days in advance. Store the cooled glazed cake in a cake container at room temperature or in the refrigerator.

3. With the mixer on low speed, alternately beat in flour mixture and buttermilk, making three additions of flour and two of buttermilk, and beating until incorporated. Stir in enough red food coloring to achieve your desired hue. Transfer batter to prepared baking sheet and smooth to an even layer (see tip).

4. Bake in preheated oven for 25 to 30 minutes or until top is firm and a tester inserted in center comes out clean. Let cool in pan for 10 minutes, then carefully invert cake onto a clean work surface to cool completely.

5. Using cookie cutter, cut out as many heart shapes as possible, discarding (or eating!) scraps. Place hearts on a baking sheet and freeze for 30 minutes to firm.

6. *Chocolate Cake:* Preheat oven to 350°F (180°C), or 325°F (160°C) for a dark pan.

7. In a medium bowl, whisk together flour, cocoa, baking powder and salt.

8. In stand mixer bowl, beat sugar, butter and oil at medium speed for 4 minutes or until light and fluffy. Beat in eggs, one at a time. Beat in vanilla.

9. With the mixer on low speed, alternately beat in flour mixture and buttermilk, making three additions of flour and two of buttermilk, and beating until incorporated. Transfer one-third of chocolate batter to prepared pan and smooth the top.

10. Arrange a ring of chilled heart cut-outs upside-down in pan (so that the "point" of heart is facing up). Place hearts as close together as possible, spacing each in center of pan so that there is room on both sides. There will be small gaps in between hearts to account for the round shape of the pan. (You might not need all the cut-outs.)

11. Carefully pour or spoon the remaining batter over hearts, doing your best to fill gaps in between hearts and on sides of pan. Smooth the top.

12. Bake in preheated oven for 55 to 65 minutes or until top of cake springs back when lightly pressed. Let cool in pan for 10 minutes, then carefully invert cake onto a wire rack to cool completely (see tip).

13. Pour glaze over the cooled cake, letting it drip down the sides. Let glaze set for at least 15 minutes before serving.

Variation

Instead of hearts, try making this Bundt with "Surprise Inside" stars, Christmas trees, shamrocks or any other shape that will fit, tinting the vanilla cake the appropriate festive color.

Hot Cross Bun(dt)s

"Hot cross buns. Hot cross buns. One-a-penny. Two-a-penny. Hot cross buns!" I cannot see these fluffy, sweet, fruit-studded rolls without thinking about the first (and only, for that matter!) song I learned to play on my recorder. Baked into a Bundt pan, these hot cross bun(dt)s fall into both the pull-apart and holiday categories. Commonly served on Easter or Good Friday, the spiced buns mark the end of Lent and are decorated with an icing crisscross on top.

MAKES 12 TO 16 BUNS (1 TO 2 PER SERVING)

Tips

It's best to knead one-third of the filling into dough at a time, to distribute evenly; otherwise, it tends to clump together.

The easiest way to roll dough into a smooth ball is to place it between the palm of your hand and a lightly floured work surface. Cup the ball slightly and roll in circles, pressing down lightly.

For an even crisscross shape, transfer glaze to a piping bag fitted with a small round tip or a sealable plastic bag with a snipped corner and pipe glaze onto Bundt.

Make Ahead

Dough can be prepared up through step 4, then punched down in bowl, covered with plastic wrap and refrigerated overnight for a "slow rise." Let dough stand at room temperature for 30 minutes before proceeding with step 5.

- Large bowl, lightly coated with oil
- Minimum 15-cup Bundt pan, sprayed and lightly coated with granulated sugar

DOUGH

1	package (¼ oz/8 g) active dry yeast	1
1 tsp	granulated sugar	5 mL
⅓ cup	warm water (see box, page 25)	75 mL
⅓ cup	granulated sugar	75 mL
1¼ cups	buttermilk, warmed	300 mL
6 tbsp	unsalted butter, melted and cooled to warm	90 mL
2 tbsp	vegetable oil	30 mL
4¼ cups	all-purpose flour	1.06 L
1 tsp	salt	5 mL

FILLING

½ cup	dried cranberries	125 mL
½ cup	golden raisins	125 mL
½ cup	dried currants	125 mL
1½ tsp	ground cinnamon	7 mL
¾ tsp	ground cardamom	3 mL
¼ tsp	ground nutmeg	1 mL
	Grated zest of 1 large orange	
¼ cup	freshly squeezed orange juice	60 mL

TOPPING

½ cup	unsalted butter, melted	125 mL
¼ cup	granulated sugar	60 mL
½	recipe Lemon Glaze (page 272)	½

1. *Dough:* In a small bowl, stir together yeast, 1 tsp (5 mL) sugar and water. Let stand for 10 minutes or until foamy.

2. In the stand mixer bowl with paddle attachment, beat ⅓ cup (75 mL) sugar, buttermilk, butter and oil on medium-low speed. Beat in yeast mixture. On low speed, add flour and salt and beat until a soft dough forms.

3. Replace paddle with dough hook. Knead on medium speed for 6 to 8 minutes or until dough is smooth, elastic and slightly sticky.

4. Gather dough into a ball and transfer to prepared bowl, turning to coat. Cover bowl with plastic wrap and let dough rise in a warm, draft-free place for 1 hour or until doubled in bulk.

Make Ahead

Hot cross buns are best served the day they are baked, but you can prepare them up to 2 days in advance. Wrap glazed cooled buns in plastic wrap or store in a cake container at room temperature. Warm buns in the microwave for a few seconds or wrapped in foil in a 300°F (150°C) oven for 10 to 15 minutes.

5. *Filling:* In a medium bowl, stir together cranberries, raisins, currants, cinnamon, cardamom, nutmeg, orange zest and orange juice.

6. On a lightly floured work surface, gradually knead filling mixture into dough until evenly distributed (see tip). Divide dough into 24 even pieces. Using your hands, roll each piece into a smooth ball (see tip).

7. *Topping:* Place melted butter in a shallow bowl. Place sugar in another. Dip each ball in butter, turning to coat, and roll evenly in sugar. Place balls in layers in prepared pan, spacing as evenly as possible. Cover pan with plastic wrap and let dough rise in a warm, draft-free place for 1 hour.

8. Preheat oven to 350°F (180°C), or 325°F (160°C) for a dark pan.

9. Uncover pan and bake for 40 to 50 minutes or until top is puffed, firm and golden brown and springs back when pressed (see tip). Let cool in pan for 10 minutes, carefully invert Bundt onto a plate, then carefully invert it a second time so that the braided, puffed side is facing up. Let cool completely.

10. Drizzle or pipe (see tip) glaze over the cooled cake in a crisscross pattern to mimic hot cross buns. Let glaze set for at least 15 minutes before serving.

Lemon and Rosemary Olive Oil Bundt

Olive oil cakes are common in both Italian cooking (for obvious reasons) and during Jewish holidays such as Passover, when the olive oil is used as a replacement for butter. Although you might think that olive oil would make a cake heavy and dense, the result is airy and very moist. Rosemary grows everywhere where I live (I'm not sure why they still sell it in our stores!), and we grow lemons in our backyard, so I combined the two in this Bundt, which has a slightly crunchy texture due to the addition of cornmeal. This would be a deliciously simple and lighter ending to a heavy or complex meal.

MAKES 12 TO 14 SERVINGS

Tips

If you don't have cake flour, you can make a substitute. See page 16 for more information.

Select an olive oil that is mild or fruity, rather than earthy, grassy or bitter.

If you see air bubbles in the batter, firmly tap the pan a few times on the counter before baking.

One medium lemon usually yields about 1 tbsp (15 mL) zest.

For best results, wrap the cooled cake tightly in plastic wrap and store at room temperature or in the refrigerator overnight before glazing.

Make Ahead

You can prepare this cake up to 2 days in advance. Store the cooled glazed cake in a cake container at room temperature or in the refrigerator.

- Preheat oven to 350°F (180°C); dark pan, 325°F (160°C)
- Minimum 10-cup Bundt pan, sprayed

2 cups	cake flour, sifted	500 mL
½ cup	yellow cornmeal	125 mL
1½ tsp	baking powder	7 mL
½ tsp	salt	2 mL
1½ cups	granulated sugar	375 mL
1 cup	extra virgin olive oil (see tip)	250 mL
6	large eggs, at room temperature	6
	Grated zest of 2 lemons (see tip)	
¼ cup	freshly squeezed lemon juice	60 mL
2 tsp	chopped fresh rosemary	10 mL
1	recipe Lemon Glaze (page 272)	1

1. In a medium bowl, whisk together flour, cornmeal, baking powder and salt.
2. In the stand mixer bowl, beat sugar and oil on medium speed for 2 minutes or until blended and light. Beat in eggs, one at a time, then beat for 3 minutes. Beat in lemon zest, lemon juice and rosemary.
3. With the mixer on low speed, add flour mixture in three additions, beating until just blended and smooth. Transfer batter to prepared pan and smooth the top (see tip).
4. Bake in preheated oven for 35 to 45 minutes or until a tester inserted in the center comes out clean. Let cool in pan for 10 minutes, then carefully invert cake onto a wire rack to cool completely (see tip).
5. Pour glaze over the cooled cake, letting it drip down the sides. Let glaze set for at least 15 minutes before serving.

Variation

Use orange zest and juice in place of lemon, and use Orange Glaze (variation, page 272).

Funfetti Birthday Bundt

When I was a kid, you only found sprinkles *on* your sweets: ice cream, cupcakes, doughnuts and cakes. Now, sprinkles can be found *inside* every dessert imaginable, thanks to the invention of the Funfetti Cake, a fluffy white cake with the addition of colored sprinkles in the batter, about 20 years ago by Pillsbury. And why not? Funfetti cupcakes, doughnuts, cake pops and, of course, Bundts are a surefire way to turn any occasion into a colorful celebration.

MAKES 12 TO 14 SERVINGS

Tips

Don't use nonpareil sprinkles, which are the colored tiny round variety. Use the sprinkle variety shaped like short cylinders, sometimes called "jimmies." Fold sprinkles gently into batter to avoid coloring the batter.

Use a clean, dry bowl in step 4 to ensure the egg whites firm up as they are beaten. For best results, use a stainless steel, copper or glass bowl, as plastic and wooden bowls can absorb oils and water, which can inhibit the whipping process. Also make sure your beaters are clean and oil-free before whipping.

Make Ahead

You can prepare this cake up to 2 days in advance. Store the cooled glazed cake in a cake container at room temperature or in the refrigerator.

- Preheat oven to 350°F (180°C); dark pan, 325°F (160°C)
- Handheld electric mixer
- Minimum 10-cup Bundt pan, sprayed

2½ cups	cake flour, sifted	625 mL
1 tsp	baking powder	5 mL
1 tsp	baking soda	5 mL
½ tsp	salt	2 mL
1¼ cups	granulated sugar	300 mL
1 cup	unsalted butter, softened	250 mL
¼ cup	vegetable oil	60 mL
2	large eggs, at room temperature	2
1 tbsp	vanilla extract	15 mL
1 cup	buttermilk	250 mL
2	large egg whites, at room temperature	2
½ cup	rainbow sprinkles (see tip)	125 mL
1	recipe White Chocolate Glaze (page 270)	1
	Additional rainbow sprinkles	

1. In a medium bowl, whisk together flour, baking powder, baking soda and salt.

2. In the stand mixer bowl, beat sugar, butter and oil at medium speed for 4 minutes or until light and fluffy. Beat in whole eggs, one at a time. Beat in vanilla.

3. With the mixer on low speed, alternately beat in flour mixture and buttermilk, making three additions of flour and two of buttermilk, and beating until incorporated.

4. In another medium bowl (see tip), using the handheld mixer, beat egg whites on medium-low speed until foamy. Gradually increase to high speed and beat until firm peaks form.

5. Using a spatula, carefully fold whites into batter in two additions. Fold in sprinkles (see tip). Transfer batter to prepared pan and smooth the top.

6. Bake in preheated oven for 45 to 55 minutes or until a tester inserted in the center comes out clean. Let cool in pan for 10 minutes, then carefully invert cake onto a wire rack to cool completely (see tip, page 170).

7. Pour glaze over the cooled cake, letting it drip down the sides. Decorate with more sprinkles. Let glaze set for at least 20 minutes before serving.

Retro Cranberry Mold

A few years ago, my mother gave me my grandmother's old recipe box, filled with handwritten recipes on index cards and clippings from newspapers and magazines. I had so much fun going through its contents, marveling at how cooking and entertaining have changed so much over the years. One thing that stood out was how many gelatin-based mold and salad recipes were in her collection. Apparently they were all the rage, although the only gelatin I remember being asked to eat at my grandparents' house was lime green. This recipe takes my favorite modern-day cranberry sauce, featuring cherries, cinnamon and Port, and turns it into a vibrant red gelatin mold. Garnished with fresh cranberries, herbs and cinnamon sticks, it can easily serve as an edible centerpiece for your holiday table. I think Grandma would have approved.

MAKES 12 TO 14 SERVINGS

Tips

To avoid an ugly white film on the jelly after unmolding, do not use nonstick baking spray with flour for this recipe.

Fresh cranberries are usually available September through December. Store in an airtight container in the refrigerator for up to 1 month or in the freezer for up to 1 year. One bag yields 3 cups (750 mL). An equal amount of frozen cranberries will also work in this recipe.

Make Ahead

For best results, serve this recipe the day it is unmolded, but you can prepare it up to 2 days in advance. Store in an airtight container or covered in plastic wrap in the refrigerator.

- Minimum 10-cup Bundt pan, sprayed with nonstick cooking spray

1½ cups	port wine	375 mL
3	cinnamon sticks	3
1 cup	dried cranberries	250 mL
1	bag (12 oz/340 g) fresh cranberries (see tip)	1
12 oz	frozen cherries (about 1½ cups/375 mL), coarsely chopped	375 g
1 cup	packed light brown sugar	250 mL
¼ tsp	salt	1 mL
3 cups	cranberry juice cocktail, divided	750 mL
3	envelopes (each ¼ oz/7 g) unflavored gelatin powder	3

1. In a large saucepan, bring port, cinnamon sticks and dried cranberries to a boil over medium heat. Reduce heat and simmer for 10 to 12 minutes or until port is reduced by two-thirds.

2. Stir in fresh cranberries, cherries, brown sugar, salt and 2½ cups (625 mL) cranberry juice cocktail. Bring to a boil over medium-high heat, stirring occasionally. Reduce heat to medium-low, cover and simmer, stirring occasionally, for 8 to 10 minutes or until mixture thickens and cranberries burst.

3. In a medium bowl, sprinkle gelatin over the remaining cranberry juice cocktail. Let stand for about 5 minutes or until gelatin softens.

4. Whisk about 1 cup (250 mL) of the hot juices from cranberry mixture into the gelatin mixture until gelatin has dissolved. Add gelatin mixture to the saucepan, whisking until blended.

5. Carefully pour hot cranberry mixture into prepared pan and let cool to room temperature. Cover with plastic wrap and refrigerate for at least 8 hours or overnight, until set.

6. Submerge bottom of chilled pan in a bowl of warm water for 30 to 45 seconds. Using a thin knife or the tip of an offset spatula, separate the top inner and outer rims of the Bundt from the pan to loosen and release the suction. Carefully invert Bundt onto a plate or platter, giving it a few minutes to unmold if it doesn't pop out right away. Serve chilled.

Cheddar Bacon Jalapeño Cornbread Bundt

Why stick to plain Jane cornbread for your holiday dinner when you can give it a smoky, spicy and cheesy twist? This Southwestern-style version comes together in a snap and gives your taste buds a flavor fiesta in every bite — guaranteed to change the mind of anyone who thinks of cornbread as "boring." Serve it alongside rolls or biscuits as an interesting addition to your holiday bread basket, or make it during the summer to accompany your backyard barbecue.

MAKES 12 TO 14 SERVINGS

Tips

You can make your own version of buttermilk by stirring together 1 cup (250 mL) milk (not fat-free) and 1 tbsp (15 mL) white or apple cider vinegar; let stand at room temperature for 15 minutes before using.

Drain cooked bacon on paper towels before crumbling to avoid incorporating excess grease into batter.

This cornbread has a bit of a kick to it. Use only 1 jalapeño if you aren't a fan of spicy food.

Make Ahead

You can prepare this Bundt up to 3 days in advance. Tightly wrap the cooled Bundt in plastic wrap and store at room temperature. For best results, warm slices in the microwave for a few seconds or wrapped in foil in a 300°F (150°C) oven for 15 minutes.

- Preheat oven to 375°F (190°C); dark pan, 350°F (180°C)
- Minimum 10-cup Bundt pan, sprayed

1½ cups	all-purpose flour	375 mL
1 cup	yellow cornmeal (preferably stone-ground)	250 mL
1½ tsp	baking powder	7 mL
½ tsp	baking soda	2 mL
½ tsp	salt	5 mL
3	large eggs, lightly beaten	3
1 cup	buttermilk	250 mL
½ cup	unsalted butter, melted	125 mL
¼ cup	liquid honey	60 mL
6 oz	sliced smoked bacon, cooked crisp and crumbled (see tip)	175 g
4	green onions, trimmed and minced	4
2	jalapeño peppers, seeded and minced (see tip)	2
1 cup	finely shredded sharp (old) Cheddar cheese	250 mL

1. In a large bowl, whisk together flour, cornmeal, baking powder, baking soda and salt.
2. Make a well in center of flour mixture. Add eggs, buttermilk, butter and honey; mix together until blended and smooth.
3. Stir in bacon, green onions, jalapeños and cheese until evenly distributed. Spoon or pour batter into prepared pan and smooth the top.
4. Bake in preheated oven for 30 to 35 minutes or until a tester inserted in the center comes out clean. Let cool in pan for 10 minutes, then carefully invert Bundt onto a wire rack. Serve warm or at room temperature.

Variations

Substitute Monterey Jack or pepper Jack cheese for the Cheddar.

Substitute ½ red bell pepper, chopped, for the jalapeños to add some color but not the spice.

Raspberry Truffle Challah Bundt

Challah is a lightly sweetened, braided bread, usually eaten on Sabbath and other Jewish holidays. It used to be hard to source, but thanks to its popularity for use in French toast and bread pudding, you can now find it in the bakery sections of most well-stocked grocery stores. The most common challahs I've seen are either plain or cinnamon-raisin-flavored, but for this recipe, I've incorporated my mom's favorite flavor combination: dark chocolate and raspberry, braiding them together so that they are beautifully swirled throughout each and every slice.

MAKES 12 TO 16 SERVINGS

Tips

Water for proofing yeast should be about 100°F to 110°F (38°C to 43°C). If the water is too hot, it will kill the yeast, but it needs to be warm to activate the yeast. If your yeast mixture still doesn't foam after 10 minutes, your yeast could be too old or the water wasn't the right temperature.

Use leftover challah (at least 1 day old works best) as the base for French toast or bread pudding.

To make this recipe dairy-free, substitute oil for the butter in the dough, substitute non-dairy butter alternative or margarine for the butter in the filling, and use a dairy-free chocolate.

- Large bowl, lightly coated with oil
- Minimum 15-cup Bundt pan, sprayed

CHALLAH DOUGH

1	package (¼ oz/8 g) active dry yeast	1
¾ cup	warm water (see tip)	175 mL
1 tsp	liquid honey	5 mL
6 tbsp	unsalted butter, melted	90 mL
⅓ cup	liquid honey	75 mL
3	large eggs, at room temperature	3
2	large egg yolks, at room temperature	2
4¼ cups	all-purpose flour	1.06 L
1½ tsp	salt	7 mL

FILLING

½ cup	raspberry jam	125 mL
2 tbsp	unsalted butter, softened	30 mL
2 tbsp	granulated sugar	30 mL
⅓ cup	dark or semisweet chocolate, chopped	75 mL

EGG WASH

1	large egg	1
1 tbsp	water	15 mL
	Granulated sugar	

1. *Challah Dough:* In the stand mixer bowl, stir together yeast, water and 1 tsp (5 mL) honey. Let stand for 10 minutes or until foamy.

2. Attach paddle to mixer. With mixer on medium-low speed, beat in butter until blended. Beat in remaining honey. Beat in eggs and egg yolks, one at a time. Beat in flour and salt until fully blended.

3. Replace paddle with dough hook. Knead on medium speed for 6 to 8 minutes or until dough is smooth, slightly sticky and elastic.

4. Gather dough into a ball and transfer to prepared bowl, turning to coat. Cover bowl with plastic wrap and let rise in a warm, draft-free place for 1½ to 2 hours or until doubled in bulk.

5. On a lightly floured work surface, using a rolling pin, roll dough out into a 24- by 16-inch (60 by 40 cm) rectangle. Cut dough lengthwise into three equal strips.

Make Ahead

Challah is best served the day it is baked, but you can prepare it up to 3 days in advance. Tightly wrap challah in plastic wrap or store in a cake container at room temperature. Warm slices in the toaster oven for 5 to 10 minutes.

6. *Filling:* Spread ¼ cup (60 mL) raspberry jam on each of two strips, leaving a ½-inch (1 cm) border. Spread butter in an even layer on third strip, leaving a ½-inch (1 cm) border. Sprinkle sugar and chopped chocolate over butter, pressing to adhere.

7. Roll each strip into a tight cylinder to enclose filling, pinching seams to seal. Place cylinders side by side on work surface, joining them together at the end farthest from you and pinching to seal. Braid cylinders together as snugly as possible, pinching ends to seal. Bring ends of braid together to create a loop, overlapping slightly and scrunching together as necessary to fit into pan. Transfer braided loop to prepared pan.

8. *Egg Wash:* In a small bowl, whisk egg and water until blended. Using a pastry brush, brush top of braid with egg wash. Cover pan with plastic wrap and let rise in a warm, draft-free place for 1 hour or until almost doubled in bulk.

9. Preheat oven to 350°F (180°C), or 325°F (160°C) for a dark pan.

10. Brush braid again with egg wash and sprinkle lightly with sugar. Bake for 40 to 50 minutes or until deep golden brown and firm and a tester inserted in the center comes out clean. Let cool in pan for 10 minutes, carefully invert cake onto a plate, then carefully invert it a second time so that the puffed braided side is facing up. Let cool completely.

Spiced Pumpkin Bundt with Salted Caramel Glaze

I was once invited to audition for a big television cooking show. For the audition, we were asked to bring a "signature dish" for the judges to taste. When I arrived, I was surrounded by beautifully plated pasta, chicken, lamb and fish, resting in swirls of colorful sauces. What did I bring? A cake. A huge four-layer cake. A spiced pumpkin layer cake with salted caramel icing and spiced pecans. Yes, I received odd looks from the other participants (*Who brings an entire bulky cake to something like this?*). Yes, I was the only person to whom the judges returned three times to polish off every last bite of their slices! My cake earned me a spot in the next few rounds of auditions, although I never actually made it onto the show. This is that generously spiced cake reinvented as a Bundt, topped with an addictive salted caramel glaze.

MAKES 12 TO 14 SERVINGS

Tips

For best results, wrap the cooled cake tightly in plastic wrap and store at room temperature or in the refrigerator overnight before glazing.

The glaze may need some coaxing down the sides of the Bundt. Firmly tap the cake-topped plate or wire rack on the counter a few times, which should do the trick while creating a smooth surface.

Make Ahead

You can prepare this cake up to 3 days in advance. Store the cooled glazed cake in a cake container at room temperature or in the refrigerator.

- Preheat oven to 325°F (160°C)
- Minimum 10-cup Bundt pan, sprayed

2¼ cups	all-purpose flour	560 mL
1½ tsp	baking powder	7 mL
1 tsp	salt	5 mL
½ tsp	baking soda	2 mL
2½ tsp	ground cinnamon	12 mL
2 tsp	ground ginger	10 mL
¾ tsp	ground allspice	3 mL
¼ tsp	ground nutmeg	1 mL
¾ cup	granulated sugar	175 mL
¾ cup	packed light brown sugar	175 mL
¾ cup	vegetable oil	175 mL
4	large eggs, at room temperature	4
1½ cups	pumpkin purée (not pie filling)	375 mL
⅔ cup	unsweetened applesauce	150 mL
2 tsp	vanilla extract	10 mL
1	recipe Salted Caramel Glaze (page 273)	1

1. In a medium bowl, whisk together flour, baking powder, salt, baking soda, cinnamon, ginger, allspice and nutmeg.

2. In the stand mixer bowl, beat granulated sugar, brown sugar and oil at medium speed for 2 minutes or until blended and light. Beat in eggs, one at a time, then beat for 3 minutes. Beat in pumpkin, applesauce and vanilla.

3. With the mixer on low speed, add flour mixture in three additions, beating until blended and smooth. Transfer batter to prepared pan and smooth the top.

4. Bake in preheated oven for 45 to 55 minutes or until a tester inserted in the center comes out clean. Let cool in pan for 10 minutes, then carefully invert cake onto a wire rack to cool completely (see tip).

5. Pour glaze over the cooled cake, letting it drip down the sides (see tip). Let glaze set for at least 15 minutes before serving.

Peppermint Chocolate Mocha Bundt

Everyone knows it's not *truly* the holiday season until the local coffee shop starts selling its signature holiday drinks, my favorite of which is the peppermint chocolate mocha. Inspired by that popular drink, this chocolate mocha Bundt has a luscious chocolate peppermint mousse filling and a velvety white chocolate peppermint ganache.

MAKES 12 TO 14 SERVINGS

Tips

Use a clean, dry bowl in step 8 to ensure the cream firms up as it is beaten. For best results, use a stainless steel, copper or glass bowl, as plastic and wooden bowls can absorb oils and water, which can inhibit the whipping process. Also make sure your beaters are clean and oil-free before whipping.

For best results, wrap the cooled cake tightly in plastic wrap and store at room temperature or in the refrigerator overnight before filling.

It's sometimes easier to transfer mousse to a piping bag fitted with a large round tip (at least ¾ inch/2 cm) and pipe it into the center of the Bundt.

After filling cake, it's best to invert it onto a serving plate instead of a wire rack. Because sections of the cake have been removed and replaced, the cake should be moved as little as possible.

- Preheat oven to 350°F (180°C); dark pan, 325°F (160°C)
- Minimum 10-cup Bundt pan, sprayed
- Food processor
- Handheld electric mixer

CAKE

2½ cups	all-purpose flour	625 mL
¼ cup	unsweetened cocoa powder, sifted	60 mL
2 tsp	baking powder	10 mL
½ tsp	salt	2 mL
¼ tsp	baking soda	1 mL
2¼ cups	granulated sugar	560 mL
¾ cup	vegetable oil	175 mL
3	large eggs, at room temperature	3
6 oz	chopped dark or semisweet chocolate, melted and slightly cooled	175 g
1 cup	brewed very strong coffee, cooled	250 mL
¾ cup	full-fat sour cream	175 mL

CHOCOLATE PEPPERMINT MOUSSE FILLING

6 oz	dark or semisweet chocolate, chopped	175 g
1 tsp	vanilla extract	5 mL
⅛ tsp	salt	0.5 mL
1½ cups	heavy or whipping (35%) cream, chilled, divided	375 mL
¼ cup	granulated sugar	60 mL
1 tsp	peppermint extract	5 mL
1	White Chocolate Peppermint Ganache (page 277)	1
	Crushed peppermint candies	

1. *Cake:* In a medium bowl, whisk together flour, cocoa, baking powder, salt and baking soda.
2. In the stand mixer bowl, beat sugar and oil at medium speed until blended. Beat in eggs, one at a time, then beat for 3 minutes. Beat in chocolate until blended.
3. With the mixer on low speed, alternately beat in flour mixture, coffee and sour cream, making three additions of flour and one each of coffee and sour cream, and beating until incorporated. Transfer batter to prepared pan and smooth the top.
4. Bake in preheated oven for 45 to 60 minutes or until a tester inserted in the center comes out clean. Let cool in pan for 10 minutes, then carefully invert cake onto a wire rack to cool completely (see tip).

Tip

Brewed espresso can be used in place of the coffee.

Make Ahead

Mousse can be prepared up to 1 day in advance.

You can prepare this cake up to 2 days in advance. Store the glazed filled cake in a cake container in the refrigerator. Let cake stand at room temperature for 1 hour before serving.

5. *Filling:* At least 4 hours before serving, in food processor, combine chocolate, vanilla and salt; pulse to chop chocolate.

6. In a small saucepan, bring ½ cup (125 mL) cream to a boil over medium-low heat.

7. With food processor running, pour warmed cream through its feed tube, blending until melted and smooth. Transfer to a medium bowl and let cool to room temperature.

8. In another medium bowl, using the handheld mixer, beat sugar and the remaining cream on medium-high speed until stiff peaks form.

9. Using a spatula, gently fold cream mixture into chocolate mixture in two additions until fully incorporated. Stir in peppermint extract. Cover and refrigerate for at least 3 hours.

10. Return cooled cake to its cleaned and dried pan. Stir chilled mousse and fill cake with mousse as described on page 88. Carefully invert cake onto a serving plate (see tip).

11. Pour ganache over the filled cake, letting it drip down the sides. Sprinkle top with crushed peppermint candies. Let ganache set for at least 20 minutes before serving.

Gingerbread Pear Bundt

Growing up, I always associated gingerbread with the cookie. One year, my mom even threw a "gingerbread house party" for my friends and me. She built 12 miniature houses and set out icing and bowls full of toppings so that each of us could have our own gingerbread masterpiece. I always loved the rich and spicy flavors of the cookie, so as I started baking, it was a mission of mine to create the perfect gingerbread cake: one that has depth of flavor but is also light and moist. Fresh pears folded into the batter are a natural match for the gingerbread, and are little juicy bursts of sweetness in every bite.

MAKES 12 TO 14 SERVINGS

Tip

This is a very versatile cake, just as delicious warm as it is chilled. Chilled slices are dense, almost pudding-like, with a concentrated gingerbread flavor. Or warm slices in the microwave for a few seconds or wrapped in foil in a 300°F (150°C) oven for 10 to 15 minutes and serve with a scoop of vanilla ice cream on top.

Make Ahead

You can prepare this cake up to 4 days in advance. Wrap the cooled cake tightly in plastic wrap and store at room temperature or in the refrigerator. The flavor of the gingerbread will develop and intensify over time. Dust cake with confectioners' sugar just before serving.

- Preheat oven to 350°F (180°C); dark pan, 325°F (160°C)
- Minimum 10-cup Bundt pan, sprayed

2¼ cups	all-purpose flour	560 mL
1 tbsp	unsweetened cocoa powder, sifted	15 mL
1 tsp	baking powder	5 mL
½ tsp	baking soda	2 mL
½ tsp	salt	2 mL
4 tsp	ground ginger	20 mL
1½ tsp	ground cinnamon	7 mL
½ tsp	ground nutmeg	2 mL
¼ tsp	ground cloves	1 mL
¼ tsp	ground allspice	1 mL
¾ cup	packed dark brown sugar	175 mL
½ cup	unsalted butter, softened	125 mL
¼ cup	vegetable oil	60 mL
3	large eggs, at room temperature	3
¾ cup	dark (cooking) molasses	175 mL
1 cup	stout beer, at room temperature	250 mL
2	ripe but firm pears (such as Bosc or Anjou), peeled and diced	2
	Confectioners' (icing) sugar, sifted	

1. In a medium bowl, whisk together flour, cocoa, baking powder, baking soda, salt, ginger, cinnamon, nutmeg, cloves and allspice.
2. In the stand mixer bowl, beat brown sugar, butter and oil at medium speed for 4 minutes or until light and fluffy. Beat in eggs, one at a time. Add molasses and beat for 3 minutes.
3. With the mixer on low speed, alternately beat in flour mixture and stout, making three additions of flour and two of stout, and beating until incorporated.
4. Using a spatula, fold in pears. Transfer batter to prepared pan and smooth the top.
5. Bake in preheated oven for 50 to 60 minutes or until a tester inserted in the center comes out clean. Let cool in pan for 10 minutes, then carefully invert cake onto a wire rack to cool completely.
6. Dust cake with confectioners' sugar and serve chilled, warm or at room temperature.

Holiday Eggnog Bundt

Eggnog, also called the "egg flip" in Great Britain, is traditionally used as a toast to one's health — an interesting choice for what is essentially dessert in a cup! "Nog" is an old English word to describe strong beer. Eggnog is derived from a hot drink called posset, which consists of eggs, milk and ale, and cultures around the world have adapted it to fit their tastes: bourbon in the South, rum in the Caribbean, Mexican cinnamon and vanilla in Mexico, and beer in Germany. I've always had it served with a sprinkle of freshly grated nutmeg, which you will taste in both the cake and glaze of this Bundt.

MAKES 12 TO 14 SERVINGS

Tips

To grate whole nutmeg, use a nutmeg grater or a rasp grater and gently grate the nutmeg over the surface. Freshly grated nutmeg has a more intense flavor than pre-ground, so use about ¼ tsp (1 mL) freshly grated in this recipe.

Store-bought eggnog is perfect for this recipe — no need to make your own! Look for it during the holiday season in your grocery store's refrigerator case, next to the milk.

For best results, wrap the cooled cake tightly in plastic wrap and store at room temperature or in the refrigerator overnight before glazing.

Make Ahead

You can prepare this cake up to 3 days in advance. Store the cooled glazed cake in a cake container in the refrigerator.

- Preheat oven to 325°F (160°C)
- Minimum 10-cup Bundt pan, sprayed

2½ cups	cake flour, sifted	625 mL
1½ tsp	baking powder	7 mL
1 tsp	salt	5 mL
¼ tsp	baking soda	1 mL
½ tsp	ground or freshly grated nutmeg (see tip)	2 mL
¾ cup	granulated sugar	175 mL
¾ cup	packed light brown sugar	175 mL
½ cup	unsalted butter, softened	125 mL
½ cup	vegetable oil	125 mL
4	large eggs, at room temperature	4
1 tsp	rum extract	5 mL
1 tsp	vanilla extract	5 mL
1 cup	eggnog	250 mL
1	recipe Eggnog Glaze (variation, page 271)	1

1. In a medium bowl, whisk together flour, baking powder, salt, baking soda and nutmeg.
2. In the stand mixer bowl, beat granulated sugar, brown sugar, butter and oil at medium speed for 4 minutes or until blended and light. Beat in eggs, one at a time. Add rum extract and vanilla extract; beat for 2 minutes.
3. With the mixer on low speed, alternately beat in flour mixture and eggnog, making three additions of flour and two of eggnog, and beating until incorporated. Transfer batter to prepared pan and smooth the top.
4. Bake in preheated oven for 45 to 65 minutes or until a tester inserted in the center of cake comes out clean. Let cool in pan for 10 minutes, then carefully invert cake onto a wire rack to cool completely (see tip).
5. Pour glaze over the cooled cake, letting it drip down the sides. Let glaze set for at least 15 minutes before serving.

Variation

The rum extract can be replaced with 2 tbsp (30 mL) dark rum.

Spiced Citrus Fruitcake Bundt

Poor fruitcake. It takes a beating every holiday season, serving as the focus of jokes due to its heavy, dense texture, relatively long shelf life, and polarizing appeal (people either love it or they claim to hate it, even if they've never tried it). I'm in the former group and am a huge fan of any cake that is packed with a festival of jewel-toned, tart dried fruit plumped in liqueur, citrus notes and spice. I love the fact that, for its complex flavor and texture, fruitcake is easy to make, and it keeps well for weeks, making it the perfect holiday gift to prepare in advance or to give out at a moment's notice. Still not convinced? Give this recipe a try. I think it will change your mind.

MAKES 12 TO 16 SERVINGS

Tip

You can use any combination of dried fruits, including golden raisins, cranberries, currants, chopped dates, figs, apricots or cherries, blueberries or diced pineapple, in any proportions you like. Just make sure to keep the total volume to 4½ cups (1.125 L).

Make Ahead

This cake can be made up to 3 weeks in advance. Wrap the cooled (undusted) cake tightly in plastic wrap, then foil, and store in the refrigerator. Let Bundt stand at room temperature for 1 hour before serving. Dust with confectioners' sugar just before serving.

- Preheat oven to 325°F (160°C)
- Minimum 10-cup Bundt pan, sprayed

4½ cups	mixed dried fruit (see tip)	1.125 L
1 cup	dark rum or brandy (approx.), divided	250 mL
	Grated zest of 1 large lemon	
	Grated zest and juice of 1 large orange	
2½ cups	all-purpose flour	625 mL
1 tsp	baking soda	5 mL
½ tsp	salt	2 mL
1 tsp	ground cinnamon	5 mL
1 tsp	ground ginger	5 mL
½ tsp	ground allspice	2 mL
¼ tsp	ground cloves	1 mL
1½ cups	packed light brown sugar	375 mL
1 cup	unsalted butter, softened	250 mL
3	large eggs, at room temperature	3
3 tbsp	dark (cooking) molasses	45 mL
	Confectioners' (icing) sugar, sifted	

1. In a medium saucepan, stir together dried fruit and ½ cup (125 mL) rum. Bring to a simmer over medium heat, stirring occasionally. Remove from heat and stir in lemon zest, orange zest and orange juice. Let stand for 30 minutes.

2. Meanwhile, in a medium bowl, whisk together flour, baking soda, salt, cinnamon, ginger, allspice and cloves.

3. In the stand mixer bowl, beat brown sugar and butter on medium speed for 4 minutes or until light and fluffy. Beat in eggs, one at a time. Beat in molasses.

4. With the mixer on low speed, beat in flour mixture in three additions until incorporated. Add fruit mixture, including any unabsorbed liquid. On low speed, beat until fruit is evenly blended. Transfer batter to prepared pan and smooth the top.

5. Bake in preheated oven for 65 to 80 minutes or until a tester inserted in the center of cake comes out clean. Let cool in pan for 10 minutes, then carefully invert cake onto a wire rack.

6. Using a pastry brush, brush top and sides of warm cake with ¼ cup (60 mL) rum, letting it soak in before you add up to ¼ cup (60 mL) more. Let cool completely. Dust with confectioners' sugar before serving.

Sweet Belgian Craquelin

International Bundts

Sweet Belgian Craquelin

I first tried craquelin in the quaint medieval town of Bruges, Belgium, which my mom and I visited as a day excursion during our visit to Paris. Although the country is known for their chocolate (we tried plenty of it!), the buttery, fluffy brioche pastry filled with sweet candied orange peel and topped with pearl sugar was by far the best thing I ate. In this recipe, I've reworked an individual craquelin recipe into one large Bundt, which can be cut into tall, pillowy slices and served with coffee.

MAKES 12 TO 16 SERVINGS

Tips

Pearl sugar, also called nib sugar, is coarse, hard and opaque, and it does not melt during the baking process. You usually see it atop European pastries such as sweet rolls, and it makes a pretty garnish for muffins and quick breads. Look for it in the baking aisle of specialty food stores or online.

Candied orange peel is orange peel that has been cooked in sugar syrup and then dried. It has a slightly bittersweet taste and a chewy texture, similar to dried fruit. Look for it in the bulk foods section of specialty food stores or online.

Water for proofing yeast should be about 100 to 110°F (38 to 43°C). If the water is too hot, it will kill the yeast, but it needs to be warm to activate the yeast. If your yeast mixture still doesn't foam after 10 minutes, your yeast could be too old or the water wasn't the right temperature.

- **Large bowl, lightly coated with oil**
- **Minimum 14-cup Bundt pan, sprayed**

FILLING

1½ cups	pearl sugar, chilled	375 mL
1 cup	candied orange peel, chopped	250 mL
	Juice of 1 orange (about ¼ cup/60 mL)	

DOUGH

1 tbsp	active dry yeast	15 mL
1 tsp	granulated sugar	5 mL
½ cup	warm water (see tip)	125 mL
2¼ cups	all-purpose flour	560 mL
2 cups	cake flour, sifted	500 mL
½ cup	granulated sugar	125 mL
2 tsp	salt	10 mL
7	large eggs, at room temperature	7
1¼ cups	unsalted butter, cut into 10 pieces and softened	300 mL

EGG WASH

1	large egg	1
1 tbsp	water	15 mL
	Additional pearl sugar	
¼ cup	sliced almonds	60 mL

1. *Filling:* In a medium bowl, mix pearl sugar and orange peel. Cover and refrigerate up to 4 hours.
2. *Dough:* In a small bowl, stir together yeast, 1 tsp (5 mL) sugar and water. Let stand for 10 minutes, until foamy.
3. In the stand mixer bowl, beat all-purpose flour, cake flour, sugar and salt on medium-low speed until blended. Beat in eggs, one at a time. Beat for 2 minutes on medium-low speed, scraping down the sides as needed.
4. Replace paddle with dough hook. Slowly add yeast mixture and knead for 5 minutes. Stop the machine, scrape any dough off the hook, then knead on medium speed for 5 minutes.

Tips

If you don't have cake flour, you can make a substitute. See page 16 for more information.

A good, draft-free place for dough to rise is in your oven. Turn the oven on for 30 seconds, just to infuse a little bit of warmth, then turn it off before placing the bowl or pan in the oven.

Make Ahead

This cake is best enjoyed the day it is baked, but you can prepare it up to 3 days in advance. Store the cooled craquelin in a cake container at room temperature.

See a photograph of this Bundt on page 190.

5. With the mixer on low speed, add butter, one piece at a time, kneading for about 1 minute after each addition so that the butter disappears into the dough before adding more. Increase speed to medium and beat for 10 to 12 minutes or until dough is silky, sticky and glossy. Increase speed to medium-high and beat for 1 minute.

6. Transfer dough to prepared large bowl, turning to coat, and cover with plastic wrap. Let rise in a warm, draft-free place for 1½ to 2 hours or until doubled in bulk.

7. Turn dough out onto a lightly floured work surface and dust with flour. Using your hands, gently deflate dough by kneading it a few times, adding flour as needed (dough will be sticky). Return dough to bowl, cover with plastic wrap and chill for at least 6 hours or overnight.

8. Stir orange juice into chilled pearl sugar mixture, tossing to coat. Let rest for 10 minutes.

9. Turn dough out onto a lightly floured work surface. Using a rolling pin, roll dough out into a 24- by 12-inch (60 by 30 cm) rectangle, with a long side facing you. Spread pearl sugar and orange mixture evenly over the top two-thirds of dough, pressing lightly to adhere.

10. Fold bottom third of dough up over the center third, covering half of orange mixture. Fold top third of dough down over center third, envelope-style, so that you have a rectangle about 24 by 4 inches (60 by 10 cm).

11. Using a sharp knife, cut dough crosswise into 10 even pieces. Arrange pieces around prepared pan in a ring so that they are leaning outward, spaced evenly, with cut sides overlapping slightly. Cover pan with plastic wrap and let dough rise in a warm, draft-free place for 1½ to 2 hours or until puffy and almost doubled.

12. Preheat oven to 350°F (180°C), or 325°F (160°C) for a dark pan.

13. *Egg Wash:* In a small bowl, whisk egg and water until blended. Using a pastry brush, brush top of dough evenly with wash, then sprinkle evenly with pearl sugar and almonds.

14. Bake for 35 to 45 minutes or until puffed and golden brown and a tester inserted in the center comes out clean. Let cool in pan for 10 minutes, then carefully invert onto a plate and carefully invert again so that the garnished side is facing up.

Variation

If you can't find pearl sugar, simply chop or crush regular sugar cubes into peppercorn-sized pieces.

Mexican Hot Chocolate Piñata Bundt

A piñata Bundt? That sounds fun! Indeed. This Bundt is full of surprises and guaranteed to turn any occasion into an instant fiesta. Cut into the whole cake, pull out the first slice and you're met with a cascade of colored chocolate candies spilling out onto your plate. Take your first bite, and what you thought was a standard chocolate cake hits you with notes of cinnamon and spicy cayenne. Whether or not you hit the dance floor, your taste buds will definitely be doing the salsa!

MAKES 12 TO 14 SERVINGS

Tips

After filling cake, it's best to invert it onto a serving plate instead of a wire rack. Because sections of the cake have been removed and replaced, the cake should be moved as little as possible.

The ganache thickens quickly once poured over the cake. To coax it down the sides, firmly tap the cake-topped plate or wire rack on the counter a few times.

Make Ahead

You can prepare this cake up to 2 days in advance. Store the cooled glazed filled cake in a cake container in the refrigerator.

- Preheat oven to 350°F (180°C); dark pan, 325°F (160°C)
- Minimum 12-cup Bundt pan, sprayed

2½ cups	all-purpose flour	625 mL
1 cup	unsweetened cocoa powder (see tip, page 198), sifted	250 mL
1 tsp	baking soda	5 mL
1 tsp	salt	5 mL
1 tbsp	ground cinnamon	15 mL
¼ to ½ tsp	cayenne pepper	1 to 2 mL
2¼ cups	granulated sugar	560 mL
¾ cup	vegetable oil	175 mL
3	large eggs, at room temperature	3
1 tbsp	coffee-flavored liqueur (such as Kahlúa)	15 mL
2 tsp	vanilla extract	10 mL
1½ cups	buttermilk	375 mL
1¾ cups	mini candy-coated chocolate pieces (such as M&Ms), about 11 oz (330 g)	425 mL
1	recipe Mexican Chocolate Ganache (page 277)	1

1. In a medium bowl, whisk together flour, cocoa, baking soda, salt, cinnamon and cayenne.

2. In the stand mixer bowl, beat sugar and oil on medium speed until blended. Beat in eggs, one at a time. Beat in liqueur and vanilla.

3. With the mixer on low speed, alternately beat in flour mixture and buttermilk, making three additions of flour and two of buttermilk, and beating until incorporated. Transfer batter to prepared pan and smooth the top.

4. Bake in preheated oven for 50 to 60 minutes or until puffed and a tester inserted in the center comes out clean. Let cool in pan for 10 minutes, then carefully invert cake onto a wire rack to cool completely (see second tip, page 182).

5. Prepare cake for filling as directed on page 88. Pour candies into the "moat," filling it to about ½ inch (1 cm) from the top. Trim cut-out cake sections so that they fit snugly back together on top of the candies, pressing to adhere and completely covering up candies. Carefully invert cake onto a serving plate.

6. Pour ganache over the cake, letting it drip down the sides (see tip). Let ganache set for at least 20 minutes before serving.

Tres Leches Bundt

This classic Latin American cake is named *tres leches* (meaning "three milks") because, after baking, it is soaked in a rich, sweet combination of evaporated milk, sweetened condensed milk and cream. Prepared 1 day in advance and chilled, the cake is given more time to absorb the trio, resulting in a denser, more luscious cake. Although this Bundt would be hard to resist served immediately after unmolding, I've taken it over the top with whipped cream frosting and colorful fresh berries.

MAKES 12 TO 14 SERVINGS

Tips

Evaporated milk and sweetened condensed milk are both shelf-stable milk products from which most of the water has been removed. Sweetened condensed milk has a thicker texture and is caramel in color, while unsweetened evaporated milk is creamy and has an off-white or ivory shade. Use full-fat varieties whenever possible in baking, but lower-fat varieties can be substituted in a pinch.

Mixing the "tres leches" in a bowl or measuring cup with a spout makes it easier to pour evenly over top of cake.

If cake doesn't unmold easily once pan is inverted, use a thin knife or offset spatula to loosen the cake around its edges.

- Preheat oven to 350°F (180°C); dark pan, 325°F (160°C)
- Handheld electric mixer
- Minimum 10-cup Bundt pan, sprayed

CAKE

2 cups	cake flour, sifted	500 mL
½ tsp	baking powder	2 mL
½ tsp	salt	2 mL
½ tsp	ground cinnamon	2 mL
1½ cups	granulated sugar	375 mL
¾ cup	unsalted butter, softened	175 mL
6	large eggs, at room temperature, separated	6
1 tsp	vanilla extract	5 mL
2 tbsp	granulated sugar	30 mL
1	can (12 oz or 370 mL) evaporated milk (see tip)	1
1	can (14 oz or 300 mL) sweetened condensed milk	1
¼ cup	heavy or whipping (35%) cream	60 mL
1 tbsp	dark rum	15 mL

TOPPING

1½ cups	heavy or whipping (35%) cream	375 mL
2 tbsp	granulated sugar	30 mL
	Mixed fresh berries	

1. *Cake:* In a medium bowl, whisk together flour, baking powder, salt and cinnamon.

2. In the stand mixer bowl, beat 1½ cups (375 mL) sugar and butter on medium speed for 4 minutes or until light and fluffy. Beat in egg yolks, one at a time. Beat in vanilla.

3. With the mixer on low speed, add flour mixture in three additions, beating until incorporated.

4. In another medium bowl (see tip, page 172), using the handheld mixer, beat egg whites with 2 tbsp (30 mL) sugar on medium-low speed until foamy. Gradually increase to high speed and beat until firm peaks form.

5. Using a spatula, carefully fold egg white mixture into batter in three additions. Transfer batter to prepared pan and smooth the top.

Make Ahead

This cake is best
enjoyed the day it
is frosted, but you
can prepare it up to
2 days in advance.
Store the cooled
frosted cake in a cake
container store in
the refrigerator.

6. Bake in preheated oven for 35 to 45 minutes or until puffed and
golden brown and a tester inserted in the center comes out
clean. Let cool in pan for 10 minutes.

7. Meanwhile, in a large glass measuring cup or medium bowl
(see tip), whisk together evaporated milk, sweetened condensed
milk, cream and rum until blended.

8. Using a long, thin skewer, poke warm cake 30 to 40 times,
reaching to the bottom of the pan. Pour or spoon milk mixture
evenly over cake. Cover pan with plastic wrap and refrigerate,
letting milk soak into cake, for at least 6 hours or overnight.

9. *Topping:* In a medium bowl, using handheld mixer, beat cream
on medium speed until soft peaks form. Add sugar, increase
speed to medium-high and beat until stiff peaks form.

10. Carefully invert the chilled cake onto a plate or platter. Spread
topping in an even layer over cake. Garnish with fresh berries.

Chocolate-Covered Stout Bundt

As in the Gingerbread Pear Bundt (page 184), the dark, molasses-like stout beer in this cake adds depth to and intensifies the chocolate flavor. I first made a version of this cake for May May, my husband's Irish grandmother, when we visited her in Massachusetts soon after he and I were engaged. The dense cake not only traveled well, but the flavor noticeably improved from the time we tasted the first slice to the next day, when we came back for seconds. Glazed in a rich Irish cream ganache, this cake is ideal for St. Paddy's Day — or, in our family, a Red Sox World Series victory!

MAKES 12 TO 14 SERVINGS

Tips

Because unsweetened cocoa is the dominant flavor in the cake, the quality of the ingredient will shine through in the finished product. Premium cocoa powder is generally 22% to 24% fat, which you can verify on nutritional labels. Look for cocoa that contains at least 1 gram of fat per 5-gram serving. It's important to sift cocoa before adding it to batter, to avoid bitter-tasting clumps.

Look for candied ginger in the bulk foods or natural foods sections of well-stocked grocery stores.

Make Ahead

You can prepare this cake up to 2 days in advance. Store the cooled glazed cake in a cake container at room temperature or in the refrigerator.

- Preheat oven to 350°F (180°C); dark pan, 325°F (160°C)
- Minimum 10-cup Bundt pan, sprayed

2¼ cups	all-purpose flour	560 mL
1 cup	unsweetened cocoa powder (see tip), sifted	250 mL
1 tsp	baking powder	5 mL
½ tsp	baking soda	2 mL
½ tsp	salt	2 mL
1½ cups	packed light brown sugar	375 mL
1 cup	unsalted butter, softened	250 mL
3	large eggs, at room temperature	3
½ cup	dark (cooking) molasses	125 mL
1½ cups	stout beer (such as Guinness), at room temperature	375 mL
¾ cup	full-fat sour cream	175 mL
1	recipe Irish Cream Ganache (page 277)	1
	Chopped candied ginger (optional)	

1. In a medium bowl, whisk together flour, cocoa, baking powder, baking soda and salt.

2. In the stand mixer bowl, beat brown sugar and butter on medium speed for 4 minutes or until light and fluffy. Beat in eggs, one at a time. Beat in molasses.

3. With the mixer on low speed, beat in beer until blended. Alternately beat in flour mixture and sour cream, making three additions of flour and two of sour cream, and beating until incorporated. Transfer mixture to prepared pan and smooth the top.

4. Bake in preheated oven for 40 to 50 minutes or until puffed and a tester inserted in the center comes out clean. Let cool in pan for 10 minutes, then carefully invert cake onto a wire rack to cool completely (see last tip, page 186).

5. Pour ganache over the cooled cake, letting it drip down the sides. Garnish with candied ginger (if using). Let ganache set for at least 20 minutes before serving.

Baba au Rhum Bundts

A baba au rhum is an individually sized yeast-raised cake that is soaked in a rum sugar mixture and glazed with apricot jam before serving. With their very short baking time at a higher temperature, these baby cakes puff up high, ready to absorb all of the sweet flavored syrup.

MAKES 10 TO 12 MINI BUNDTS

Tips

If you are working with one Bundt pan, halve the recipe or prepare the cakes in two batches. Cover and chill the remaining batter until ready to use.

Milk for proofing yeast should be about 100 to 110°F (38 to 43°C). If the milk is too hot, it will kill the yeast, but it needs to be warm to activate the yeast. If your yeast mixture still doesn't foam after 10 minutes, your yeast could be too old or the milk wasn't the right temperature.

To make lightly sweetened whipped cream, using a handheld electric mixer, beat ½ cup (125 mL) heavy or whipping (35%) cream on medium speed until soft peaks form. Add 1 to 2 tbsp (15 to 30 mL) granulated sugar, increase speed to medium-high and beat until stiff peaks form.

• **1 to 2 mini Bundt pans (see tip), sprayed**

CAKES

½ cup	golden raisins	125 mL
½ cup	dried currants	125 mL
¼ cup	dark rum	60 mL
1	package (¼ oz/8 g) active dry yeast	1
7 tsp	granulated sugar, divided	35 mL
¼ cup	warm milk (see tip)	60 mL
4	large eggs, at room temperature	4
2½ cups	all-purpose flour	625 mL
1 tsp	salt	5 mL
	Grated zest of 1 orange	
6 tbsp	unsalted butter, cut into 1 tbsp (15 mL) pieces and softened	90 mL

SOAKING SYRUP

2½ cups	granulated sugar	625 mL
4 cups	water	1 L
¾ cup	dark rum	175 mL
2 tsp	vanilla extract	10 mL
¾ cup	apricot jam, warmed	175 mL
	Lightly sweetened whipped cream (see tip)	
	Fresh berries	

1. *Cakes:* In a small saucepan, bring raisins, currants and rum to a boil over medium heat, stirring occasionally. Immediately remove from heat and set aside.

2. In the stand mixer bowl, stir together yeast, 1 tsp (5 mL) sugar and milk. Let stand for 5 to 10 minutes or until foamy.

3. Attach paddle to mixer. On medium-low speed, beat in the remaining sugar. Beat in eggs, one at a time. Beat in flour and salt until blended and smooth. Beat in orange zest.

4. Replace paddle with dough hook. With mixer on medium-low speed, add butter, one piece at a time, kneading for about 1 minute after each addition so that the butter disappears into the dough before adding more. Increase speed to medium and knead for 5 minutes or until dough is soft and elastic. Cover bowl with plastic wrap and let dough rise in a warm, draft-free place for 1 hour or until doubled in bulk.

5. Preheat oven to 400°F (200°C).

6. Using a spatula or wooden spoon, mix rum-soaked fruit into dough. Fill each prepared pan about half full with batter, smoothing tops.

Tip

To warm jam, in a small saucepan, heat jam over medium-low heat, stirring, until warmed through.

Make Ahead

This cake is best enjoyed the day it is baked, but you can prepare it up to 2 days In advance. Store the cooled cake in a cake container at room temperature or in the refrigerator.

7. Bake for 5 minutes. Reduce oven temperature to 350°F (180°C) and bake for 15 minutes or until golden brown and puffed and a tester inserted in the centers comes out clean. Let cool in pan for 10 minutes, then carefully invert babas onto a wire rack to cool completely.

8. *Soaking Syrup:* In a medium saucepan, bring sugar and water to a boil over medium heat, stirring occasionally until sugar is dissolved. Boil for 10 minutes. Remove from heat and stir in rum and vanilla.

9. Using a slotted spoon or ladle, in batches as necessary, carefully place babas in hot syrup, and cook, turning several times to coat and letting them swell up and absorb the syrup, for 30 to 45 seconds. Transfer to a wire rack or serving plate. Discard leftover syrup.

10. Using a pastry brush, brush each cake with apricot jam. Serve immediately with lightly sweetened whipped cream and fresh berries.

Chocolate Cherry Almond Gugelhupf

A gugelhupf, or kugelhupf, is a European sweet yeast bread swirled with raisins or other dried fruit, nuts, citrus or, in this case, chocolate. Traditionally baked in a decorative tube pan or in its uniquely shaped namesake Bundt pan, the finished bread with a pretty marbled interior needs nothing more than a simple vanilla glaze on top.

MAKES 12 TO 16 SERVINGS

Tips

One medium orange yields about 2 tbsp (30 mL) zest.

The liquid for proofing yeast should be about 100 to 110°F (38 to 43°C). If the liquid is too hot, it will kill the yeast, but it needs to be warm to activate the yeast. If your yeast mixture still doesn't foam after 10 minutes, your yeast could be too old or the mixture wasn't the right temperature.

If you don't have a dough hook, dough can also be kneaded by hand for 8 to 10 minutes on a lightly floured work surface.

A good, draft-free place for dough to rise is in your oven. Turn the oven on for 30 seconds, just to infuse a little bit of warmth, then turn it off before placing the bowl or pan of dough in the oven.

- Large bowl, lightly coated with oil
- Minimum 10-cup Bundt pan, sprayed and lightly coated with granulated sugar

DOUGH

1 cup	whole milk	250 mL
½ cup	unsalted butter, cubed	125 mL
½ cup	granulated sugar	125 mL
2 tbsp	grated orange zest	30 mL
2 tsp	vanilla extract	10 mL
1	package (¼ oz/8 g) active dry yeast	1
4 to 4½ cups	all-purpose flour, divided	1 to 1.125 L
½ tsp	salt	2 mL
4	large eggs, at room temperature	4

FILLING

⅔ cup	dried cherries (either sour or sweet)	150 mL
¼ cup	orange liqueur (such as Grand Marnier) or dark rum	60 mL
½ cup	packed light brown sugar	125 mL
¾ cup	finely chopped almonds	175 mL
¾ cup	chopped dark or semisweet chocolate	175 mL
1 tbsp	grated orange zest	15 mL
¼ cup	unsalted butter, melted	60 mL
1	recipe Vanilla Glaze (page 271)	1

1. *Dough:* In a medium saucepan, bring milk and butter to a simmer over medium heat, stirring occasionally, until butter has almost melted. Remove from heat and stir in sugar, zest and vanilla.

2. Transfer mixture to the stand mixer bowl and let cool to warm (see tip). Sprinkle yeast over milk mixture and let stand for 5 minutes, until foamy.

3. With the mixer on low speed, beat in 2½ cups (625 mL) flour and salt until combined. Beat in eggs, one at a time. Gradually beat in 1½ cups (375 mL) flour until combined.

4. Replace paddle with dough hook. With the mixer on medium-low speed, knead dough, adding up to ½ cup (125 mL) more flour if dough is too sticky, for 5 to 6 minutes or until dough is soft, smooth and only slightly sticky.

5. Transfer dough to prepared bowl, turning to coat. Cover bowl with plastic wrap and let rise in a warm, draft-free place for 1 to 1½ hours or until doubled in bulk.

6. *Filling:* Meanwhile, in a small bowl, stir together cherries and orange liqueur. Let stand for 1 hour to plump cherries; drain, discarding excess liquid.

7. In a medium bowl, stir together brown sugar, almonds, chocolate, orange zest and butter. Stir in cherries.

8. Punch down dough and turn it out onto a lightly floured work surface. Gently knead a few times. Using a rolling pin, roll dough out into a 22- by 14-inch (55 by 35 cm) rectangle, with a long side facing you. Sprinkle filling evenly over top, leaving a 1-inch (2.5 cm) border.

9. Carefully roll up dough into a cylinder, pinching seam to seal. Using a sharp knife, cut dough crosswise into 12 even slices.

10. Place a ring of slices around outer wall of prepared pan, with cut sides touching the pan. Place the remaining slices, cut sides facing each other, in a ring around center of pan. Cover bowl with plastic wrap and let dough rise in a warm, draft-free place for 1 to 2 hours or until doubled in bulk.

11. Preheat oven to 350°F (180°C), or 325°F (160°C) for a dark pan.

12. Bake for 40 to 50 minutes or until puffed and golden brown and a tester inserted in the center comes out clean. Let cool in pan for 10 minutes, then carefully invert bread onto a wire rack to cool completely.

13. Pour glaze over the cooled bread, letting it drip down the sides. Let glaze set for at least 15 minutes before serving.

Panettone Bundt

Italian panettone is a sweet, fruit-studded, yeast-raised bread that originated in Milan. It is typically enjoyed during the holiday season, when you can find it in specialty markets and as a gift suggestion in gourmet catalogs. The dough, which has similarities to sourdough, has a longer-rising (or "proofing") process than other doughs in this book, so be sure to start the panettone at least 2 (preferably 3) days before you plan to serve it.

MAKES 12 TO 16 SERVINGS

Tips

A starter, also known as a *biga* in Italian baking, is a long pre-fermentation process that creates a light texture and adds tangy complexity to a bread's flavor. Breads made with biga generally have a longer rising time, which also enhances their taste.

Candied orange peel is orange peel that has been cooked in sugar syrup and then dried. It has a slightly bittersweet taste and a chewy texture, similar to dried fruit. Look for it in the bulk foods section of specialty food stores or online.

For best results, wrap the cooled panettone tightly in plastic wrap and store at room temperature overnight before serving.

Try slices toasted and spread with European butter or turn them into French toast for a memorable holiday breakfast.

- Minimum 10-cup Bundt pan, sprayed

STARTER

1 cup	all-purpose flour	250 mL
⅛ tsp	active dry yeast	0.5 mL
½ cup	buttermilk, at room temperature	125 mL

FRUIT

½ cup	golden raisins	125 mL
½ cup	dried cranberries	125 mL
½ cup	chopped dried apricots	125 mL
½ cup	diced candied orange peel	125 mL
½ cup	orange liqueur (such as Grand Marnier)	125 mL

DOUGH

3 cups	all-purpose flour	750 mL
2¼ tsp	active dry yeast	11 mL
1 tsp	salt	5 mL
3	large eggs, at room temperature	3
1	large egg yolk, at room temperature	1
¾ cup	buttermilk, at room temperature	175 mL
¾ cup	granulated sugar	175 mL
	Grated zest of 1 orange (about 2 tbsp/30 mL)	
2 tsp	vanilla extract	10 mL
¾ cup	unsalted butter, cut into 1-tbsp (15 mL) pieces and softened	175 mL

EGG WASH

1	large egg	1
1 tbsp	water	15 mL

1. *Starter:* In a small bowl, stir together flour, yeast and buttermilk to form a shaggy dough. Cover bowl with plastic wrap and let rise at room temperature for 8 to 12 hours or until doubled in bulk.

2. *Fruit:* In a medium saucepan, bring raisins, cranberries, apricots, orange peel and orange liqueur to a boil over medium heat, stirring often. Immediately remove from heat and set aside at room temperature, stirring occasionally, until fruit is plump and liquid has been absorbed, at least 1 hour or overnight.

3. *Dough:* In the stand mixer bowl, beat starter, flour, yeast, salt, eggs, egg yolk and buttermilk on medium-low speed for 3 to 4 minutes or until blended and smooth. Add sugar, orange zest and vanilla; beat for 3 minutes. Increase speed to medium and beat for 4 minutes or until dough is sticky and elastic.

Make Ahead

You can prepare panettone up to 1 week in advance. Tightly wrap cooled bread in plastic wrap and store at room temperature. Alternatively, tightly wrap cooled bread in plastic wrap, then foil, and store in the freezer for up to 1 month. Let thaw at room temperature overnight.

4. With the mixer on medium-low speed, add butter, one piece at a time, beating for about 1 minute after each addition so that the butter disappears into the dough before adding more. Dough should be glossy, loose and elastic.

5. With the mixer on low speed, beat in reserved fruit mixture until evenly distributed. Transfer dough to prepared pan and smooth the top. Cover pan with plastic wrap and let rise in a warm, draft-free place for 8 to 12 hours or until noticeably puffed but not necessarily doubled in size.

6. Preheat oven to 375°F (190°C), or 350°F (180°C) for a dark pan.

7. *Egg Wash:* In a small bowl, whisk egg with water until blended. Using a pastry brush, brush top of panettone with egg wash.

8. Bake for 15 minutes. Reduce oven temperature to 350°F (180°C), or to 325°F (160°C) for a dark pan, and bake for 25 to 35 minutes or until deep golden brown and a tester inserted in the center comes out clean. Let cool in pan for 10 minutes, then carefully invert panettone onto a wire rack to cool completely (see tip).

Sticky Toffee Pudding Bundt

We are fortunate to have many great restaurants in Las Vegas, where I live. We are also fortunate to have many great desserts within those restaurants — and I think that I've tried just about all of them! The best dessert I've ever tasted, though, was in a restaurant owned by the famous chef Gordon Ramsay: a decadent warm sticky toffee pudding accompanied by nutty brown butter ice cream, shaped like a stick of butter. Even people who claim to not be "dessert people" find it impossible to resist. This recipe is my nod to that dessert, in the form of a Bundt. Served warm, all it's missing is Chef Ramsay's ice cream — I wonder if he'd give me the recipe?

MAKES 12 TO 14 SERVINGS

Tips

Adding baking soda to the dates and boiling water helps tenderize the dates.

Because you will be pouring sticky toffee sauce over the cake, line your counter with a baking sheet to catch any drippings (and save cleanup time!) if you invert the cake onto a wire rack.

If desired, double the toffee sauce recipe so you have more sauce to serve alongside slices of cake or over ice cream.

Make Ahead

This cake is best enjoyed the day it is baked, but you can prepare it up to 3 days in advance. Store the cooled cake in a cake container at room temperature or in the refrigerator. Serve slices chilled, at room temperature or warmed in foil in a 300°F (150°C) oven for 15 minutes.

- Preheat oven to 350°F (180°C); dark pan, 325°F (160°C)
- Minimum 12-cup Bundt pan, sprayed

1½ cups	water	375 mL
2½ cups	chopped dried dates	625 mL
1 tsp	baking soda	5 mL
2 tbsp	brandy	30 mL
2½ cups	all-purpose flour	625 mL
1½ tsp	baking powder	7 mL
1 tsp	salt	5 mL
1½ cups	packed light brown sugar	375 mL
1 cup	unsalted butter, softened	250 mL
3	large eggs, at room temperature	3
2 tsp	vanilla extract	10 mL
1	recipe Toffee Sauce (page 278)	1

1. In a medium saucepan, bring water to a boil over high heat. Add dates, baking soda and brandy and stir to mix. Remove from heat and let cool until warm and liquid is absorbed by dates, about 20 minutes.
2. In a medium bowl, whisk together flour, baking powder and salt.
3. In the stand mixer bowl, beat brown sugar and butter on medium speed for 4 minutes or until light and fluffy. Beat in eggs, one at a time. Beat in vanilla.
4. With the mixer on low speed, add flour mixture in three additions, beating until incorporated.
5. Using a spatula, fold in date mixture. Transfer batter to prepared pan and smooth the top.
6. Bake in preheated oven for 40 to 50 minutes or until puffed and a tester inserted in the center comes out clean.
7. Let cake cool in pan for 10 minutes. Carefully invert onto a plate or wire rack set over a baking sheet (see tip). Using a toothpick, poke 30 to 40 holes in top of cake. Spoon warm toffee sauce evenly over top, letting it soak into cake before adding more. For best results, serve warm.

Figgy Pudding

So bring us some figgy pudding. So bring us some figgy pudding. So bring us some figgy pudding. And bring it right here! Many of us have sung these lyrics dozens of times without knowing exactly what "figgy pudding" is. Also known as "Christmas pudding," figgy pudding is a dense, moist cake filled with dried figs, which is steamed in a large pot rather than baked. Served as the finale to holiday dinners, it is often drizzled with warm liqueur and dramatically set aflame just before serving.

MAKES 12 TO 14 SERVINGS

Tips

Candied orange peel is orange peel that has been cooked in sugar syrup and then dried. It has a slightly bittersweet taste and a chewy texture, similar to dried fruit. Look for it in the bulk foods section of specialty food stores or online.

Panko are coarsely ground Japanese bread crumbs shaped like flakes. Look for them next to the regular bread crumbs in your grocery store. Regular dry bread crumbs can be used instead.

Placing a trivet, wire rack or even a few folded-up paper towels in the bottom of the stockpot will help prevent the Bundt pan from being jostled around too much during the steaming process.

Check water levels throughout the steaming process, refilling water to at least halfway up the sides of the Bundt pan as necessary.

- Minimum 10-cup Bundt pan, sprayed and lightly coated with granulated sugar

12 oz	plump dried figs, chopped	375 g
1 cup	water	250 mL
	Grated zest of 1 lemon and 1 orange	
½ cup	freshly squeezed orange juice	125 mL
½ cup	brandy	125 mL
½ cup	golden raisins	125 mL
¼ cup	diced candied orange peel	60 mL
1½ cups	all-purpose flour	375 mL
2 tsp	baking powder	10 mL
½ tsp	salt	2 mL
2 tsp	ground cinnamon	10 mL
1½ tsp	ground ginger	7 mL
¼ tsp	ground nutmeg	1 mL
¼ tsp	ground allspice	1 mL
¾ cup	packed light brown sugar	175 mL
½ cup	unsalted butter, softened	125 mL
4	large eggs, at room temperature	4
2 tbsp	dark (cooking) molasses	30 mL
2 cups	panko bread crumbs	500 mL
1½ cups	dried cranberries	375 mL
1 cup	sliced almonds	250 mL
½ cup	sweetened shredded coconut	125 mL

1. In a medium saucepan, bring figs and water to a boil over medium heat. Reduce heat and simmer, stirring occasionally, for 6 to 8 minutes or until water has evaporated. Stir in lemon zest, orange zest, orange juice, brandy, raisins and candied orange peel. Bring mixture back to a boil, stirring occasionally, then remove pan from heat and let cool to room temperature.

2. In a medium bowl, whisk together flour, baking powder, salt, cinnamon, ginger, nutmeg and allspice.

3. In the stand mixer bowl, beat brown sugar and butter on medium speed for 3 minutes or until light and fluffy. Beat in eggs, one at a time. Beat in molasses.

4. With the mixer on low speed, beat in bread crumbs. Add flour mixture in three additions, beating until blended and smooth (batter will be thick). Beat in fig mixture.

5. Using a spatula, fold in cranberries, almonds and coconut. Transfer batter to prepared pan and smooth the top.

Make Ahead

You can prepare this pudding through step 7 up to 2 weeks in advance and store it in the refrigerator. Alternatively, tightly wrap cooled pudding in plastic wrap, then foil, and store in the freezer for up to 2 months. Let thaw at room temperature overnight before resteaming as directed in step 8.

6. Place a trivet in the bottom of a large stockpot and fill pot with enough water to reach about two-thirds of the way up the Bundt pan (see tips). Carefully place pan on trivet. Bring water to a boil over medium heat. Cover pot tightly with foil and place lid securely on top of foil. Reduce heat to a simmer and steam pudding for 2 to 2½ hours or until very firm and a tester inserted in the center comes out clean.

7. To avoid getting burned, let steam escape before you try to remove pan from stockpot. Use doubled-up paper towels or oven mitts to reach in and pull Bundt pan from pot. Transfer pan to a wire rack to cool for 10 minutes, then carefully invert pudding onto a wire rack or plate to cool completely. Wrap cake tightly in plastic wrap and store at room temperature or in the refrigerator overnight.

8. Spray Bundt pan again and return pudding to pan. Repeat step 6, steaming for 45 minutes after reducing heat to a simmer. Unmold as directed in step 7, let cool and serve.

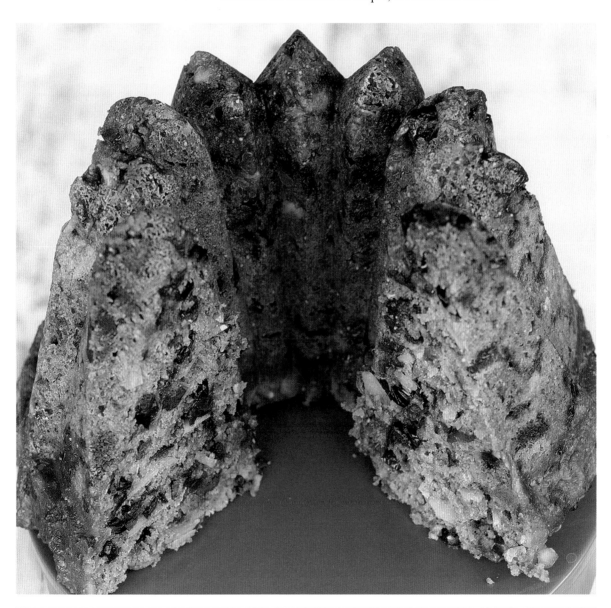

Mixed Berry Summer Pudding

The word "pudding" is used interchangeably with "dessert" in British culture, unlike the United States, where we think of it as a rich and creamy custard-like treat. This berry-filled pudding is one of a few recipes in this book that don't require an oven, making it ideal for summer months when the last thing you need is extra heat in the kitchen! Originally created at Claridge's in London, in a bowl rather than a Bundt pan, this summer pudding is held together by thin slices of regular white bread, which soak up the berries' juices and bright colors overnight, making it lighter than a traditionally prepared cake.

MAKES 10 TO 12 SERVINGS

Tips

Use a colorful combination of blueberries, raspberries, blackberries and chopped strawberries. While fresh berries work best in this recipe, they can be replaced with an equal amount of frozen berries (unthawed).

If you can't find a plate with some weight to it, you can weigh the plate down by placing a soup can or similar canned food on top.

For best results, serve pudding the day it is unmolded, garnished with lightly sweetened whipped cream (see tip, page 200) and fresh berries.

Make Ahead

You can prepare this pudding up to 2 days in advance. Store in a cake container in the refrigerator.

- **Minimum 10-cup Bundt pan, sprayed**

12 to 15	slices white sandwich bread, crusts trimmed	12 to 15
1	package (¼ oz/7 g) unflavored gelatin	1
2 tbsp	cold water	30 mL
8 cups	mixed fresh berries	2 L
¾ cup	granulated sugar	175 mL
½ cup	freshly squeezed orange juice	125 mL
1 tbsp	freshly squeezed lemon juice	15 mL

1. Line interior of prepared Bundt pan with plastic wrap, with a 1- to 2-inch (2.5 to 5 cm) overhang.
2. Using a rolling pin, flatten bread slices to about half their original thickness.
3. In a small bowl, sprinkle gelatin over water; let soak for 5 to 10 minutes or until softened.
4. In a large saucepan, bring berries, sugar, orange juice and lemon juice to a boil over medium heat, stirring often. Boil for 1 to 2 minutes or until berries soften. Remove from heat and stir in gelatin mixture until dissolved.
5. Pour or ladle about ½ cup (125 mL) berry mixture into prepared pan. Line bottom and sides of pan with flattened bread, trimming and overlapping a bit if necessary so that entire pan is covered.
6. Pour or ladle about half of the remaining berry mixture over bread slices and top with another layer of flattened bread, cutting pieces to fit. Repeat with the remaining berry mixture and bread.
7. Cover pan tightly with plastic wrap. Weigh plastic wrap down with an inverted plate that fits inside the outer edge of the pan. Chill for 8 hours or overnight.
8. Uncover Bundt and carefully invert onto a large serving plate, tugging gently on ends of plastic liner if necessary, to coax pudding from pan.

Apple Bread Pudding with Brandied Butterscotch Sauce

Bread pudding was originally created as a use for stale bread. Today's bread pudding is significantly more decadent, often made using premium breads like challah, brioche, croissants or even Italian panettone. This autumn-inspired bread pudding features brown sugar–spiced apples and is topped with a rich brandied butterscotch sauce.

MAKES 12 TO 14 SERVINGS

Tips

Other good apple choices would be Gala, Braeburn or Crispin.

Challah bread is a fluffy, sweet, braided egg bread often used for bread pudding. Day-old bread is drier than fresh and absorbs more custard.

In step 2, I've found it's best to toss the ingredients together using clean hands, rather than a spoon or spatula. This helps prevent the bread cubes from breaking up too much.

Make Ahead

This pudding is best enjoyed the day it is baked, but can be prepared up to 3 days in advance. Store cooled pudding, covered in plastic wrap, in the refrigerator. If desired, warm slices in the microwave for a few seconds or wrapped in foil in a 300°F (150°C) oven for 10 to 15 minutes.

- Minimum 10-cup Bundt pan, sprayed and lightly coated with granulated sugar

APPLES

6 tbsp	unsalted butter	90 mL
½ cup	packed light brown sugar	125 mL
2 tsp	ground cinnamon	10 mL
½ tsp	ground nutmeg	2 mL
¼ tsp	salt	1 mL
3	large Granny Smith apples, peeled and diced	3

CUSTARD

¾ cup	packed light brown sugar	175 mL
3	large eggs	3
4	large egg yolks	4
3 cups	half-and-half (10%) cream	750 mL
2 tbsp	brandy	30 mL
1 tsp	vanilla extract	5 mL
¼ tsp	salt	1 mL
1 lb	challah bread, cut into ¾-inch (2 cm) cubes	500 g
1	recipe Brandied Butterscotch Sauce (page 278)	1

1. *Apples:* In a nonstick skillet, melt butter over medium heat. Stir in brown sugar, cinnamon, nutmeg and salt until sugar has dissolved. Add apples and cook, stirring, for 5 to 7 minutes or until butter mixture is syrupy. Let cool.

2. *Custard:* In a large bowl, whisk together brown sugar, eggs and egg yolks until blended. Whisk in cream, brandy, vanilla and salt until blended. Using your hands, add bread to bowl and toss gently until evenly coated (see tip). Gently mix in caramelized apples with your hands until blended.

3. Transfer bread mixture to prepared pan, pressing down to compact. Cover pan with plastic wrap and refrigerate for at least 4 hours or overnight so that bread can fully absorb custard.

4. Preheat oven to 350°F (180°C), or 325°F (160°C) for a dark pan.

5. Uncover pan and bake for 50 to 60 minutes or until puffed and golden brown and a paring knife inserted in the center comes out clean. Let cool in pan for 15 minutes, then carefully invert pudding onto a plate.

6. Serve bread pudding slices warm, at room temperature or even chilled, with warm brandied butterscotch sauce.

Dark Chocolate Mocha Bread Pudding

Find the chocolate lover in your life and make them this recipe! Dense and fudgy, especially when chilled, this bread pudding contains a healthy dose of chopped chocolate enhanced with both unsweetened cocoa and espresso powder. Featured in both the pudding and the sauce, coffee liqueur adds a smooth coffee undertone, which, as we all know, goes hand in hand with chocolate (think: mochas).

MAKES 12 TO 14 SERVINGS

Tips

Look for espresso powder in the coffee section or baking aisle of your grocery store or at specialty baking retailers. If you can't find it, substitute ¾ tsp (3 mL) instant powdered coffee.

Brioche is a rich, buttery yeast bread with a tender crumb. Look for it in the bakery section of your grocery store. If you can't find brioche, you can substitute challah or any firm white bread.

In step 3, I've found it's best to toss the ingredients together using clean hands, rather than a spoon or spatula. This helps prevent the bread cubes from breaking up too much.

Make Ahead

You can prepare this pudding up to 3 days in advance. Tightly wrap the cooled pudding in plastic wrap or store in a cake container and store in the refrigerator.

- **Minimum 10-cup Bundt pan, sprayed and lightly coated with granulated sugar**

8 oz	dark or semisweet chocolate, chopped	250 g
½ tsp	espresso powder	2 mL
1½ cups	heavy or whipping (35%) cream	375 mL
1¾ cups	granulated sugar	425 mL
¼ cup	unsweetened cocoa powder, sifted	60 mL
8	large eggs	8
1 cup	whole milk	250 mL
⅓ cup	coffee-flavored liqueur (such as Kahlúa)	75 mL
2 tsp	vanilla extract	10 mL
⅛ tsp	salt	0.5 mL
1 lb	brioche bread, cut into ½-inch (1 cm) cubes	500 g
1	recipe Coffee Crème Anglaise (page 279)	1

1. In a medium saucepan, stir together chocolate, espresso powder and cream over medium-low heat; heat, stirring often, until melted and smooth.

2. In a large bowl, whisk together sugar and cocoa. Whisk in eggs, then milk, until blended. Whisk in liqueur, vanilla and salt. Slowly add melted chocolate mixture, whisking constantly, until blended.

3. Using your hands, add bread to bowl and toss gently until evenly coated (see tip).

4. Transfer bread mixture to prepared pan, pressing lightly to compact. Cover pan with plastic wrap and refrigerate for at least 4 hours or overnight so that bread can fully absorb custard.

5. Preheat oven to 350°F (180°C), or 325°F (160°C) for a dark pan.

6. Uncover pan and bake for 40 to 50 minutes or until puffed and a paring knife inserted in the center comes out clean. Let cool in pan for 15 minutes, then carefully invert pudding onto a plate. Serve warm, at room temperature or even chilled, with coffee crème Anglaise.

Variation

Add a dash of cinnamon and cayenne to the custard for a Mexican chocolate twist.

Chocolate Orange Croissant Bread Pudding with Orange Caramel Sauce

Bread pudding is perfect just the way it is, traditionally made with challah or brioche. That said, I don't think *anybody* would complain if you decided to change things up a bit and serve them bread pudding made from buttery, flaky French croissants! The result is a creamier texture with notes of toast in the flavor. In this recipe, I've combined chocolate and orange (one of my favorite combinations), which play off each other with their deeply sweet and slightly bitter flavors. A vibrant orange caramel sauce spooned on top of each slice creates a pretty presentation.

MAKES 12 TO 14 SERVINGS

Tips

Croissants come in different sizes. You want to have enough torn pieces to fill up your Bundt pan when lightly packed (minimum 10 cups). Croissant pieces will condense when mixed with custard.

In step 3, I've found it's best to toss the ingredients together using clean hands, rather than a spoon or spatula. This helps prevent the bread cubes from breaking up too much.

Make Ahead

You can prepare this pudding up to 3 days in advance. Tightly wrap the cooled pudding in plastic wrap or store in a cake container and store in the refrigerator.

• **Minimum 10-cup Bundt pan, sprayed and lightly coated with granulated sugar**

8 to 10	day-old croissants (see tip)	8 to 10
1¼ cups	chopped dark or semisweet chocolate (7½ oz/225 g)	300 mL
1 cup	granulated sugar	250 mL
7	large eggs	7
⅓ cup	orange marmalade	75 mL
½ tsp	ground cinnamon	2 mL
2¼ cups	half-and-half (10%) cream	560 mL
1 tbsp	orange liqueur (such as Grand Marnier), optional	15 mL
2 tsp	vanilla extract	10 mL
1	recipe Orange Caramel Sauce (page 279)	1

1. Cut or tear croissants into 1-inch (2.5 cm) pieces and place in a large bowl. Add chopped chocolate and toss to combine.

2. In another large bowl, whisk together sugar and eggs until blended. Whisk in marmalade and cinnamon. Gradually add cream, whisking, until blended. Whisk in orange liqueur (if using) and vanilla. Pour custard over croissant mixture.

3. Using your hands, gently toss mixture until evenly coated (see tip).

4. Transfer croissant mixture to prepared pan, pressing mixture down lightly to compact. Cover pan with plastic wrap and refrigerate for 2 hours or overnight so that croissants can fully absorb custard.

5. Preheat oven to 350°F (180°C), or 325°F (160°C) for a dark pan.

6. Uncover pan and bake for 40 to 50 minutes or until puffed and golden and a paring knife inserted in the center comes out clean. Let cool in pan for 15 minutes, then carefully invert pudding onto a plate.

7. Serve pudding slices warm, at room temperature or even chilled, with orange caramel sauce.

Variation

You can substitute 1 tbsp (15 mL) freshly squeezed orange juice for the orange liqueur.

Chocolate Chip Cookie Bundts

Mini Bundts

Lemon Poppy Seed Bundts

These bright and cheerful buttermilk Bundts are lovely to serve year-round, but they are particularly nice in the spring and summer months, when dining al fresco is in full swing. Light in texture and flavor with a tart lemon glaze, these Bundts also make a good dessert to serve after a heavier meal, complemented by some fresh berries.

MAKES 10 TO 12 MINI BUNDTS

Tips

If you are working with one mini Bundt pan, halve the recipe or prepare the cakes in two batches. Cover and chill the remaining batter until ready to use.

If needed, use a pastry brush or paper towel to make sure the baking spray gets into the crevices of the Bundt pans so the cakes don't stick.

You can make your own version of buttermilk by stirring together ½ cup (125 mL) milk (not fat-free) and 1½ tsp (7 mL) white or apple cider vinegar; let stand at room temperature for 15 minutes before using.

For best results, wrap the cooled cakes tightly in plastic wrap and store at room temperature or in the refrigerator overnight before glazing.

Make Ahead

You can prepare the glazed cakes up to 3 days in advance. Store in a cake container at room temperature.

- Preheat oven to 350°F (180°C); dark pan, 325°F (160°C)
- Two 6-cake mini Bundt pans, sprayed (see tips)

2 cups	cake flour, sifted	500 mL
½ tsp	baking powder	2 mL
½ tsp	baking soda	2 mL
½ tsp	salt	2 mL
1½ cups	granulated sugar	375 mL
⅔ cup	vegetable oil	150 mL
2	large eggs, at room temperature	2
2	large egg yolks, at room temperature	2
2 tbsp	poppy seeds	30 mL
2 tbsp	grated lemon zest	30 mL
¼ cup	freshly squeezed lemon juice	60 mL
½ cup	buttermilk	125 mL
1	recipe Lemon Glaze (page 272)	1

1. In a medium bowl, whisk together flour, baking powder, baking soda and salt.

2. In the stand mixer bowl, beat sugar and oil on medium speed for 2 minutes. Beat in eggs and egg yolks, one at a time. Add poppy seeds, lemon zest and lemon juice; beat for 2 minutes.

3. With the mixer on low speed, alternately beat in flour mixture and buttermilk, making three additions of flour and two of buttermilk, and beating until incorporated. Fill each prepared pan half to two-thirds full with batter, smoothing tops.

4. Bake in preheated oven for 20 minutes or until a tester inserted in the centers comes out clean. Let cool in pan for 10 minutes, then carefully invert cakes onto a wire rack to cool completely (see tip).

5. Spoon glaze evenly over Bundts, letting it drip down the sides. Let glaze set for at least 15 minutes before serving.

Variation

Replace the lemon glaze in this recipe with "Crispy" Lemon Glaze (variation, page 272).

Chocolate Malt and Sour Cherry Bundts with Cherry Vanilla Bean Glaze

Many years ago, I appeared on a Food Network cake competition, during which we had to create two recipes — one layer cake and one smaller cake or cupcake. I ended up winning the episode, thanks in part to my Double-Chocolate Malt Shop Cupcakes with Cherry Vanilla Buttercream. I based the recipe concept on an old-fashioned malt you would have found at a classic American soda fountain. That recipe inspired these Bundts. I've added plumped dried cherries to the batter, and a simple cherry vanilla glaze on top replaces the buttercream on the cupcakes.

MAKES 10 TO 12 MINI BUNDTS

Tips

It's worth investing in a high-quality cocoa powder, as I've found it creates a more chocolaty flavor in this recipe. It's important to sift cocoa powder before adding to dry ingredients, to avoid bitter-tasting clumps.

Look for malted milk powder (such as Carnation) in the baking or cereal aisle of your grocery store.

For best results, wrap the cooled cakes tightly in plastic wrap and store at room temperature or in the refrigerator overnight before glazing.

Make Ahead

You can prepare these glazed cakes up to 3 days in advance. Store in a cake container at room temperature.

- Preheat oven to 350°F (180°C); dark pan, 325°F (160°C)
- Two 6-cake mini Bundt pans, sprayed (see tips, page 220)

⅔ cup	coarsely chopped dried sour cherries	150 mL
¾ cup	whole milk	175 mL
2 cups	all-purpose flour	500 mL
¾ cup	unsweetened cocoa powder, sifted	175 mL
¾ cup	malted milk powder	175 mL
½ tsp	baking soda	2 mL
½ tsp	baking powder	2 mL
½ tsp	espresso powder	2 mL
½ tsp	salt	2 mL
1¼ cups	granulated sugar	300 mL
3	large eggs, at room temperature	3
1 cup	sour cream (not fat-free)	250 mL
¾ cup	vegetable oil	175 mL
½ cup	mini dark or semisweet chocolate chips	125 mL
1	recipe Cherry Vanilla Bean Glaze (variation, page 271)	1

1. In a small saucepan, stir together cherries and milk. Bring to a simmer over medium heat. Remove from heat and set aside, letting cherries plump up.

2. In a medium bowl, whisk together flour, cocoa, malted milk powder, baking soda, baking powder, espresso powder and salt.

3. In a large bowl, whisk together sugar, eggs, sour cream and oil until blended. Stir in flour mixture in three additions until fully incorporated. Stir in cherry mixture and chocolate chips. Fill each prepared pan about two-thirds full with batter, smoothing tops.

4. Bake in preheated oven for 20 to 25 minutes or until puffed and a tester inserted in the centers comes out clean. Let cool in pan for 10 minutes, then carefully invert cakes onto a wire rack to cool completely (see tip).

5. Pour glaze evenly over Bundts, letting it drip down the sides. Let glaze set for at least 15 minutes before serving.

Autumn Apple Bundts with Spiced Cider Glaze

I am always so inspired by the quintessential flavors of fall — butternut squash, pumpkin, ginger and, of course, apple. These mini spiced apple Bundts make me think of my childhood orchard visits, carrying home bushels of freshly picked apples and a few gallons of cider. The tart cider glaze for this recipe takes a little extra time to prepare, but the resulting flavor is worth it!

MAKES 10 TO 12 MINI BUNDTS

Tips

This recipe was created using Granny Smith apples, but any firm, tart apple, such as Gala or Braeburn, would be a good choice.

For best results, wrap the cooled cakes tightly in plastic wrap and store at room temperature or in the refrigerator overnight before glazing.

Make Ahead

You can prepare these glazed cakes up to 2 days in advance. Store in a cake container at room temperature.

- Preheat oven to 350°F (180°C); dark pan, 325°F (160°C)
- Two 6-cake mini Bundt pans, sprayed (see tips, page 220)

3 cups	grated peeled tart apples (about 3)	750 mL
3 tbsp	unsalted butter	45 mL
1 cup	granulated sugar, divided	250 mL
2 cups	all-purpose flour	500 mL
½ tsp	baking powder	2 mL
½ tsp	baking soda	2 mL
½ tsp	salt	2 mL
2 tsp	ground cinnamon	10 mL
1 tsp	ground ginger	5 mL
¼ tsp	ground nutmeg	1 mL
¾ cup	packed light brown sugar	175 mL
¾ cup	vegetable oil	175 mL
4	large eggs, at room temperature	4
2 tsp	vanilla extract	10 mL
1	recipe Spiced Cider Glaze (page 275)	1

1. Using your hands, squeeze juice from the grated apples into a glass measuring cup or bowl.

2. In a large skillet, melt butter over medium heat, stirring, until it becomes golden brown and fragrant. Add apples and ¼ cup (60 mL) granulated sugar; toss to coat. Add reserved apple juice to skillet. Cook, stirring occasionally, for 8 to 10 minutes or until all liquid has evaporated and apples are golden. Let cool slightly.

3. In a medium bowl, whisk together flour, baking powder, baking soda, salt, cinnamon, ginger and nutmeg.

4. In stand mixer bowl, beat apple mixture, the remaining granulated sugar and brown sugar on medium speed until blended. Beat in oil. Beat in eggs, one at a time. Beat in vanilla.

5. With the mixer on low speed, gradually beat in flour mixture in three additions until fully incorporated. Fill each prepared pan about three-quarters full with batter, smoothing tops.

6. Bake in preheated oven for 20 to 25 minutes or until puffed and a tester inserted in the centers comes out clean. Let cool in pan for 10 minutes, then carefully invert cakes onto a wire rack to cool completely (see tip).

7. Pour glaze evenly over Bundts, letting it drip down the sides. Let glaze set for at least 15 minutes before serving.

Chocolate Chip Cookie Bundts

I've seen hundreds of variations on the chocolate chip cookie. I've seen the dough baked in a skillet. I've seen the cookies crushed and used as a crust for pie. I've even seen the dough stuffed with *another* cookie and baked. But I have not seen a chocolate chip cookie mini Bundt — so *why not?* These minis are based on a recipe I have been making for years, tweaked enough to make it "Bundt-friendly." The oats give the cookies more texture, and the spices complement both the bittersweet chocolate and the buttery brown sugar batter. Like all chocolate chip cookies, these Bundts are best served warm, fresh from the oven, with a glass of ice-cold milk.

MAKES 10 TO 12 MINI BUNDTS

Tip

It's best to keep these Bundts slightly underbaked (with a few moist crumbs attached to a tester), as this will result in that optimal "freshly baked chocolate chip cookie" texture.

Make Ahead

These Bundts are best eaten still warm, but they are also delicious at room temperature. You can prepare them up to 2 days in advance. When serving, warm them for a few seconds in the microwave or wrapped in foil in a 300°F (150°C) oven for 10 to 15 minutes.

Batter can be prepared up to 1 week in advance and stored in an airtight container in the refrigerator or freezer. Bring to room temperature before filling prepared pans and baking.

- Preheat oven to 350°F (180°C); dark pan, 325°F (160°C)
- Food processor
- Two 6-cake mini Bundt pans, sprayed (see tips, page 220)

2 cups	all-purpose flour	500 mL
1½ cups	large-flake (old-fashioned) rolled oats	375 mL
1 cup	chopped pecans (optional)	250 mL
1 tsp	baking powder	5 mL
½ tsp	baking soda	2 mL
½ tsp	salt	2 mL
1 tsp	ground cinnamon	5 mL
½ tsp	ground ginger	2 mL
¼ tsp	ground nutmeg	1 mL
¾ cup	granulated sugar	175 mL
¾ cup	packed dark brown sugar	175 mL
1 cup	unsalted butter, softened	250 mL
4	large eggs, at room temperature	4
1 tsp	vanilla extract	5 mL
6 tbsp	milk	90 mL
1½ cups	dark or semisweet chocolate chunks	375 mL
1	recipe Vanilla Glaze (page 271; optional)	1

1. In food processor, combine flour, oats, pecans (if using), baking powder, baking soda, salt, cinnamon, ginger and nutmeg; pulse 5 or 6 times or just until oats and nuts are slightly chopped.

2. In the stand mixer bowl, beat granulated sugar, brown sugar and butter on medium speed for 5 minutes or until very light and fluffy. Beat in eggs, one at a time. Beat in vanilla.

3. With the mixer on low speed, alternately beat in flour mixture and milk, making three additions of flour and two of milk, and beating until incorporated. Beat in chocolate chunks. Fill each prepared pan two-thirds to three-quarters full with batter, smoothing tops.

4. Bake in preheated oven for about 20 minutes or until browned and a tester inserted in the centers comes out with a few moist crumbs attached (see tip). Let cool in pan for 10 minutes, then carefully invert Bundts onto a wire rack to cool. Serve warm from the oven or at room temperature.

5. If desired, pour glaze evenly over Bundts, letting it drip down the sides. Let glaze set for at least 10 minutes before serving.

Orange-Glazed Rum Raisin Bundts

Soaking the raisins in rum before adding them to the batter not only plumps them up, it also ensures the rum shines through in every bite. A hint of orange zest in the cakes, in addition to the sweet orange glaze, serves as a bright contrast to these tender, lightly spiced treats.

MAKES 10 TO 12 MINI BUNDTS

Tips

Use all dark or all golden raisins instead of a combination.

You can make your own version of buttermilk by stirring together ½ cup (125 mL) milk (not fat-free) and 1½ tsp (7 mL) white or apple cider vinegar; let stand at room temperature for 15 minutes before using.

For best results, wrap the cooled cakes tightly in plastic wrap and store overnight at room temperature before glazing.

The orange glaze should be thin enough so that it is slightly translucent when set — not opaque.

Make Ahead

You can prepare these cakes up to 1 day in advance. Store in a cake container at room temperature.

• **Two 6-cake mini Bundt pans, sprayed (see tips, page 220)**

½ cup	dark raisins	125 mL
½ cup	golden raisins	125 mL
½ cup	dark rum	125 mL
2 cups	all-purpose flour	500 mL
½ tsp	baking soda	2 mL
½ tsp	baking powder	2 mL
½ tsp	salt	2 mL
1 tsp	ground cinnamon	5 mL
½ tsp	ground cardamom	2 mL
1½ cups	packed light brown sugar	375 mL
1 cup	unsalted butter, softened	250 mL
4	large eggs, at room temperature	4
2 tsp	grated orange zest	10 mL
½ cup	buttermilk	125 mL
1	recipe Orange Glaze (variation, page 272)	1

1. In a small saucepan, stir together dark raisins, golden raisins and rum. Bring mixture to a simmer over medium heat. Remove from heat and set aside for 30 minutes, letting raisins absorb the rum.

2. Meanwhile, preheat oven to 350°F (180°C), or 325°F (160°C) for a dark pan.

3. In a large bowl, whisk together together flour, baking soda, baking powder, salt, cinnamon and cardamom.

4. In the stand mixer bowl, beat brown sugar and butter on medium speed for 3 to 4 minutes or until light and fluffy. Beat in eggs, one at a time. Add orange zest and beat for 3 minutes.

5. With the mixer on low speed, beat in raisin mixture. Alternately beat in flour mixture and buttermilk, making three additions of flour and two of buttermilk, and beating until incorporated. Fill each prepared pan about three-quarters full with batter, smoothing tops.

6. Bake for 20 to 25 minutes or until puffed and a tester inserted in the centers comes out clean. Let cool in pan for 10 minutes, then carefully invert cakes onto a wire rack to cool completely (see tip).

7. Pour glaze evenly over Bundts, letting it drip down the sides. Let glaze set for at least 15 minutes before serving.

"World's Best" Brownie Bundts

It's a pretty bold statement to call a brownie "world's best." When I had my bakery, we even went as far as making T-shirts that said, "We don't call it the World's Best Brownie for nothing!" Our customers agreed. Fudgy, dense and over-the-top chocolaty, our brownies were our #1 best-selling item. These Bundts, a slight variation on my original brownie, are the closest I've come to divulging my closely guarded "secret recipe." One is rich enough to share, but I've seen plenty of people polish off the entire mini Bundt by themselves!

MAKES 12 TO 14 MINI BUNDTS

Tips

These Bundts are supposed to be slightly underbaked, which is why the tester should come out with a few moist crumbs attached.

These Bundts can be served warm or at room temperature, but (in my opinion) they are best cooled to room temperature and then chilled for 4 hours, which gives them a rich and fudgy texture.

Make Ahead

You can prepare these Bundts up to 3 days in advance. Tightly wrap the cooled Bundts in plastic wrap and store in the refrigerator. Dust with confectioners' sugar just before serving.

- Preheat oven to 350°F (180°C); dark pan, 325°F (160°C)
- Two 6-cake mini Bundt pans, sprayed (see tips, page 220)

1¾ cups	cake flour, sifted	425 mL
1 cup	unsweetened cocoa powder (see tip, page 198), sifted	250 mL
½ tsp	baking powder	2 mL
½ tsp	salt	2 mL
12 oz	dark chocolate, chopped	375 g
1 cup + 6 tbsp	unsalted butter	340 mL
7	large eggs, at room temperature	7
3 cups	granulated sugar	750 mL
	Confectioners' (icing) sugar (optional)	

1. In a medium bowl, whisk together flour, cocoa, baking powder and salt.

2. In a large saucepan, melt chocolate and butter over medium-low heat, stirring constantly, until smooth. Remove from heat and let cool for 5 minutes.

3. Rapidly whisk eggs into chocolate mixture, one at a time. Whisk until thickened to a glossy, almost pudding-like consistency.

4. Stir in granulated sugar. Gradually stir in flour mixture in four additions until fully incorporated. Fill each prepared pan about two-thirds full with batter, smoothing tops.

5. Bake in preheated oven for about 25 minutes or until puffed and a tester inserted in the centers comes out with a few moist crumbs attached (see tip). Let cool in pan for 10 minutes, then carefully invert cakes onto a wire rack to cool for 10 minutes more.

6. If desired, dust with confectioners' sugar before serving.

Zucchini Apple Nut Bundts

If you're looking for a way to get your fruits and vegetables while satisfying your sweet tooth, these spiced mini Bundts are an excellent choice! Four generous cups (1 L) of grated apples and zucchini keep the texture moist and the flavor sweet, although my favorite part is the "crispy" lemon glaze on top, created by mixing granulated and confectioners' sugars with lemon juice. Serve these Bundts with afternoon coffee or as part of a weekend breakfast.

MAKES 10 TO 12 MINI BUNDTS

Tips

You can use peeled or unpeeled apples in this recipe. Any firm, tart apple, such as Granny Smith, Braeburn or Gala, would be a good choice.

Try substituting finely grated peeled sweet potatoes for the apples or zucchini.

For best results, wrap the cooled cakes tightly in plastic wrap and store overnight at room temperature before glazing.

Make Ahead

You can prepare these cakes up to 2 days in advance. Store in a cake container at room temperature.

- Preheat oven to 350°F (180°C); dark pan, 325°F (160°C)
- Two 6-cake mini Bundt pans, sprayed (see tips, page 220)

2 cups	grated zucchini (unpeeled)	500 mL
2 cups	grated apples	500 mL
2 cups	all-purpose flour	500 mL
1 tsp	baking soda	5 mL
½ tsp	salt	2 mL
¼ tsp	baking powder	1 mL
1 tbsp	ground cinnamon	15 mL
1 tsp	ground ginger	5 mL
¾ tsp	ground cardamom	3 mL
¼ tsp	ground nutmeg	1 mL
1½ cups	granulated sugar	375 mL
½ cup	packed light brown sugar	125 mL
¾ cup	vegetable oil	175 mL
3	large eggs, at room temperature	3
1 tsp	vanilla extract	5 mL
1½ cups	chopped walnuts or pecans	375 mL
1	recipe "Crispy" Lemon Glaze (variation, page 272)	1

1. Over a sink, using your hands, gently squeeze the water out of grated zucchini and apples.

2. In a medium bowl, whisk together flour, baking soda, salt, baking powder, cinnamon, ginger, cardamom and nutmeg.

3. In the stand mixer bowl, beat granulated sugar, brown sugar and oil on medium speed for 1 minute. Beat in eggs, one at a time. Beat in vanilla. Gradually beat in zucchini and apples, separating the strands as you add them so that they are not in clumps.

4. With the mixer on low speed, gradually beat in flour mixture, mixing until just incorporated. Beat in walnuts. Fill prepared pans two-thirds to three-quarters full with batter, smoothing tops.

5. Bake in preheated oven for 25 to 30 minutes or until puffed and a tester inserted in the centers comes out clean. Let cool in pan for 10 minutes, then carefully invert cakes onto a wire rack to cool completely (see tip).

6. Pour glaze evenly over Bundts, letting it drip down the sides. Let glaze set for at least 15 minutes before serving.

Pineapple Upside-Down Bundts

There is no better use for canned pineapple rings than these mini Bundts. The rings fit perfectly around the classically shaped Bundt molds, which creates a beautiful presentation when the Bundts are popped out of the pan and garnished with a cherry. The cakes are very light, allowing the buttery topping and caramelized pineapple to be the stars of the show.

**MAKES
12 MINI BUNDTS**

Tips

If the pineapple rings don't fit perfectly around the centers of the Bundt molds, cut them in half and arrange on the topping, overlapping slightly if needed.

Every once in a while, the topping will bubble over the Bundt pans while baking. Line the bottom of your oven with foil or place a large rimmed baking sheet on the rack below the Bundt pan to prevent a potential smoky mess!

Make Ahead

These Bundts are best enjoyed the day they are baked, but you can prepare them up to 1 day in advance. Tightly wrap the cooled Bundts in plastic wrap and store at room temperature. If desired, warm Bundts in the microwave for a few seconds or wrapped in foil in a 250°F (120°C) oven for 10 to 15 minutes.

- Preheat oven to 350°F (180°C); dark pan, 325°F (160°C)
- Two 6-cake mini Bundt pans, sprayed (see tips, page 220)

TOPPING

¾ cup	unsalted butter	175 mL
¾ cup	packed dark brown sugar	175 mL
¼ tsp	ground cinnamon	1 mL
¼ tsp	salt	1 mL
1 tbsp	dark rum (optional)	15 mL

CAKES

2 cups	all-purpose flour	500 mL
½ tsp	baking powder	2 mL
¼ tsp	salt	1 mL
½ tsp	ground cinnamon	2 mL
¾ cup	granulated sugar	175 mL
¾ cup	packed dark brown sugar	175 mL
½ cup	unsalted butter, softened	125 mL
¼ cup	vegetable oil	60 mL
4	large eggs, at room temperature	4
2 tsp	vanilla extract	10 mL
12	drained canned pineapple rings	12
12	maraschino cherries	12

1. *Topping:* In a small saucepan, melt butter over medium-low heat. Add brown sugar, cinnamon and salt. Cook, stirring, for 2 minutes. Remove from heat. If desired, stir in rum.

2. *Cakes:* In a medium bowl, whisk together flour, baking powder, salt and cinnamon.

3. In the stand mixer bowl, beat granulated sugar, brown sugar, butter and oil on medium speed for 2 minutes. Beat in eggs, one at a time. Beat in vanilla.

4. With the mixer on low speed, gradually add flour mixture, beating until just incorporated.

5. Spoon 1½ tbsp (22 mL) topping into each prepared mold. Place 1 pineapple ring into each mold, fitting each around the mold's center (see tip). Divide batter evenly on top, smoothing tops, so that pans are about two-thirds to three-quarters full.

6. Bake in preheated oven for 20 to 25 minutes or until a tester inserted in the centers comes out clean. Let cool in pan for 10 minutes, then carefully invert cakes onto a platter to cool for 5 minutes. For best results, serve warm, garnished with a maraschino cherry in the center of each Bundt.

Chai-Spiced Bundts with Spiced Vanilla Glaze

Did you know that chai (rhymes with "tie") is the word for "tea" in many cultures? In India, chai is a spiced, sweetened tea with milk, which has gained popularity around the world, appearing on menus in popular coffee houses and in recipes all over the Internet. Although chai spice combinations vary, most of them tend to include cinnamon, cardamom, cloves and ginger (I've added nutmeg too). These mini Bundts are generously spiced, both in the batter and in the sweet vanilla glaze, which makes them smell heavenly while baking.

MAKES 10 TO 12 MINI BUNDTS

Tips

If you are working with one mini Bundt pan, halve the recipe or prepare the cakes in two batches. Cover and chill the remaining batter until ready to use.

If needed, use a pastry brush or paper towel to make sure the baking spray gets into the crevices of the Bundt pan so the cakes don't stick.

For best results, wrap the cooled Bundts tightly in plastic wrap and store at room temperature overnight before glazing.

For a less intense chai flavor, use Vanilla Glaze (page 271) instead of Spiced Vanilla Glaze.

Make Ahead

You can prepare these cakes up to 2 days in advance. Store in a cake container at room temperature.

- Preheat oven to 350°F (180°C); dark pan, 325°F (160°C)
- Two 6-cake mini Bundt pans, sprayed (see tips)

2½ cups	all-purpose flour	625 mL
¾ tsp	baking powder	3 mL
½ tsp	baking soda	2 mL
½ tsp	salt	2 mL
1 tbsp	ground cinnamon	15 mL
1 tbsp	ground cardamom	15 mL
1 tbsp	ground ginger	15 mL
½ tsp	ground nutmeg	2 mL
½ tsp	ground cloves	2 mL
1 cup	packed light brown sugar	250 mL
½ cup	unsalted butter, softened	125 mL
½ cup	vegetable oil	125 mL
½ cup	liquid honey	125 mL
3	large eggs, at room temperature	3
2 tsp	vanilla extract	10 mL
1 cup	whole milk	250 mL
1	recipe Spiced Vanilla Glaze (variation, page 271)	1

1. In a medium bowl, whisk together flour, baking powder, baking soda, salt, cinnamon, cardamom, ginger, nutmeg and cloves.

2. In the stand mixer bowl, beat brown sugar, butter and oil on medium speed for 4 minutes or until very light and fluffy. Beat in honey. Beat in eggs, one at a time. Beat in vanilla.

3. With the mixer on low speed, alternately beat in flour mixture and milk, making three additions of flour and two of milk, and beating until incorporated. Fill prepared pans two-thirds to three-quarters full with batter, smoothing tops.

4. Bake in preheated oven for 20 minutes or until puffed and a tester inserted in the centers comes out clean. Let cool in pan for 10 minutes, then carefully invert cakes onto a wire rack to cool completely (see tip).

5. Pour glaze evenly over Bundts, letting it drip down the sides. Let glaze set for at least 15 minutes before serving.

Bananas Foster Monkey Bread Bundts

These individually sized versions of pull-apart monkey bread would be a fun dessert for either a dinner party or a brunch buffet. Instead of everyone picking pieces from one large Bundt, each person receives his or her own mini Bundt, consisting of six brown sugar– and spice-coated balls topped with a sticky-sweet blend of caramelized bananas, walnuts and orange. Serve these warm, while the dough is still pillow-soft inside, alongside a scoop of vanilla ice cream.

**MAKES
10 MINI BUNDTS**

Tips

If needed, use a pastry brush or paper towel to make sure the baking spray gets into the crevices of the Bundt pan so the cakes don't stick.

Store the unused half of Monkey Bread Dough in an airtight container in the freezer for up to 1 month. Thaw overnight in the refrigerator before using.

A good, draft-free place for dough to rise is in your oven. Turn the oven on for 30 seconds, just to infuse a little bit of warmth, then turn it off before placing the pan of dough in the oven.

These Bundts can be messy while baking! Line your oven with foil to save yourself a cleaning headache — and a smoky kitchen! Or place a rimmed baking sheet on the rack below.

- **Two 6-cake mini Bundt pans, sprayed (see tip)**

1	recipe Monkey Bread Dough (page 142)	1
BANANA TOPPING		
½ cup	unsalted butter	125 mL
	Grated zest of 1 orange	
1 cup	packed light brown sugar	250 mL
3 tbsp	dark rum	45 mL
2 tbsp	banana liqueur	30 mL
2	ripe but firm bananas, diced	2
¾ cup	finely chopped walnuts	175 mL
BROWN SUGAR TOPPING		
1 cup	packed light brown sugar	250 mL
1 tsp	ground cinnamon	5 mL
½ tsp	ground nutmeg	2 mL
¼ tsp	ground allspice	1 mL
¼ tsp	salt	1 mL
½ cup	unsalted butter, melted	125 mL

1. Prepare dough through step 4. Divide dough in half, freezing one half for another use (see tip).

2. *Banana Topping:* In a medium skillet, melt butter over low heat. Stir in orange zest and brown sugar until sugar dissolves. Stir in rum and banana liqueur. Bring to a simmer over medium heat. Cook, stirring constantly, for 2 minutes. Add bananas and cook, stirring gently, for 1 minute. Stir in walnuts and remove from heat. Let cool completely.

3. *Brown Sugar Topping:* In a medium shallow bowl, whisk together brown sugar, cinnamon, nutmeg, allspice and salt.

4. Turn dough out onto a lightly floured work surface and dust with flour. Using the rolling pin, roll dough out into a (roughly) 10- by 6-inch (25 by 15 cm) rectangle. Using a sharp knife, cut rectangle crosswise into 10 equal slices, about 1 inch (2.5 cm) thick. Cut each slice crosswise into six 1-inch (2.5 cm) pieces, so that you have 60 pieces.

5. Divide banana topping among prepared Bundt pans.

6. Using your hands, roll each piece of dough into a ball. Dip each ball in melted butter, then roll it in brown sugar topping to coat. Place six balls around each Bundt pan so that they fit together. Cover pans loosely with plastic wrap and let dough rise in a warm, draft-free place for 30 minutes.

Make Ahead

These Bundts are best enjoyed the day they are baked, but you can prepare them up to 1 day in advance. Store cooled Bundts in a cake container at room temperature. If desired, warm Bundts in the microwave for a few seconds.

7. Meanwhile, preheat oven to 350°F (180°C), or 325°F (160°C) for a dark pan (see tip).

8. Uncover pans and bake for 25 to 30 minutes or until puffed and deep golden brown, and banana topping is bubbling underneath. Let cool in pan for 15 minutes, then carefully invert cakes onto a platter or a wire rack set over a large rimmed baking sheet. Serve warm or at room temperature.

Variation

Replace 2 tbsp (30 mL) banana liqueur with 1 tbsp (15 mL) vanilla extract and 2 tsp (10 mL) banana flavoring.

Baked Sausage Rigatoni Bundt

Savory Bundts

Spaghetti Carbonara Pie Bundt

Ask a group of people what their favorite pasta dish is, and I'm willing to bet at least a handful of them will tell you it's spaghetti carbonara. Although the concept of this dish is fairly simple — crisp, salty pancetta mixed with eggs, cheese, black pepper and spaghetti — the resulting flavors and textures are anything but, which is why it is very easy to devour a generous portion, leaving nothing on the plate. Carbonara pasta is traditionally prepared in a skillet, but in this recipe, I have baked it into a Bundt, creating a crispy-edged exterior, perfect for cutting into slices.

MAKES 10 TO
12 SERVINGS

Tips

Similar to bacon, pancetta is made from cured pork belly, usually with spices and/or black pepper added. Look for it at the deli counter of your grocery store. In a pinch, you can substitute a good quality thick-cut bacon (diced) for the pancetta in this recipe.

Spaghetti can be broken in half before boiling. This will make it easier to arrange the noodles in the pan before baking.

Make Ahead

This Bundt is best enjoyed the day it is baked, but you can prepare it up to 2 days in advance. Cover with plastic wrap and store in the refrigerator. To reheat slices, microwave on High in a covered microwave-safe container for 45 to 60 seconds or wrap in foil and heat in a 325°F (160°C) oven for 15 to 20 minutes.

- Preheat oven to 400°F (200°C)
- Minimum 12-cup Bundt pan, sprayed

1 lb	dried spaghetti	500 g
1 tbsp	extra virgin olive oil	15 mL
6 oz	diced pancetta	175 g
1 tbsp	chopped garlic	15 mL
4	large eggs	4
¼ cup	chopped fresh flat-leaf (Italian) parsley	60 mL
1½ cups	whole milk	375 mL
1 tsp	salt	5 mL
1 tsp	freshly ground black pepper	5 mL
6 oz	fontina cheese, finely shredded	175 g
6 oz	provolone cheese, finely shredded	175 g
¾ cup	grated pecorino-Romano cheese, divided	175 mL

1. In a large pot of boiling salted water, cook spaghetti, stirring occasionally, for 8 to 10 minutes or until al dente. Drain.

2. In a large skillet, heat oil over medium heat. Add pancetta and cook, stirring, for 5 minutes or until crisp and fat has rendered. Add garlic and cook, stirring, for 30 seconds. Remove from heat and add drained spaghetti, tossing to coat.

3. In a large bowl, whisk together eggs, parsley, milk, salt and pepper until blended. Stir in fontina, provolone and ½ cup (125 mL) pecorino-Romano. Add spaghetti mixture, tossing to evenly distribute ingredients.

4. Sprinkle the remaining pecorino-Romano in prepared pan, shaking to coat evenly. Transfer spaghetti mixture to pan, arranging in an even layer and pressing lightly to compact.

5. Bake in preheated oven for 30 to 40 minutes or until golden brown and bubbling. Let cool in pan for 10 to 15 minutes, then carefully invert Bundt onto a plate. For best results, serve warm.

Variation

You can substitute an equal amount of a different long, thin pasta, such as linguini, fettuccini or angel hair, for the spaghetti; adjust cooking time according to package directions.

Macaroni and Four-Cheese Bundt

A good test for any savory recipe that I create is how much of it my husband eats. After he enjoyed three helpings of this macaroni and cheese for dinner, followed by two rewarmed slices the next day, I knew I had a winner. Coating a casserole pan (in this case, the Bundt) with a combination of bread crumbs and cheese is a trick that I learned to create an extra-golden, crispy crust to contrast the rich, tangy and cheesy filling.

MAKES 10 TO 12 SERVINGS

Tip

Gradually adding hot liquid to eggs heats them slowly, or tempers them, to ensure they don't scramble in the milk mixture.

Make Ahead

This Bundt is best enjoyed the day it is baked, but you can prepare it up to 2 days in advance. Cover with plastic wrap and store in the refrigerator. To reheat slices, microwave on High in a covered microwave-safe container for 45 to 60 seconds or wrap in foil and heat in a 325°F (160°C) oven for 15 to 20 minutes. You can also brown slices under a broiler, flipping once so that both sides are warmed through.

- Preheat oven to 375°F (190°C)
- Minimum 12-cup Bundt pan, sprayed

COATING

2 tbsp	panko bread crumbs	30 mL
2 tbsp	grated Parmesan cheese	30 mL

CASSEROLE

1 lb	dried elbow macaroni	500 g
3	large eggs	3
¼ cup	unsalted butter	60 mL
1 tbsp	chopped fresh rosemary	15 mL
3 tbsp	dry white wine	45 mL
¼ cup	all-purpose flour	60 mL
2 cups	whole milk, warmed	500 mL
½ tsp	salt	2 mL
½ tsp	smoked paprika	2 mL
¼ tsp	freshly ground black pepper	1 mL
6 oz	sharp (old) Cheddar cheese, shredded	175 g
6 oz	Gruyère cheese, shredded	175 g
6 oz	fontina cheese, shredded	175 g
½ cup	grated Parmesan cheese	125 mL
1 cup	panko bread crumbs (see tip, page 246)	250 mL

1. *Coating:* In a small bowl, stir together bread crumbs and Parmesan. Sprinkle over the prepared pan, shaking to coat evenly. Chill pan in the freezer while you prepare the casserole.
2. *Casserole:* In a large pot of boiling salted water, cook macaroni, stirring occasionally, for 6 to 8 minutes or until al dente. Drain.
3. Meanwhile, in a medium heatproof bowl, whisk eggs until blended.
4. In a medium saucepan, melt butter over medium heat. Add rosemary and cook, stirring, for 30 seconds or until fragrant. Whisk in wine and cook, stirring occasionally, for 1 to 2 minutes or until reduced. Sprinkle in flour and cook, whisking constantly, for 1 minute.
5. Gradually pour in milk, whisking constantly; cook, whisking, for 8 to 10 minutes or until mixture is smooth, bubbly and thickened. Slowly pour half the milk mixture into the eggs, whisking constantly. Return egg mixture to the saucepan and cook, stirring, for 1 minute, until slightly thickened. Whisk in salt, paprika and pepper. Remove from heat.

6. One handful at a time, add cheeses to the sauce, stirring until almost melted before adding more. Once all the cheeses have been added, stir until smooth. Stir in panko and macaroni. Transfer macaroni and cheese to chilled pan, arranging in an even layer and pressing lightly to compact.

7. Bake in preheated oven for 35 to 40 minutes or until deep golden brown and bubbling. Let cool in pan for 15 to 20 minutes, then carefully invert Bundt onto a plate. For best results, serve warm.

Variation

For a spicy kick, add a few dashes of hot pepper sauce or a generous pinch of cayenne pepper to the cheese sauce with the spices.

Southwestern Mac and Cheese Bundt

We love spicy foods in our house. In our refrigerator, you'll find several brands of hot sauce, and you'll never find salsa that is labeled "mild" or "medium." In our desert garden, we grow jalapeño, serrano and habanero peppers, although I drew the line at ghost peppers (one of the world's hottest varieties). Yes, I love heat in my food, but I'm not crazy! Naturally, Southwestern cuisine, with its spicy tendencies, is a good match for my family. This Bundt takes the ingredients of a well-seasoned, slightly spicy beef taco and translates them into a gooey, zesty macaroni and cheese.

MAKES 10 TO 12 SERVINGS

Tips

Panko are coarsely ground Japanese bread crumbs shaped like flakes. They bake up lighter and crispier than traditional bread crumbs, which makes them an excellent choice for coating the Bundt. Look for them next to the regular bread crumbs in your grocery store. Regular bread crumbs can be used in place of the panko.

When slicing a spicy pepper such as a jalapeño, it's best to use kitchen gloves, as heat from the ribs and seeds is likely to stay on your hands and will be painful should it come into contact with your eyes and face.

Gradually adding hot liquid to eggs heats them slowly, or tempers them, to ensure they don't scramble in the milk mixture.

- Preheat oven to 375°F (190°C)
- Minimum 12-cup Bundt pan, sprayed

1¼ cups	panko bread crumbs, divided	300 mL
1 lb	dried elbow macaroni	500 g
1 tbsp	extra virgin olive oil	15 mL
1	small onion, finely chopped	1
1 tbsp	chopped garlic	15 mL
1	small red bell pepper, chopped	1
1	jalapeño pepper, seeded and minced	1
12 oz	lean ground beef	375 g
1 tbsp	chili powder	15 mL
1 tbsp	ground cumin	15 mL
1 tbsp	smoked paprika	15 mL
2 tsp	salt	10 mL
½ tsp	freshly ground black pepper	2 mL
¼ tsp	cayenne pepper	1 mL
1 cup	drained canned diced tomatoes	250 mL
3	large eggs	3
¼ cup	unsalted butter	60 mL
¼ cup	all-purpose flour	60 mL
2 cups	whole milk, warmed	500 mL
8 oz	sharp (old) Cheddar cheese, finely shredded	250 g
8 oz	Monterey Jack cheese, finely shredded	250 g

1. Sprinkle ¼ cup (60 mL) panko over prepared pan, shaking to coat. Chill pan in the freezer while you prepare the macaroni and cheese.

2. In a large pot of boiling salted water, cook macaroni, stirring occasionally, for 6 to 8 minutes or until al dente. Drain.

3. Meanwhile, in a large skillet, heat oil over medium-high heat. Add onion and cook, stirring occasionally, for 4 to 5 minutes or until softened. Add garlic, red pepper and jalapeño; cook, stirring occasionally, for 2 minutes.

4. Add beef, chili powder, cumin, paprika, salt, pepper and cayenne; cook, breaking up beef with a spoon, until no longer pink. Stir in tomatoes. Transfer mixture to a plate lined with paper towels to drain.

5. In a medium heatproof bowl, whisk eggs until blended.

6. In a large saucepan, melt butter over medium heat. Sprinkle in flour and cook, whisking constantly, for 2 minutes or until thick and bubbly. Gradually pour in milk, whisking constantly; cook, whisking, for 8 to 10 minutes or until mixture is smooth, bubbly and thickened.

7. Slowly pour half the milk mixture into the eggs, whisking constantly. Return egg mixture to the saucepan and cook, stirring, for 1 minute, until slightly thickened. Remove from heat.

8. One handful at a time, add cheeses to the sauce, stirring until almost melted before adding more. Once all the cheeses have been added, stir until smooth. Stir in the remaining panko, beef mixture and macaroni until blended. Transfer mixture to prepared pan, arranging in an even layer.

9. Bake in preheated oven for 30 to 40 minutes or until deep golden brown and bubbling. Let cool in pan for 15 minutes, then carefully invert Bundt onto a plate. For best results, serve warm.

Variation

For additional smoky, slightly sweet flavor with mild to medium heat, substitute an equal amount of ancho chile powder for the regular chili powder.

Baked Sausage Rigatoni Bundt

This hearty Italian baked pasta Bundt would be right at home on a red-and-white-checked tablecloth alongside a basket of buttery garlic bread, a tossed Caesar salad and a full-bodied Barolo. Wider than penne, tube-shaped rigatoni surround bits of sweet Italian sausage, tomato, mushrooms and cheese in every bite. The top bakes up golden brown and bubbly, making it nearly impossible to resist taking a few bites straight from the pan. (Go ahead. I won't tell!)

MAKES 10 TO 12 SERVINGS

Tip

Gradually adding hot liquid to eggs heats them slowly, or tempers them, to ensure they don't scramble in the milk mixture.

Make Ahead

This Bundt is best enjoyed the day it is baked, but you can prepare it up to 2 days in advance. Cover with plastic wrap and store in the refrigerator. To reheat slices, microwave on High in a covered microwave-safe container for 45 to 60 seconds or wrap in foil and heat in a 325°F (160°C) oven for 15 to 20 minutes.

- Preheat oven to 400°F (200°C)
- Minimum 12-cup Bundt pan, sprayed

1 lb	dried rigatoni pasta	500 g
1 lb	sweet Italian turkey sausage (bulk or casings removed)	500 g
1	small onion, chopped	1
8 oz	thinly sliced mushrooms	250 g
¼ cup	chopped fresh flat-leaf (Italian) parsley	60 mL
1 tbsp	chopped garlic	15 mL
½ tsp	salt	2 mL
¼ tsp	freshly ground black pepper	1 mL
½ tsp	hot pepper flakes	2 mL
6 tbsp	unsalted butter	90 mL
⅓ cup	all-purpose flour	75 mL
3 cups	whole milk, warmed	750 mL
1 cup	tomato sauce	250 mL
2 tbsp	tomato paste	30 mL
4 oz	fontina cheese, finely grated	125 g
4 oz	mozzarella cheese, finely grated	125 g
1 cup	grated pecorino-Romano cheese, divided	250 mL

1. In a large pot of boiling salted water, cook rigatoni, stirring occasionally, for 8 to 10 minutes or until al dente. Drain.

2. In a large skillet, cook sausage over medium heat, breaking it up with a spoon, until no longer pink. Add onion and cook, stirring often, for 3 to 4 minutes or until softened. Add mushrooms and cook, stirring, for 5 minutes or until browned and cooked through. Add parsley, garlic, salt, pepper and hot pepper flakes; cook, stirring, for 1 minute. Transfer sausage mixture to a plate lined with paper towels and let drain.

3. In a large saucepan, melt butter over medium heat. Sprinkle in flour and cook, whisking, for 2 minutes or until thick and bubbly. Gradually whisk in milk; cook, whisking, for 10 to 12 minutes or until mixture is smooth, bubbly and thickened.

4. Whisk in tomato sauce and tomato paste and cook, whisking, for 2 minutes or until smooth. Remove from heat.

5. One handful at a time, add fontina and mozzarella to the sauce, stirring until almost melted before adding more. Whisk in ½ cup (125 mL) pecorino-Romano. Once all of the cheeses have been added, stir until smooth. Transfer sauce to a large bowl and stir in sausage mixture and rigatoni until evenly distributed.

Tip

For lighter results, replace the whole milk with low-fat (not non-fat/skim) milk.

6. Sprinkle ¼ cup (60 mL) pecorino-Romano over prepared pan, shaking to coat. Transfer rigatoni mixture to pan, arranging into an even layer, pressing lightly to compact. Sprinkle the remaining pecorino-Romano on top.

7. Bake in preheated oven for 35 to 45 minutes or until deep golden brown and bubbling. Let cool in pan for 10 to 15 minutes, then carefully invert Bundt onto a plate. For best results, serve warm.

Variation

For spicier results, replace the sweet Italian turkey sausage with an equal amount of a hot variety. You can also choose pork or chicken sausage, if desired.

Layered Italian Turkey Meatloaf Bundt

When I ran my little café, we had a hot and cold daily sandwich special. One morning, we had leftover turkey meatloaf from the previous night's dinner, so we created an impromptu turkey meatloaf sandwich on crusty ciabatta, covered with marinara sauce and melted provolone cheese. A hit with customers, the sandwich quickly turned into a permanent menu item. This Bundt is a layered version of that meatloaf, featuring the marinara in the middle along with my homemade basil pesto. It's delicious warm from the oven, but also great the next day, reheated and served as a sandwich.

MAKES 10 TO 12 SERVINGS

Tip

For best results, use regular (85%) or lean (93%) ground turkey, not extra-lean (99%) turkey.

Make Ahead

This meatloaf is best enjoyed the day it is baked, but you can prepare it up to 3 days in advance. Tightly wrap the cooled Bundt in plastic wrap and store in the refrigerator. To reheat slices, microwave on High in a covered microwave-safe container for 30 to 45 seconds or wrap in foil and heat in a 325°F (160°C) oven for 15 to 20 minutes.

You can prepare the pesto up to 1 week in advance. Store in an airtight container in the refrigerator, with plastic wrap pressed directly on the surface.

- Preheat oven to 375°F (190°C)
- Food processor
- Minimum 12-cup Bundt pan, sprayed

PESTO

1½ cups	lightly packed fresh basil leaves	375 mL
3	cloves garlic, peeled	3
6 tbsp	extra virgin olive oil	90 mL
3 tbsp	pine nuts	45 mL
½ cup	grated pecorino-Romano cheese	125 mL
1 tsp	salt	5 mL
½ tsp	freshly ground black pepper	2 mL

MEATLOAF

2 tbsp	extra virgin olive oil	30 mL
2 cups	finely chopped onion	500 mL
2 tbsp	minced garlic	30 mL
1	red bell pepper, finely chopped	1
8 oz	cremini mushrooms, finely chopped	250 g
1 tsp	dried oregano	5 mL
1 tsp	salt	5 mL
½ tsp	freshly ground black pepper	2 mL
½ cup	minced fresh flat-leaf (Italian) parsley	125 mL
2 tbsp	balsamic vinegar	30 mL
2 tbsp	Worcestershire sauce	30 mL
2 cups	panko bread crumbs (see tip, page 246)	500 mL
¾ cup	whole milk	175 mL
4	large eggs, beaten	4
1 cup	grated pecorino-Romano cheese	250 mL
2½ lbs	ground turkey	1.25 kg
¾ cup	marinara sauce	175 mL

1. *Pesto:* In food processor, pulse basil and garlic several times to roughly chop. With the motor running, pour oil through the feed tube in a steady stream, stopping to scrape down the sides of the bowl as necessary. Add pine nuts, cheese, salt and pepper; process for 30 seconds or until well blended and smooth.

In step 3, I've found that it's easiest to mix ingredients together using clean, moist hands (rather than a spoon or spatula), as this allows you to thoroughly blend ingredients. Be sure not to overwork the meat, to prevent dense, tough meatloaf.

2. *Meatloaf:* In a large skillet, heat oil over medium heat. Add onion and garlic; cook, stirring, for 3 to 4 minutes or until onion is softened. Add red pepper and cook, stirring, for 2 minutes. Add mushrooms, oregano, salt and pepper; cook, stirring occasionally, for 8 to 10 minutes or until mushrooms are tender and golden and liquid has evaporated. Stir in parsley, vinegar and Worcestershire sauce. Transfer to a bowl and let cool.

3. In a large bowl, stir together panko and milk. Stir in eggs and cheese, then cooled mushroom mixture. Add turkey mixture and, using your hands, gently combine to evenly incorporate ingredients (see tip).

4. Transfer half of turkey mixture to prepared pan and arrange in an even layer. Spread pesto in an even layer over turkey mixture. Spread marinara sauce over pesto. Top with the remaining turkey mixture and smooth the top.

5. Bake in preheated oven for 60 to 70 minutes or until browned and an instant-read thermometer inserted in the thickest part registers 170°F (77°C). Let cool in pan for 10 to 15 minutes, then carefully invert meatloaf onto a plate. For best results, serve warm.

Cheesy Two-Potato Gratin Bundt

This savory side dish Bundt pulls double duty. Featuring both regular potatoes and sweet potatoes, it eliminates the need for two separate casseroles on your dinner or holiday table. Alternating orange and white layers, bound together by melted Gruyère and cream, creates a pretty presentation when the Bundt is sliced, although you can certainly use all sweet potatoes or regular potatoes, depending on your preference.

MAKES 10 TO 12 SERVINGS

Tips

Grocery stores often label yams and sweet potatoes interchangeably, though true yams are a dry, starchy vegetable with white flesh with dark skin — and not what you want here. For this recipe, look for sweet potatoes that have orange flesh and light brown or red skin.

For evenly sliced potatoes, it's best to use a mandoline, but you can use a sharp knife instead, keeping an eye on uniformity. Try to slice potatoes no thicker than ⅛ inch (3 mm) thick.

Make Ahead

This Bundt is best enjoyed the day it is baked, but you can prepare it up to 2 days in advance. Tightly wrap the cooled Bundt in plastic wrap and store in the refrigerator. To reheat slices, wrap Bundt in foil and heat in a 350°F (180°C) oven for 25 to 30 minutes.

- Preheat oven to 375°F (190°C)
- Minimum 10-cup Bundt pan, sprayed

2½ cups	shredded Gruyère cheese	625 mL
1¼ cups	grated Parmesan cheese, divided	300 mL
1½ tbsp	chopped fresh thyme	22 mL
1 tsp	salt	5 mL
½ tsp	freshly ground black pepper	2 mL
2	large eggs, lightly beaten	2
2½ cups	half-and-half (10%) cream	625 mL
1½ lbs	yellow-fleshed potatoes, peeled and very thinly sliced (see tip)	750 g
½ cup	unsalted butter, melted	125 mL
1½ lbs	sweet potatoes, peeled and very thinly sliced	750 g
¼ cup	panko bread crumbs (see tip, page 246)	60 mL

1. In a medium bowl, stir together Gruyère and 1 cup (250 mL) Parmesan until blended.

2. In small bowl, combine thyme, salt and pepper.

3. In another medium bowl, whisk together eggs and cream until blended.

4. Arrange a layer of potatoes in prepared pan. Using a pastry brush, brush potatoes with a thin coating of melted butter. Top with a layer of sweet potatoes and brush with butter. Sprinkle with about 1 tsp (5 mL) thyme mixture and ½ cup (125 mL) cheese mixture. Drizzle about ½ cup (125 mL) egg mixture over cheese.

5. Repeat layers four or five times. Sprinkle with panko and the remaining Parmesan, and drizzle any remaining butter over the top. Cover pan with foil.

6. Bake in preheated oven for 35 minutes. Remove foil and bake for 35 to 40 minutes or until golden brown and bubbling and a knife is easily inserted into the center. Let cool in pan for 15 minutes, then carefully invert Bundt onto a plate. For best results, serve warm.

Dried Cherry, Apple, Pecan and Sausage Stuffing Bundt

Every year, I say that I am going to try a new stuffing recipe for Thanksgiving dinner… and every year, I end up making the same stuffing. My husband loves it. My guests love it. I love it. You know what they say: "If it ain't broke, don't fix it!" With this Bundt, I've found a way to change the stuffing — not in the way it tastes, but in the way it is presented. Baked into one large Bundt, it adds a little bit of variety to a holiday table among a sea of casserole dishes, allowing guests to take a big or small slice, depending on what their plates (and stomachs!) allow.

MAKES 10 TO 12 SERVINGS

Tips

Other good apple varieties to use in this recipe would be Gala, Braeburn or Crispin.

For a more rustic look, leave chopped apples unpeeled.

Make Ahead

This recipe can be prepared up through step 5 and chilled overnight. Store in an airtight container in the refrigerator.

This Bundt is best enjoyed the day it is baked, but you can prepare it up to 1 day in advance. Tightly wrap the cooled Bundt in plastic wrap and store in the refrigerator. To reheat slices, wrap in foil and heat in a 325°F (160°C) oven for 15 to 20 minutes.

- Preheat oven to 350°F (180°C); dark pan, 325°F (160°C)
- Minimum 12-cup Bundt pan, sprayed

1 lb	loaf white bread, cut into ¾-inch (2 cm) cubes	500 g
1 lb	sweet or hot Italian turkey sausage (bulk or casings removed)	500 g
3 tbsp	unsalted butter	45 mL
2 cups	chopped sweet onions	500 mL
2	large Granny Smith apples, peeled and chopped (see tips)	2
1½ cups	chopped celery	375 mL
1½ tbsp	chopped fresh rosemary (or 1½ tsp/7 mL dried)	22 mL
1½ tbsp	chopped fresh sage (or 1½ tsp/7 mL dried)	22 mL
½ tsp	ground nutmeg	2 mL
2 tsp	salt	10 mL
1 tsp	freshly ground black pepper	5 mL
1 cup	dried cherries (sweet or sour)	250 mL
¾ cup	lightly toasted pecans, chopped	175 mL
½ cup	chopped fresh flat-leaf (Italian) parsley	125 mL
1¼ cups	ready-to-use reduced-sodium chicken broth	300 mL
4	large eggs, lightly beaten	4

1. Spread bread cubes in an even layer on a baking sheet. Toast in preheated oven for 15 minutes, tossing halfway through, until lightly browned and dry. Let cool.

2. Increase oven temperature to 375°F (190°C).

3. In a large skillet over medium-high heat, cook sausage, breaking it up with a spoon, for 6 to 8 minutes or until no longer pink. Using a slotted spoon, transfer sausage to a plate lined with paper towels to drain. Drain fat from pan.

4. In the same skillet (no need to clean it), melt butter over medium heat. Add onions and cook, stirring, for 4 to 5 minutes or until soft. Add apples, celery, rosemary, sage, nutmeg, salt and pepper; cook, stirring, for 5 minutes.

5. Transfer mixture to a large bowl. Stir in sausage, cherries, pecans and parsley. With clean hands, mix in bread cubes. Drizzle broth evenly over top and toss. Add eggs and mix with your hands until evenly incorporated.

Tip

To toast pecan halves, spread in an even layer on a baking sheet and bake in a 350°F (180°C) oven, stirring occasionally, for 8 to 10 minutes or until golden brown.

6. Transfer stuffing to prepared pan, packing firmly. Cover pan with foil.

7. Bake for 30 minutes. Remove foil and bake for 30 to 45 minutes or until puffed and deep golden brown. Let cool in pan for 15 minutes, then carefully invert Bundt onto a plate. For best results, serve warm.

Rosemary, Apple and Cheddar Beer Bread Bundt

Beer bread is a simple "dump and stir" quick bread that, as the name implies, contains a bottle of beer as an ingredient. Many beer bread recipes fall on the minimalist side, containing only beer, sugar and flour, and ingredients usually result in a dense, mild-tasting loaf. In this recipe, I've doctored up the basic bread with fragrant rosemary, sharp Cheddar and tart apple, which helps to keep the texture moist. Slice and serve warm from the oven with a bowl of tomato soup or, to stick with the theme, stout beef stew!

MAKES 12 TO 14 SERVINGS

Tips

I used a large Granny Smith apple for this recipe. Other good choices would be Gala, Braeburn or Crispin.

Although it is best to use fresh herbs when cooking, the fresh rosemary in this recipe can be replaced with 1 tsp (5 mL) dried rosemary.

Make Ahead

This Bundt is best enjoyed the day it is baked, but you can prepare it up to 3 days in advance. Tightly wrap the cooled Bundt in plastic wrap and store at room temperature or in the refrigerator. Reheat slices in a toaster oven or wrap in foil and heat in a 300°F (150°C) oven for 10 to 15 minutes.

- Preheat oven to 375°F (190°C); dark pan, 350°F (180°C)
- Minimum 10-cup Bundt pan, sprayed

1	large tart apple, grated	1
3 cups	all-purpose flour	750 mL
¼ cup	packed light brown sugar	60 mL
1 tbsp	baking powder	15 mL
1 tsp	salt	5 mL
¼ tsp	freshly ground black pepper	1 mL
1 tbsp	chopped fresh rosemary	15 mL
¼ tsp	cayenne pepper	1 mL
1½ cups	finely shredded sharp (old) Cheddar cheese	375 mL
1	bottle (12 oz/341 mL) lager-style beer	1
5 tbsp	unsalted butter, melted, divided	75 mL

1. To remove excess juice from apples, gently squeeze handfuls of grated apple over a bowl or sink. Separate the pieces of grated apple with your fingers so there are no clumps.

2. In a large bowl, whisk together flour, brown sugar, baking powder, salt, pepper, rosemary and cayenne.

3. Make a well in center of flour mixture and add apple, cheese, beer and 3 tbsp (45 mL) butter. Using a wooden spoon or spatula, stir until blended (mixture will be very thick).

4. Transfer batter to prepared Bundt pan and smooth the top. Drizzle the remaining butter evenly over batter.

5. Bake in preheated oven for 40 to 45 minutes or until a tester inserted in the center comes out clean. Let cool in pan for 10 minutes, then carefully invert bread onto a wire rack to cool completely. For best results, serve warm or at room temperature.

Croque Monsieur Strata Bundt

Originating in French cafés as a lunch or afternoon snack, the croque monsieur is a ham sandwich, usually served on buttery brioche bread, with broiled Gruyère or Comte cheese on top. The name of the sandwich derives from the French words *croquer*, to bite, and *monsieur*, mister. The croque madame, its counterpart, takes the already satisfying sandwich another step by placing a fried egg on top! Inspired by the croque monsieur, slices of this savory strata feature layers of Black Forest ham and nutty Gruyère cheese and need only a simple green salad and a glass of sauvignon blanc for a perfect weekend brunch.

MAKES 10 TO 12 SERVINGS

Tip

It is important to cut the bread into small enough cubes so that it can thoroughly absorb the egg mixture. If desired, buy your bread a day in advance so that it has a chance to dry out a bit.

Make Ahead

This strata is best enjoyed the day it is baked, but you can prepare it up to 3 days in advance. Tightly wrap the cooled Bundt in plastic wrap and store in the refrigerator. If desired, reheat a slice in the microwave on High for 30 to 45 seconds or wrap in foil, heat in a 300°F (150°C) oven and sandwich between two pieces of buttered whole-grain toast (or a sliced croissant!) for an extra-special breakfast on the go.

- **Minimum 12-cup Bundt pan, sprayed**

9	large eggs	9
3 cups	half-and-half (10%) cream	750 mL
2 tbsp	grainy mustard	30 mL
1 tsp	salt	5 mL
½ tsp	freshly ground black pepper	2 mL
Pinch	cayenne pepper	Pinch
1 lb	Black Forest ham slices, chopped	500 g
2 cups	finely shredded Gruyère cheese	500 mL
¼ cup	minced green onions	60 mL
1½ tbsp	chopped fresh rosemary (or 1½ tsp/7 mL dried)	22 mL
1 lb	loaf rustic white bread, cut into ¾-inch (2 cm) cubes (see tip)	500 g

1. In a large bowl, whisk eggs until blended. Whisk in cream, mustard, salt, pepper and cayenne.

2. In a medium bowl, toss together ham, cheese, green onions and rosemary. If necessary, using your hands, separate pieces to break up any clumps and create a uniform mixture.

3. Place one-third of the bread cubes in prepared Bundt pan. Top with half the ham mixture, sprinkling in an even layer. Repeat with half the remaining bread and the remaining ham mixture. Arrange the remaining bread on top, pressing down gently.

4. Slowly pour egg mixture evenly over the layers, letting it soak in as you pour. Cover pan with plastic wrap and refrigerate for 8 hours or overnight to allow bread to absorb egg mixture.

5. Preheat oven to 375°F (190°C).

6. Uncover pan and bake for 55 to 65 minutes or until puffed and golden brown and a paring knife inserted in the center comes out clean. Let cool in pan for 15 minutes, then carefully invert strata onto a plate. For best results, serve warm or at room temperature.

Variation

To make this recipe a bit lighter, substitute whole milk or low-fat milk (not non-fat) for the cream.

Mushroom Risotto Bundts

Delicious risotto isn't hard to make; it just takes a little extra time and a little extra patience. Arborio rice, traditionally used in risotto, is an Italian short-grain white rice that becomes creamy and chewy as it slowly absorbs liquid. Keeping an eye on the rice and stirring it constantly ensure even cooking and luscious, restaurant-worthy results. In this recipe, mushroom risotto is baked into individually portioned Bundts, which can be "baked to order" for your next dinner party.

MAKES 10 TO 12 MINI BUNDTS

Tips

If you are working with one Bundt pan, halve the recipe or bake the Bundts in two batches. Cover and chill the remaining risotto until ready to use.

If you can't find Arborio rice among the more common rice varietals in your grocery store, look for it in the specialty Italian foods section.

Make Ahead

Cooked risotto can be covered and refrigerated overnight before filling Bundt pans and baking.

These Bundts are best enjoyed the day they are baked, but you can prepare them up to 1 day in advance. Tightly wrap the cooled Bundts in plastic wrap on a plate and store in the refrigerator. To reheat, wrap Bundts in foil and heat in a 300°F (150°C) oven for 20 to 25 minutes.

- **Two 6-cake mini Bundt pans, sprayed (see tip)**

6 cups	ready-to-use reduced-sodium chicken broth	1.5 L
3 tbsp	unsalted butter	45 mL
2 tbsp	extra virgin olive oil, divided	30 mL
1	medium onion, finely chopped	1
1 tbsp	chopped garlic	15 mL
1 lb	cremini mushrooms, sliced	500 g
¼ cup	chopped fresh flat-leaf (Italian) parsley	60 mL
1 tbsp	chopped fresh thyme	15 mL
1 tsp	salt	5 mL
½ tsp	freshly ground black pepper	2 mL
1½ cups	Arborio rice	375 mL
½ cup	dry white wine	125 mL
½ cup	grated Parmesan cheese	125 mL
½ cup	grated pecorino-Romano cheese	125 mL

1. In a medium saucepan, warm broth over high heat until steaming. Reduce heat to low and cover to keep warm.

2. In medium skillet, heat butter and 1 tbsp (15 mL) oil over medium heat until butter is melted. Add onion and cook, stirring, for 5 minutes or until softened. Add garlic and cook, stirring, for 1 minute. Add mushrooms and cook, stirring, for 8 to 10 minutes or until mushrooms are tender and golden brown and liquid has evaporated. Stir in parsley, thyme, salt and pepper. Remove from heat.

3. In a large saucepan, heat the remaining oil over medium heat. Add rice and cook, stirring, for 1 minute or until coated. Add wine and cook, stirring constantly, until evaporated. Reduce heat to medium-low. Using a ladle or measuring cup, add warm broth, about 1 cup (250 mL) at a time, stirring constantly and waiting for broth to be absorbed before adding more, about 30 minutes total.

4. Meanwhile, preheat oven to 425°F (220°C).

5. Once broth has been absorbed (risotto should have a creamy but slightly al dente texture), add reserved mushroom mixture, Parmesan and pecorino-Romano. Cook, stirring, until cheese has melted. Transfer risotto to prepared pans, filling to the tops.

6. Bake for 30 to 40 minutes or until browned and crisp. Let cool in pan for 10 to 15 minutes, then carefully invert Bundts onto a plate or serving platter. For best results, serve warm soon after baking.

Crispy Parmesan Hash Brown Bundts

These mini breakfast potato Bundts are golden brown and crispy on the outside, fluffy and cheesy on the inside. They come together in a snap: simply mix all ingredients together in a bowl, press the mixture into Bundt molds and pop them into the oven. While the Bundts bake, whip up some scrambled eggs, toast and freshly squeezed orange juice for a hearty complete breakfast.

**MAKES
6 MINI BUNDTS**

Tips

If needed, use a pastry brush or paper towel to make sure the baking spray gets into the crevices of the Bundt pan so the cakes don't stick.

Although I prefer to use fresh herbs when cooking, the fresh rosemary in this recipe can be replaced with 1½ tsp (7 mL) dried rosemary.

Using moist fingers to press potato mixture into Bundt molds helps prevent them from sticking to the pan.

Make Ahead

These Bundts are best enjoyed the day they are baked, but you can prepare them up to 1 day in advance. Tightly wrap the cooled Bundts in plastic wrap and store in the refrigerator. To reheat, wrap Bundts in foil and heat in a 300°F (150°C) oven for 20 to 25 minutes.

- **Preheat oven to 425°F (220°C)**
- **6-cake mini Bundt pan, sprayed (see tip)**

2	large russet potatoes, peeled and grated (about 2 lbs/1 kg total)	2
¼ cup	all-purpose flour	60 mL
1½ tbsp	finely chopped fresh rosemary	22 mL
2	large eggs, beaten	2
1½ cups	grated Parmesan cheese	375 mL
1 tsp	salt	5 mL
½ tsp	freshly ground black pepper	2 mL

1. To remove liquid from potatoes, gently squeeze handfuls of grated potatoes over a bowl or sink.
2. In a large bowl, stir together potatoes, flour, rosemary, eggs, cheese, salt and pepper until ingredients are well blended.
3. Using your hands, divide mixture among prepared Bundt molds, packing firmly with moist fingers.
4. Bake in preheated oven for 30 to 40 minutes or until deep golden brown and sizzling. Let cool in pan for 10 minutes, then carefully invert Bundts onto a plate or serving platter. For best results, serve warm soon after baking.

Mushroom and Herb Stuffing Bundts

These Bundts are similar to "stuffing muffins," which you may have seen prepared on food-related TV segments or featured online during the holidays as an alternative to traditional casserole-style stuffing. Perfectly portioned for one and packed with herbs and mushrooms, these Bundts can be drizzled with gravy or served as they are, warm from the oven as a vegetarian side.

MAKES
12 MINI BUNDTS

Tips

To clean leek, slice off the dark green end, trimming to the part where the color is pale green; discard dark green end or reserve for stock. Slice the leek in half lengthwise. Run halves under water, separating the layers slightly to help clean out any dirt; drain well, then slice crosswise.

Use any blend of cremini, shiitake, oyster and portobello mushrooms. If you can't source these mushrooms, an equal amount of regular white button mushrooms will also work.

Make Ahead

These Bundts are best enjoyed the day they are baked, but you can prepare them up to 1 day in advance. Tightly wrap the cooled Bundts in plastic wrap and store in the refrigerator. To reheat, wrap Bundts in foil and heat in a 325°F (160°C) oven for 20 to 25 minutes.

- Preheat oven to 350°F (180°C)
- Two 6-cake mini Bundt pans, sprayed

8 cups	cubed whole-grain bread (½-inch/ 1 cm cubes)	2 L
½ cup	unsalted butter	125 mL
1	large leek (white and light green parts only), thinly sliced	1
1 lb	mixed mushrooms, thinly sliced	500 g
2	cloves garlic, minced	2
½ cup	chopped celery	125 mL
½ cup	chopped fresh flat-leaf (Italian) parsley	125 mL
1 tbsp	chopped fresh sage	15 mL
1 tbsp	chopped fresh thyme	15 mL
1½ tsp	salt	7 mL
½ tsp	freshly ground black pepper	2 mL
¼ cup	dry white wine	60 mL
1½ cups	ready-to-use reduced-sodium chicken broth	375 mL
3	large eggs, lightly beaten	3

1. Spread bread cubes in an even layer on a baking sheet. Toast in preheated oven for 15 minutes, tossing halfway through, until lightly browned and dry. Let cool.

2. Increase oven temperature to 375°F (190°C).

3. In a large skillet, melt butter over medium heat. Add leek and cook, stirring, for 3 minutes or until softened. Add mushrooms and cook, stirring, for 8 to 10 minutes or until tender and golden brown and liquid has evaporated. Add garlic, celery, parsley, sage, thyme, salt and pepper; cook, stirring, for 3 minutes. Add wine and cook, stirring occasionally, for 2 to 3 minutes or until evaporated. Remove from heat.

4. Transfer bread cubes to a large bowl. Add mushroom mixture and toss until blended. Drizzle broth evenly over top and toss to coat. Add eggs and mix with clean hands until evenly incorporated.

5. Divide mixture among prepared Bundt pan molds, packing firmly. Cover pans with foil.

6. Bake for 15 minutes. Remove foil and bake for 15 to 25 minutes or until puffed and deep golden brown. Let cool in pan for 10 minutes, then carefully invert Bundts onto a wire rack and immediately invert them again so that the golden brown, textured sides are facing up. For best results, serve warm.

Baked Brie and Spicy Raspberry Jam Bundts

One of our favorite local restaurants used to have a wonderful baked Brie appetizer on their menu: individually portioned wedges of Brie topped with sun-dried tomato jam that were wrapped in puff pastry and baked until they were flaky and golden brown on the outside, gooey on the inside. Unfortunately, they took it off the menu — the nerve! Fortunately, I've created a mini Bundt version of this dish, featuring four buttery pull-apart pieces of pastry filled with melted Brie and spicy raspberry jam in each bundle. These would be a great first course for a dinner party, served atop a lightly dressed bed of mixed greens.

MAKES
8 MINI BUNDTS

Tips

If you are working with one Bundt pan, halve the recipe or prepare the Bundts in two batches. Cover and chill the remaining puff pastry pieces, Brie and jam separately until ready to use.

When cubing Brie pieces, it's fine to leave pieces of the rind on (it's edible), but you can trim the rind, if preferred.

It's okay if some of the filling "breaks" through the puff pastry while baking. This creates a crispy, caramelized cheesy "crust" that adds a nice contrasting texture to the soft, buttery baked pastry.

If Bundts don't immediately turn out of pans, use a paring knife or offset spatula to loosen them around the rims.

- Two 6-cake mini Bundt pans, sprayed (see tip)

	All-purpose flour (for dusting work surface)	
1	box (17.3 oz/490 g) puff pastry, thawed	1
⅓ cup	raspberry jam	75 mL
¼ to ½ tsp	cayenne pepper	1 to 2 mL
8 oz	Brie cheese, cut into 1-tsp (5 cm) cubes	250 g
1	large egg	1
1 tbsp	water	15 mL

1. On a lightly floured work surface, using a rolling pin, roll out 1 sheet (half) of puff pastry into a 16- by 14-inch (40 by 36 cm) rectangle, with a long side facing you. Keep the other sheet under a damp kitchen towel so it doesn't dry out.

2. Using a knife, cut rectangle into 4 equal quadrants (each about 8 by 7 inches/20 by 18 cm). Cut each quadrant into 4 more equal quadrants, so that you have 16 pieces of puff pastry.

3. In a small bowl, stir together jam and cayenne to taste.

4. In another small bowl, whisk together egg and water until blended.

5. Spoon about ½ tsp (2 mL) jam mixture into the center of one piece of pastry. Top with a cube of Brie. Fold one corner of pastry over filling to the center of the rectangle. Using a pastry brush, brush the top of point with egg wash. Fold adjacent corner of pastry over filling, overlapping the first corner. Brush point with egg wash. Repeat with the remaining two corners, until filling is completely enclosed. Pinch any seams to seal and brush top of pastry with egg wash. Transfer bundle to a prepared mini Bundt mold, with the seam side facing inward.

6. Repeat step 5 until you have 8 bundles divided between the two pans. Brush tops of bundles with egg wash. Tightly cover pans with plastic wrap and freeze for at least 30 minutes or up to 2 days.

7. Meanwhile, preheat oven to 400°F (200°C).

8. Uncover pan and bake for 20 to 25 minutes or until golden brown and puffed and filling is bubbly. Let cool in pan for 10 minutes, then carefully invert bundles onto a wire rack or serving platter. For best results, serve warm.

Rainbow Swirl Bundt

BONUS RECIPES

Glazes and Sauces

Chocolate Glaze

MAKES ENOUGH FOR A CAKE
BAKED IN A 10- TO 12-CUP PAN

5 oz	semisweet chocolate, chopped	150 g
½ cup	heavy or whipping (35%) cream	125 mL
1½ tbsp	light (white or golden) corn syrup	22 mL
1 tsp	vanilla extract	5 mL

1. In a small saucepan, stir together chocolate, cream and corn syrup over medium-low heat until melted and smooth. Remove from heat and stir in vanilla. Let cool slightly before drizzling over the cake.

Chocolate Hazelnut Glaze

MAKES ENOUGH FOR A CAKE
BAKED IN A 10- TO 12-CUP PAN

1½ cups	confectioners' (icing) sugar, sifted	375 mL
3 to 4 tbsp	whole milk	45 to 60 mL
3 tbsp	chocolate hazelnut spread, warmed	45 mL
1 tbsp	hazelnut liqueur (such as Frangelico), optional	15 mL

1. In a medium bowl, whisk together sugar, 3 tbsp (45 mL) milk, chocolate hazelnut spread and liqueur (if using) until blended and smooth. Whisk in more milk if necessary, 1 tsp (5 mL) at a time, until glaze is thick but pourable.

Tip

Chocolate hazelnut spread is quite thick. Warm it in its packaging (if in glass) or in a microwave-safe bowl in the microwave in 15-second intervals, or transfer to a small saucepan and heat over medium-low heat, stirring occasionally, until heated through.

Vegan Chocolate Glaze

MAKES ENOUGH FOR A CAKE
BAKED IN A 10- TO 15-CUP PAN

2 cups	confectioners' (icing) sugar, sifted	500 mL
½ cup	unsweetened cocoa powder, sifted	125 mL
5 to 7 tbsp	full-fat coconut milk	75 to 105 mL
1 tbsp	light (white or golden) corn syrup	15 mL
1 tsp	vanilla extract	5 mL

1. In a medium bowl, whisk together sugar and cocoa. Add 5 tbsp (75 mL) coconut milk, corn syrup and vanilla, whisking until smooth. Whisk in more coconut milk if necessary, 1 tsp (5 mL) at a time, until glaze is thick but pourable.

Tip

Whisk the can of coconut milk well before measuring to make sure you evenly blend the cream and the milk, which tend to separate in the can.

Variation

You can replace the coconut milk with unsweetened plain almond milk, although the coconut milk provides a slightly richer, more moist texture due to its higher fat content.

White Chocolate Glaze

MAKES ENOUGH FOR A CAKE
BAKED IN A 10- TO 12-CUP PAN

8 oz	white chocolate, chopped	250 g
⅓ cup	half-and-half (10%) cream	75 mL
⅛ tsp	salt	0.5 mL
1 to 1½ cups	confectioners' (icing) sugar, sifted	250 to 375 mL

1. In a small saucepan, stir together white chocolate, cream and salt over medium-low heat until melted and smooth. Whisk in 1 cup (250 mL) sugar. Whisk in more sugar if necessary, 2 tbsp (30 mL) at a time, until glaze is thick but pourable.

Vanilla Glaze

MAKES ENOUGH FOR A CAKE
BAKED IN A 10- TO 15-CUP PAN

2 cups	confectioners' (icing) sugar, sifted	500 mL
Pinch	salt	Pinch
3 to 5 tbsp	half-and-half (10%) cream	45 to 75 mL
1 tsp	vanilla extract	5 mL

1. In a medium bowl, whisk together sugar, salt, 3 tbsp (45 mL) cream and vanilla until smooth. Whisk in more cream if necessary, 1 tsp (5 mL) at a time, until glaze is thick but pourable.

Tip

Whole or low-fat milk can be used in place of the cream. The result will be a slightly thinner and less opaque glaze.

....

Variations

Buttery Vanilla Glaze: Omit the salt, substitute whole milk for the cream, and add ¼ cup (60 mL) unsalted butter, softened, with the vanilla. (I like a thicker glaze for this recipe, as it melts when spread over a warm Bundt, so keep that in mind when whisking in any additional milk.)

Spiced Vanilla Glaze: Replace the salt with ¼ tsp (1 mL) each ground cinnamon, ginger and cardamom, and replace the cream with 3 to 4 tbsp (45 to 60 mL) whole milk.

Cinnamon Glaze: Replace the salt with ½ tsp (1 mL) ground cinnamon, and replace the half-and-half cream with 4 to 5 tbsp (60 to 75 mL) heavy or whipping (35%) cream. Start by adding 4 tbsp (60 mL) cream, then whisk in more as needed.

Eggnog Glaze: Replace the salt with ground nutmeg (or a small pinch of freshly grated nutmeg), and replace the cream with 4 to 5 tbsp (60 to 75 mL) eggnog. Start by adding 4 tbsp (60 mL) eggnog, then whisk in more as needed.

Vanilla Bean Glaze

MAKES ENOUGH FOR A CAKE
BAKED IN A 10- TO 12-CUP PAN

½	vanilla bean	½
¼ cup	heavy or whipping (35%) cream	60 mL
1½ cups	confectioners' (icing) sugar, sifted	375 mL
1 to 2 tbsp	water	15 to 30 mL

1. Using a paring knife, split the vanilla bean down its length. Press the tip of the bean against a cutting board. Use the dull side of knife to scrape seeds from pod, moving from the tip down the length, flattening the bean as you go (discard pod or reserve for another use).

2. In a medium bowl, stir together vanilla seeds and cream, breaking up any clumps with the back of a spoon. Stir in sugar and 1 tbsp (15 mL) water until smooth. Stir in more water if necessary, 1 tsp (5 mL) at a time, until glaze is thick but pourable.

Tip

Ground vanilla bean (also called vanilla bean powder) is available in jars in specialty baking and spice shops and makes a good substitute for whole vanilla beans; use ¾ tsp (3 mL) ground in this glaze. Or you can substitute 1 tsp (5 mL) vanilla extract for the vanilla seeds, although I prefer the pretty black specks and deep vanilla flavor that result from using beans.

....

Variation

Cherry Vanilla Bean Glaze: Omit the cream and water, and increase the sugar to 2 cups (500 mL). Stir together vanilla seeds, sugar and 4 tbsp (60 mL) cherry juice until smooth, breaking up any clumps. Gradually stir in more cherry juice if necessary. You can use maraschino cherry juice (from a jar of maraschino cherries), which will be sweeter, or pure unsweetened cherry juice, which will be tart.

Lemon Glaze

MAKES ENOUGH FOR A CAKE
BAKED IN A 10- TO 15-CUP PAN

3 cups	confectioners' (icing) sugar, sifted	750 mL
1 tsp	grated lemon zest (optional)	5 mL
4 to 5 tbsp	freshly squeezed lemon juice	60 to 75 mL

1. In a medium bowl, whisk together sugar, lemon zest (if using) and 4 tbsp (60 mL) lemon juice until smooth. Whisk in more lemon juice if necessary, 1 tsp (5 mL) at a time, until glaze is thick but pourable.

Variations

"Crispy" Lemon Glaze: Reduce the confectioners' sugar to 1½ cups (375 mL) and add ½ cup (125 mL) granulated sugar. Omit the lemon zest and increase the lemon juice to ⅓ cup (75 mL), whisking it in all at once until evenly blended.

Key Lime Glaze: Reduce the sugar to 2 cups (500 mL), omit the lemon zest and substitute 3 to 4 tbsp (45 to 60 mL) freshly squeezed Key lime juice for the lemon juice. (Bottled Key lime juice is often easier to find than fresh Key limes, and you can use it as a substitute.)

Orange Glaze: Omit the lemon zest and substitute freshly squeezed orange juice for the lemon juice.

Blood Orange Glaze: Reduce the sugar to 2 cups (500 mL), omit the lemon zest and substitute freshly squeezed blood orange juice for the lemon juice. (If you can't find a blood orange, use a regular orange or even a ruby red grapefruit.)

Blueberry Glaze

MAKES ENOUGH FOR A CAKE
BAKED IN A 10- TO 15-CUP PAN

- **Food processor or blender**

2 to 3 cups	confectioners' (icing) sugar, sifted	500 to 750 mL
½ cup	fresh blueberries	125 mL
1 tbsp	freshly squeezed lemon juice	15 mL

1. In food processor, process 2 cups (500 mL) sugar, blueberries and lemon juice until smooth. Add more sugar if necessary, 1 tbsp (15 mL) at a time, until glaze is thick but pourable.

Tip

You can use frozen blueberries instead of fresh, but thaw and drain them before measuring. You may need to add more confectioners' sugar to achieve your preferred consistency.

Coconut Glaze

MAKES ENOUGH FOR A CAKE
BAKED IN A 10- TO 15-CUP PAN

2 cups	confectioners' (icing) sugar, sifted	500 mL
¼ cup	full-fat coconut milk	60 mL
½ tsp	coconut extract	2 mL

1. In a medium bowl, whisk together sugar, coconut milk and coconut extract until smooth.

Salted Caramel Glaze

MAKES ENOUGH FOR A CAKE
BAKED IN A 10- TO 12-CUP PAN

1 cup	granulated sugar	250 mL
1/8 tsp	cream of tartar	0.5 mL
1/4 cup	water	60 mL
1/2 cup	heavy or whipping (35%) cream	125 mL
2	large eggs	2
1 tsp	salt	5 mL
1 1/4 to 2 cups	confectioners' (icing) sugar, sifted	300 to 500 mL

1. In a medium saucepan, stir together granulated sugar, cream of tartar and water over medium heat until sugar dissolves. Increase heat to medium-high and bring to a boil, without stirring. Boil, swirling occasionally, for about 8 minutes or until syrup turns a deep amber color. Remove from heat and carefully stir in cream (mixture will bubble vigorously). Reduce heat to low, return pan to heat and stir until caramel bits dissolve.

2. In a medium heatproof bowl, whisk eggs until blended. Very gradually pour in hot caramel in a thin, steady stream, whisking constantly. Whisk in salt. Return to the saucepan and whisk constantly over medium-low heat for 2 to 3 minutes or until smooth and slightly thickened. Let cool to room temperature.

3. Whisk 1 1/4 cups (300 mL) confectioners' sugar into caramel mixture. Whisk in more sugar if necessary, 1/4 cup (60 mL) at a time, until glaze is thick but pourable.

Tip

Adding cream of tartar to caramel syrup helps prevent the sugar solution from "seizing" during the boiling process. This is an invaluable trick I learned after one too many saucepans full of rock-hard, difficult-to-clean crystallized sugar!

....

Variation

Bourbon Caramel Glaze: Stir in 2 tbsp (30 mL) bourbon (or rum, whiskey or brandy) with the salt, and decrease the confectioners' sugar to 1 cup (250 mL).

Make Ahead

Salted Caramel Glaze can be prepared up to 3 days in advance. Store in an airtight container in the refrigerator, and bring to room temperature before glazing.

Thick Caramel Glaze

MAKES ENOUGH FOR A CAKE
BAKED IN A 10- TO 12-CUP PAN

1 cup	packed dark brown sugar	250 mL
1/4 tsp	salt	1 mL
1 cup	evaporated milk	250 mL
1/2 cup	unsalted butter	125 mL
1 1/2 cups	confectioners' (icing) sugar, sifted	375 mL
3 to 4 tbsp	heavy or whipping (35%) cream	45 to 60 mL

1. In a medium saucepan, stir together brown sugar, salt, evaporated milk and butter over medium-low heat until melted and smooth. Increase heat to medium and bring to a gentle boil. Reduce heat and boil gently, stirring often, for 25 to 30 minutes or until thickened and glossy. Remove from heat and let cool to warm.

2. Whisk in confectioners' sugar and 3 tbsp (45 mL) cream until smooth. Whisk in more cream if necessary, 1 tsp (5 mL) at a time, until glaze is thick but pourable.

Tip

This glaze is thicker than most of the other glazes in this book, and it will set quickly once the confectioners' sugar is added. If the glaze needs "coaxing" down the sides of the cake, tap the plate or wire rack on the counter a few times. This will also give the glaze a smooth finish.

Butterscotch Glaze

MAKES ENOUGH FOR A CAKE
BAKED IN A 10- TO 12-CUP PAN

½ cup	packed dark brown sugar	125 mL
½ tsp	salt	2 mL
¼ cup	unsalted butter	60 mL
¼ cup	light (white or golden) corn syrup	60 mL
⅓ cup	heavy or whipping (35%) cream	75 mL
1 tbsp	Scotch or whiskey (optional)	15 mL
½ to ¾ cup	confectioners' (icing) sugar, sifted	125 to 175 mL

1. In a medium saucepan, stir together brown sugar, salt, butter and corn syrup over medium heat until sugar dissolves. Bring to a boil and cook, stirring often, for 2 minutes. Remove from heat and carefully pour in cream (mixture will bubble), stirring to blend.

2. Return saucepan to medium-low heat, add Scotch (if using) and bring to a gentle boil. Boil gently, stirring occasionally, for 3 minutes or until slightly thickened. Let cool to warm.

3. Stir in ½ cup (125 mL) confectioners' sugar. Stir in more confectioners' sugar if necessary, 1 tbsp (15 mL) at a time, until glaze is thick but pourable.

Tip

If the glaze is still too thin after you've added all of the confectioners' sugar, it's probably too warm. Let it cool a bit more to thicken.

Maple Glaze

MAKES ENOUGH FOR A CAKE
BAKED IN A 10- TO 15-CUP PAN

2 cups	confectioners' (icing) sugar, sifted	500 mL
4 tbsp	pure maple syrup	60 mL
2 to 4 tbsp	whole milk	30 to 60 mL

1. In a medium bowl, whisk together sugar, maple syrup and 2 tbsp (30 mL) milk until smooth. Whisk in more milk if necessary, 1 tsp (5 mL) at a time, until glaze is thick but pourable.

Tips

Be sure to use pure maple syrup, not imitation pancake or table syrup. Look for grade A syrup, as it will have the most concentrated maple flavor.

Using whole milk in the glaze will result in a slightly thicker, more opaque appearance, but low-fat (2%) milk can be used instead.

Spiced Cider Glaze

MAKES ENOUGH FOR A CAKE
BAKED IN A 10- TO 15-CUP PAN

2 cups	unsweetened apple cider	500 mL
8	whole cloves	8
3	cinnamon sticks	3
2	star anise pods	2
2¼ cups	confectioners' (icing) sugar, sifted	560 mL
3 to 4 tbsp	half-and-half (10%) cream	45 to 60 mL

1. In a medium saucepan, bring cider, cloves, cinnamon sticks and star anise to a boil over medium-high heat. Boil, stirring occasionally, for 10 minutes or until cider is reduced to about ⅓ cup (75 mL). Remove from heat. Using a slotted spoon, discard cloves, cinnamon and star anise. Let cider cool to room temperature.

2. In a medium bowl, whisk together sugar, cider and 3 tbsp (45 mL) cream. Whisk in more cream if necessary, 1 tsp (5 mL) at a time, until glaze is smooth and thick but pourable.

Tip

You can substitute whole or low-fat (2%) milk for the cream, but the glaze will be thinner.

Variation

If you don't have whole cloves, cinnamon sticks and/or star anise, substitute ⅛ tsp (0.5 mL) ground cloves, ¼ tsp (1 mL) ground cinnamon and/or ⅛ tsp (0.5 mL) Chinese five-spice powder stirred in with the cider.

Butter Rum Glaze

MAKES ENOUGH FOR A CAKE BAKED IN A
10- TO 12-CUP PAN

⅔ cup	granulated sugar	150 mL
6 tbsp	unsalted butter	90 mL
2 tbsp	water	30 mL
3 tbsp	dark rum	45 mL
1 tbsp	vanilla extract	15 mL

1. In a medium saucepan, combine sugar, butter and water over medium heat; bring to a boil, stirring constantly. Boil for 4 to 5 minutes or until slightly thickened and syrupy. Remove from heat and stir in rum and vanilla. Brush or drizzle over the cake while still warm.

Irish Cream Glaze

MAKES ENOUGH FOR A CAKE
BAKED IN A 10- TO 15-CUP PAN

¼ tsp	espresso powder	1 mL
2 to 3 tbsp	hot water	30 to 45 mL
2 cups	confectioners' (icing) sugar, sifted	500 mL
3 tbsp	Irish cream liqueur	45 mL

1. In a medium bowl, whisk together espresso powder and 2 tbsp (30 mL) water until espresso powder is dissolved. Whisk in sugar and liqueur until smooth. Add more water if necessary, 1 tsp (5 mL) at a time, until glaze is thick but pourable.

Tip

Look for espresso powder in the coffee section or baking aisle of your grocery store or at specialty baking retailers. If you can't find it, replace it and the water with 2 to 3 tbsp (30 to 45 mL) cooled strong brewed coffee.

Marshmallow Glaze

MAKES ENOUGH FOR A CAKE
BAKED IN A 10- TO 12-CUP PAN

½ cup	confectioners' (icing) sugar, sifted	125 mL
⅛ tsp	salt	0.5 mL
1 cup	marshmallow crème	250 mL
3 to 4 tbsp	heavy or whipping (35%) cream	45 to 60 mL

1. In the stand mixer bowl, beat sugar, salt, marshmallow crème and 3 tbsp (45 mL) cream on medium-low speed until smooth. Beat in more cream if necessary, 1 tsp (5 mL) at a time, until glaze is thick but pourable.

Tips

Look for marshmallow crème (also known as fluff) in the baking or peanut butter section of your grocery store.

Because it is so sticky, the best way to measure it is to spray or oil a liquid measuring cup beforehand.

Peanut Butter Glaze

MAKES ENOUGH FOR A CAKE
BAKED IN A 10- TO 12-CUP PAN

1⅓ cups	peanut butter chips (8 oz/250 g)	325 mL
½ cup	heavy or whipping (35%) cream	125 mL
1 tbsp	light (white or golden) corn syrup	15 mL

1. In a small saucepan, stir together peanut butter chips, cream and corn syrup over medium-low heat until melted and smooth. Let cool for 5 minutes.

Cream Cheese Glaze

MAKES ENOUGH FOR A CAKE
BAKED IN A 10- TO 15-CUP PAN

2 cups	confectioners' (icing) sugar, sifted	500 mL
⅛ tsp	salt	0.5 mL
3 oz	brick-style cream cheese, softened	90 g
2 tbsp	unsalted butter, softened	30 mL
2 tsp	vanilla extract	10 mL
4 to 6 tbsp	half-and-half (10%) cream	60 to 90 mL

1. In the stand mixer bowl, beat sugar, salt, cream cheese and butter on low speed. Increase speed to medium and beat in vanilla and 4 tbsp (60 mL) cream. Beat in more cream if necessary, 1 tsp (5 mL) at a time, until glaze is thick but pourable.

Variation

Change the flavor of the glaze by substituting ½ tsp (2 mL) almond extract or 1 tsp (5 mL) coconut extract for the vanilla.

Mexican Chocolate Ganache

MAKES ENOUGH FOR A CAKE
BAKED IN A 10- TO 12-CUP PAN

6 oz	dark or semisweet chocolate, chopped	175 g
⅓ cup	heavy or whipping (35%) cream	150 mL
1 tbsp	unsalted butter	15 mL
½ tsp	ground cinnamon	2 mL
2 to 3 tbsp	coffee-flavored liqueur (such as Kahlúa)	30 to 45 mL

1. In a small saucepan, stir together chocolate, cream and butter over medium-low heat until melted and smooth. Remove from heat and stir in cinnamon and liqueur to taste.

Tip

The ganache thickens quickly once poured over a cake. To coax it down the sides, firmly tap the cake-topped plate or wire rack on the counter a few times.

White Chocolate Peppermint Ganache

MAKES ENOUGH FOR A CAKE
BAKED IN A 10- TO 12-CUP PAN

6 oz	white chocolate, chopped	175 g
⅓ cup	heavy or whipping (35%) cream	75 mL
2 tbsp	unsalted butter	30 mL
1 tsp	peppermint extract	5 mL

1. In a small saucepan, stir together white chocolate, cream and butter over medium-low heat until melted and smooth. Stir in peppermint.

Irish Cream Ganache

MAKES ENOUGH FOR A CAKE
BAKED IN A 10- TO 12-CUP PAN

4 oz	dark or semisweet chocolate, chopped	125 g
⅓ cup + 2 tbsp	Irish cream liqueur, divided	105 mL
1 cup	confectioners' (icing) sugar, sifted	250 mL
1 tsp	vanilla extract	5 mL

1. In a small saucepan, stir together chocolate and ⅓ cup (75 mL) Irish cream over medium-low heat until melted and smooth. Remove from heat and whisk in confectioners' sugar and vanilla. Whisk in more Irish cream if necessary, 1 tbsp (15 mL) at a time, until ganache is thick but pourable.

Tip

The ganache thickens quickly once poured over a cake. To coax it down the sides, firmly tap the cake-topped plate or wire rack on the counter a few times.

White Chocolate Cream Cheese Frosting

MAKES ENOUGH FOR A CAKE BAKED IN A 10- TO 15-CUP PAN

2 cups	confectioners' (icing) sugar, sifted	500 mL
6 tbsp	brick-style cream cheese, softened	90 mL
3 oz	white chocolate, melted (see tip)	90 g
2 tsp	vanilla extract	10 mL
5 to 7 tbsp	half-and-half (10%) cream	75 to 105 mL

1. In the stand mixer bowl, beat sugar and cream cheese on medium-low speed until blended. Add melted chocolate and vanilla; increase speed to medium-high and beat until well combined. Add 5 tbsp (75 mL) cream and beat until smooth. Beat in more cream if necessary, 1 tsp (5 mL) at a time, until frosting is thick but pourable.

Tip

To melt chocolate, in a small saucepan, heat chocolate over medium-low heat, stirring often, until melted and smooth. Alternatively, place chocolate in a microwave-safe bowl and microwave on High in 15-second intervals, stirring as necessary, until smooth.

Toffee Sauce

MAKES ABOUT 1½ CUPS (375 ML)

1 cup	packed light brown sugar	250 mL
½ cup	unsalted butter	125 mL
½ cup	heavy or whipping (35%) cream	125 mL
3 tbsp	brandy	45 mL
½ tsp	salt	2 mL

1. In a medium saucepan, bring brown sugar, butter, cream, brandy and salt to a boil over medium heat, stirring constantly. Boil for 12 minutes, stirring often, then reduce heat and simmer, stirring occasionally, for 10 minutes or until thickened. Keep warm over very low heat until ready to use.

Brandied Butterscotch Sauce

MAKES ABOUT 2 CUPS (500 ML)

½ cup	unsalted butter	125 mL
1 cup	packed light brown sugar	250 mL
1 cup	heavy or whipping (35%) cream	250 mL
2 tbsp	brandy	30 mL
1 tsp	vanilla extract	5 mL
½ tsp	ground cinnamon	2 mL
¼ tsp	salt	1 mL
2	large egg yolks	2

1. In a medium saucepan, melt butter over medium heat. Add brown sugar, stirring until smooth. Whisk in cream, brandy, vanilla, cinnamon and salt until heated through.

2. In a medium heatproof bowl, whisk egg yolks until pale and slightly thickened. Very gradually whisk about half the sauce into eggs. Return mixture to saucepan and cook over medium-low heat, whisking constantly, for 3 minutes or until slightly thickened. Let cool to warm.

Tip

Gradually adding hot liquid to eggs heats them slowly, or tempers them, to ensure they don't scramble in the sauce.

Coffee Crème Anglaise

MAKES ABOUT 2 CUPS (500 ML)

½	vanilla bean	½
1 cup	whole milk	250 mL
½ cup	heavy or whipping (35%) cream	125 mL
½ cup	granulated sugar	125 mL
3	large egg yolks	3
2 tbsp	coffee-flavored liqueur	30 mL

1. Using a paring knife, split the vanilla bean down its length. Press the tip of the bean against a cutting board. Use the dull side of knife to scrape seeds from pod, moving from the tip down the length, flattening the bean as you go (discard pod or reserve for another use).

2. In a small saucepan, bring vanilla seeds, milk and cream to a simmer over medium heat, stirring often. Remove from heat.

3. In a medium heatproof bowl, whisk together sugar and egg yolks for 3 minutes or until well blended and light. Gradually pour hot milk mixture into eggs, whisking constantly, until fully incorporated and smooth.

4. Return mixture to saucepan and cook over medium heat, stirring constantly, for 4 to 5 minutes or until custard just starts to thicken and coats the back of a spoon. Whisk in liqueur and cook, stirring, for 1 minute.

5. Transfer to a bowl, place plastic wrap directly on the surface and let cool completely. Refrigerate for at least 2 hours, until cold, or for up to 3 days.

Tips

Look for a vanilla bean that is plump, glossy and fragrant, not dry. Store in an airtight container in a cool, dark place.

Gradually adding hot liquid to eggs heats them slowly, or tempers them, to ensure that they don't scramble in the sauce.

Orange Caramel Sauce

MAKES ABOUT 1¼ CUPS (300 ML)

1 cup	granulated sugar	250 mL
Pinch	cream of tartar	Pinch
⅓ cup	freshly squeezed orange juice	75 mL
½ cup	heavy or whipping (35%) cream	125 mL
2	large egg yolks	2

1. In a medium saucepan, stir together sugar, cream of tartar and orange juice over medium heat until sugar dissolves. Increase heat to medium-high and boil, swirling pan occasionally, for 8 to 10 minutes or until syrup turns a deep orange-amber color. Remove from heat and carefully stir in cream (mixture will bubble vigorously). Return saucepan to low heat and stir until the caramel bits dissolve.

2. In a medium heatproof bowl, whisk egg yolks until blended. Very gradually pour in hot caramel in a thin, steady stream, whisking constantly.

3. Return mixture to saucepan and heat over medium-low heat, whisking constantly, for 2 to 3 minutes or until sauce is slightly thickened and coats the back of a spoon. Let cool to warm.

Tip

Gradually adding hot liquid to eggs heats them slowly, or tempers them, to ensure that they don't scramble in the sauce.

German Chocolate Bundt

Acknowledgments

I want to extend a huge thank you to everyone who helped me create this book, from those who worked directly with me on the manuscript and photographs to those who gave my recipes their stamp of approval by devouring slice after slice of Bundt-shaped cakes, breads, pastries and casseroles.

To Bob Dees and the entire Robert Rose team — Martine Quibell, Nina McCreath and Marian Jarkovich — thank you for embracing the idea of a Bundt book and for trusting me in the roles of photographer and food stylist as well as author and recipe developer. I thoroughly enjoyed taking on the challenge of shooting my own photos and making sure that the recipes looked as good as they tasted!

To my meticulous editing team — Sue Sumeraj, Jennifer MacKenzie and Kelly Jones — thank you for being so responsive, flexible and easy to communicate with, even three time zones away! Your feedback was extremely valuable, and I learned so much from each of you during the process.

Thanks to Kevin Cockburn and the PageWave Graphics team for advising me on the photography and design aspect and offering so many helpful suggestions along the way.

Thank you to my dear friend Christie Vanover for taking such beautiful step-by-step photos. I'm so glad we finally collaborated on a project, and I hope we do it again in the future, as it didn't feel like work!

To Lindsay and Bjork at Food Blogger Pro, thank you for your wonderful online food photography course, which provided me with all of the tools I needed to improve my skill set behind the lens and confidently take on the role of photographer for this book.

To my taste testers — the team at Caesars' corporate offices (especially Carolyn Willis, for making sure my cake plates were always cleaned and returned!), the Las Vegas Police Department, Chef Miah, Jackson Hole Nannies, the Moys, Gloria, Jay and Jenny, Mom and Dad and the Hessions — thank you for your honest feedback and enthusiasm for my recipes.

Finally, to Eric, thanks for allowing me to move some of your things around so that I could create a Bundt pan storage shelf in our pantry and for tolerating months of a kitchen cluttered with flour bins, softening butter, measuring cups and notebooks. Thank you for your support and encouragement throughout this project and for all of those evenings and weekends when you watched Gigi so that she didn't end up underfoot while I retested recipes!

Library and Archives Canada Cataloguing in Publication

Hession, Julie Anne, author
    Beautiful bundts : 100 recipes for delicious cakes & more / Julie Anne Hession.

Includes index.
ISBN 978-0-7788-0576-2 (softcover)

    1. Cake. 2. Cookbooks. I. Title.

TX771.H48 2017   641.86'53   C2017-902808-1

Index